Letters of the Lady Brilliana Harley: Wife of Sir Robert Harley, of Brampton Bryan, Knight of the Bath

Brilliana Harley

With love to my friend Maureen from wife of Richard John Harley Enid (Henid, Holly) 2014. XXX

Nabu Public Domain Reprints:

You are holding a reproduction of an original work published before 1923 that is in the public domain in the United States of America, and possibly other countries. You may freely copy and distribute this work as no entity (individual or corporate) has a copyright on the body of the work. This book may contain prior copyright references, and library stamps (as most of these works were scanned from library copies). These have been scanned and retained as part of the historical artifact.

This book may have occasional imperfections such as missing or blurred pages, poor pictures, errant marks, etc. that were either part of the original artifact, or were introduced by the scanning process. We believe this work is culturally important, and despite the imperfections, have elected to bring it back into print as part of our continuing commitment to the preservation of printed works worldwide. We appreciate your understanding of the imperfections in the preservation process, and hope you enjoy this valuable book.

LETTERS

OF

THE LADY BRILLIANA HARLEY,

WIFE OF SIR ROBERT HARLEY,

OF BRAMPTON BRYAN, KNIGHT OF THE BATH.

WITH INTRODUCTION AND NOTES

BY

THOMAS TAYLOR LEWIS, A.M.

VICAR OF BRIDSTOW, HEREFORDSHIRE.

LONDON:
PRINTED FOR THE CAMDEN SOCIETY.

MDCCCLIII.

LONDON:
J. B. NICHOLS AND SONS, PRINTERS,
PARLIAMENT-STREET.

[NO. LVIII.]

COUNCIL

OF

THE CAMDEN SOCIETY

FOR THE YEAR 1853-4.

President,
THE RIGHT HON. LORD BRAYBROOKE, F.S.A.

WILLIAM HENRY BLAAUW, ESQ. M.A. F.S.A.
JOHN BRUCE, ESQ. Treas. S.A. *Director.*
JOHN PAYNE COLLIER, ESQ. V.P.S.A. *Treasurer.*
WILLIAM DURRANT COOPER, ESQ. F.S.A.
BOLTON CORNEY, ESQ. M.R.S.L.
PETER CUNNINGHAM, ESQ. F.S.A.
SIR HENRY ELLIS, K.H., F.R.S., Dir.S.A.
EDWARD FOSS, ESQ. F.S.A.
THE REV. JOSEPH HUNTER, F.S.A.
THE REV. LAMBERT B. LARKING, M.A.
SIR FREDERICK MADDEN, K.H. F.R.S.
FREDERIC OUVRY, ESQ. F.S.A.
THE RT. HON. LORD VISCOUNT STRANGFORD, F.R.S. F.S.A.
WILLIAM J. THOMS, ESQ. F.S.A., *Secretary.*
SIR CHARLES GEORGE YOUNG, Garter, F.S.A.

The COUNCIL of the CAMDEN SOCIETY desire it to be understood that they are not answerable for any opinions or observations that may appear in the Society's publications; the Editors of the several works being alone responsible for the same.

INTRODUCTION.

The Letters of the Lady Brilliana Harley are published from a collection of family papers in the possession of her descendant the Lady Frances Vernon Harcourt, of Brampton Bryan, Herefordshire. The MSS. had been neglected at Eywood, the seat of the Harleys in that county, until within the last few years, when they were rescued from ruin, and arranged by the Lady Frances, to whose charge they were committed by her father, Edward, the fifth Earl of Oxford. It is not improbable, that they were left at Eywood by Edward Harley, the Auditor of the Imprest, who resided there, being himself the second son of Sir Edward Harley, to whom most of the Letters are addressed, and to whose piety, no doubt, their preservation is due.

It will be remembered, that upon failure of issue male of Robert Harley, the first Earl of Oxford, by the death of his son Edward, the founder of the Harleian Library, the title passed to the son of the auditor his brother, and thence descended to the late Earl, at whose death, whilst these pages are in the press (January 1853) the title became extinct.

The present volume comprises all the Letters in the collection written by the Lady Brilliana, which are printed from transcripts made by the Editor, with scrupulous fidelity to the originals.

INTRODUCTION.

Referring to Collins' "Historical Collections of the noble families of Cavendish, Holles, Vere, Harley and Ogle," (Lond. 1752) for the earlier notices of the distinguished family of Harley, it may be well, for the illustration of these letters, to state that Sir Robert Harley, the husband of the Lady Brilliana, was the son of Thomas Harley, of Brampton Bryan Castle, by Margaret daughter of Sir Andrew Corbet, of Morton Corbet in the county of Salop, and born at Wigmore Castle, and baptised there 1st March, 1579.[a] His father, born about 1548, was sheriff 36° Elizabeth, and again in the last year of that reign and in the first of James, in which year he had the grant from the King of the honour of Wigmore Castle. He was in frequent state employments,[b] in the council of William Lord Compton, President of the Marches of Wales, and "very considerable for his affluence both of fortune and ability, and distinguished himself by the sagacity of his counsels to the King, against the measures then in pursuit, as tending to involve his Majesty or his son in a war with his people." Quitting public employment, he retired to his estate, where he lived in the exercise of a noble hospitality, and died at an advanced age, and was buried at Brampton Bryan 19th March, 1631.[c]

The mother of Sir Robert having died when he was young, his early education was entrusted to his uncle Richard Harley, an accomplished scholar. He afterwards entered Oriel college,[d] under the tutorage of the Rev. Cadwallader Owen,[e] reputed a great disputant, and commonly known as "Sic Doceo;" at which place he must have been held in high esteem, for on the motion of the Provost, 1641,[f] his arms were placed in a window of the new hall, built about this time, where they still are to be seen. Having taken the degree of Bachelor of Arts, he removed to the Inner Temple,[g] where he associated with men of the first rank and influence in that society, and remained there until the coronation of

[a] Wigmore Register.
[b] Collins, p. 197.
[c] Brampton Bryan Register.
[d] The Auditor's Notes.
[e] Wood's Fasti by Bliss, i. 455.
[f] Letter in Appendix.
[g] Collins, p. 198.

INTRODUCTION.

King James,[h] at which he was made one of the Knights of the Bath. In 16th July, 1604, he was made Forester of Boringwood or Bringwood Chase, in the county of Hereford, with the office of the Pokership (the nature of which office is now involved in obscurity), and custody of the forest or chase of Prestwood, and in the 7th of King James he obtained a grant to himself, his heirs, and assigns for ever, for a weekly market and annual fair at Wigmore.

[h] 15th July, 1603.

Authorities given in Collins.

Marrying early, in the life-time of his father,[a] he resided for some time at Stanage Lodge, in the parish of Brampton; and whilst interesting himself in rural pursuits, in the improvement of breeds of cattle, sheep, and horses, and other branches of agriculture, devoted much of his time to everything connected with the business and welfare, religious and secular, of the county of Hereford, of which he was a magistrate and deputy lieutenant. He represented the borough of Radnor in the parliament 1° and 12° James,[b] and was elected one of the knights for Herefordshire in 21° James, and in 15°, 16° of Charles, which last beginning 3rd Nov. 1640, continued sitting until 1653; a parliament which, notwithstanding the dissolution of the monarchy and the summoning of no less than four parliaments by the usurping power, was re-assembled in 1659, when a Bill was passed for its dissolution,[c] and for calling another parliament, which met 25th April, 1660, and restored the monarchy.

[a] Notice of Rectors of Brampton Bryan in Harl. MSS. Brit. Museum.

[b] Willis's Notitia Parliamentaria.

[c] 16 March, 1659-60.

Sir Robert was a man of wit, learning, and piety, but of an austere and decided character. As a patriot, he was zealous and active for the redress of the many grievances under which the people of England had too just grounds of complaint; and in his religion he was deeply imbued with the views of the Puritans, of which party he was one of the most decided and influential members.

The Journals of the House of Commons, especially during the Long Parliament, evince how incessantly and zealously he was occupied in committees of that house, and in conferences with the Lords,

viii INTRODUCTION.

on almost all the most important questions of the times. To him, in committees with others, were referred the petitions of Leighton,[a] Prynne,[b] Bastwick,[c] and other sufferers under the Star Chamber; also, the consideration of the jurisdiction of the High Commission Courts of Canterbury and York,—of the Star Chamber, and also of the court of the Council of the Marches of Wales;[d] the acts and abuses of which courts had given such great cause of discontent. He was active in the proceedings against the Lord Strafford,—in the Scotch and Irish affairs,[e]—in carrying out also the scheme of adventures for Ireland,[f]—of the joint committee of the Commons with the Lords, to receive from the Scotch Commissioners what they had to communicate to both or either house of parliament.[g] He was busily engaged in the organizing of the militia,—in providing means for carrying on the civil wars;[h] lending money and plate himself, and encouraging others to do the same, towards the support of the Parliamentary cause; in which he was of the committee for the garrison[i] of Gloucester and the security of the western counties.[k] Sir Robert was on the committee for the Great Seal;[l] and also on an ordinance of Parliament for upholding the trade and settling the government of the Company and Fellowship of Merchants trading to the East Indies, &c. and also to the Levant seas. He was chairman of the committees for Elections, for the Universities, for Emmanuel College, also of one of the subdivisions of the Grand Committee for Religion. To Sir Robert was entrusted the preparation of the order to prohibit the wearing of the surplice in cathedral, collegiate, and parish churches,[m] and for the better observing of the Lord's Day. He was of the committee to take into consideration the removing of the Communion tables in the Universities and the Inns of Court,[n] the Book of Sports, and all other matters of innovation,—of the committee for superstitious pictures,—of a committee,[o] consisting of Strode, Cromwell, Hampden, and himself, to prepare letters to be sent to the Uni-

[a] Journals of House of Com. 13 Nov. 1640.
[b] 3 Dec. 1640.
[c] 17 Dec. 1640.
[d] 23 Dec. 1640.
[e] 3 Dec. 1641. 20 Dec. 1641. 24 Feb. 1641.
[f] 20 May, 1642.
[g] 3 Feb. 1643-4.
[h] 19 Sept. 1642. 6 Dec. 1643.
[i] 23 Sept. 1643.
[k] 27 Oct. 1643.
[l] 9 Oct. 1643. 10 Feb. 1643-4.
[m] 30 Sept. 1643.
[n] 30 Aug. 1641.
[o] 11 Feb. 1641-2.

versities concerning the complaint of pressing subscriptions upon young graduates, on taking their degrees; and also of the committee on an Act to enable Members of Parliament to discharge their consciences in the proceedings of Parliament.[a] It would be tedious to refer to the very frequent connection of his name in the Journals of the House of Commons with all these matters, or with the proceedings against the Archbishop, Bishops, and other ecclesiastical persons:—The suppression of the surplice, the removal of innovations, the destruction of altars and crosses, superstitious images and inscriptions, were all highly congenial with his convictions, and not less so the rigid observance of the Sabbath, and private and public fasts. We are not surprised to find him of the committee with Pym, Strode, Nath. Fienes, Hampden and others, "to prepare a declaration of the unanimous consent and resolution of the House, for the defence of the religion established, of the King's person, and the liberty of the subject, be it by oath or any other way;"[b] and among the first of the House of Commons to take the Protestation; again, with Selden,[c] Nath. Fienes, Hampden, Sir Benjamin Rudyard and others, "to prepare and present unto the House a form of declaration, which may express the intentions of the House, for the vindicating the doctrine of the Church from the aspersions laid upon it, and concerning government, discipline, and public liturgy, and concerning consultation to be had with divines thereon, and to consider of the establishing and maintaining of a preaching ministry throughout the kingdom, and the ways and means how to do it, and renewing the Protestation of the 3 May 1641, in the Sacred Vow and Covenant of 6 June 1643; and afterwards naturally engaged busily in framing and taking the Solemn League and Covenant.[d] On the death and in place of Pym, Sir Robert was elected into the committee of the assembly of divines,[e] and zealously devoted himself to its proceedings; he reported the " amendments to the Ordinance for esta-

[a] Journals of H. of Com. 3 July, 1641.
[b] 3 May, 1641.
[c] 4 April, 1642.
[d] 25 Sept. 1643.
[e] 15 Dec. 1643.

x INTRODUCTION.

^a 12 Dec. 1644. blishing the Directory for Public Worship,"ᵃ and took an active part in almost all other deliberations of that intolerant and unconstitutional body.

He had wisdom to discern the tendency and ambitious ends of the army, and boldness to act upon his conviction. Happily he was averse to the extreme measures against the King, and was with his son Edward amongst the members made prisoners, (6 Dec. 1648,) for voting " that the King's answer to the propositions of both Houses was a ground to proceed upon in the settlement of the kingdom's peace." He had been made by Charles I. Master and Warden of

ᵇ Pat. 2 Car. I. quoted by Collins.
ᶜ Journ. Ho. of Com. 6 March, 1642-3.
3 May, 1643.
5 May, 1643.

the Mint;ᵇ subsequently displaced by the King; restored, however, by an ordinance of Parliament, 6 May, 1643,ᶜ and continued to hold the office under the proviso of " *the self-denying ordinance*," passed 3 April, 1645. After the death of the King, upon a report of the Council of State, that the Master of the Mint refused to stamp and coin with any other stamp than formerly, the House ordered a trial of the pix to be made at his expense, and he was put out of the office, and Dr. Gourdon the physician succeeded to it, with

ᵈ Whitelocke's Memorials, p. 388, ed. 1682.

a salary, according to Whitelocke,ᵈ of £4000 a-year; which is said also to have been the salary in Sir Robert's time.

ᵉ MS. Notice of Rectors of Brampton Bryan, in Harl. Coll. B. Mus.

Sir Robert sustained great losses in the civil wars;ᵉ his castles destroyed, parks and farms plundered of about 500 deer, of 800 excellent sheep, 30 goodly cows, and other cattle in proportion, with a stud of 30 breeding mares and young colts; and suffering much from the detention of his rents, and himself an object of suspicion, he retired into the country, and repaired in some degree the waste of his estate; but in his later years he was much afflicted with the gout and stone, all which troubles he bore with patience and resignation to the Divine will.

It is recorded in his funeral sermon, that about three days before his death, when he arose and went to prayer, as he constantly used to do, though not able to enlarge in prayer, because of weakness, he prayed for the ruin of Anti-Christ, and for the churches of God beyond the sea, naming Savoy, Switzerland and Germany. The persecution of the Protestants of Piedmont had recently elicited the sympathy of Cromwell himself; who, receiving the sad news on the day on which the French treaty was to have been sealed,[a] refused to sign it until the King and Cardinal undertook to assist him in getting right done to them. He had nobly sent 2,000*l.* from his own purse, and appointed a day of solemn humiliation and a general collection, on which immense sums were contributed, for their relief. On this occasion Milton wrote his sonnet:

[a] 3 June 1655. Cromwell's Letters, &c. by Carlyle, 1846. Neal's Hist. of the Puritans, vol. iv. p. 140, Toulmin's Edition.

> "Avenge, O Lord, thy slaughtered saints, whose bones
> Lie scattered on the Alpine mountains cold," &c. &c.

and Mr. Morland (afterwards Sir Samuel Morland) was sent ambassador to remonstrate with the Duke of Savoy, and on his return published "The History of the Evangelical Churches of the Valleys of Piedmont, 1658."

Sir Robert had ever been the friend and patron of learning and religion, both of which he sincerely loved; and many able ministers were settled in his neighbourhood through his influence, and found a shelter from trouble and persecution under his roof. To him were many works dedicated; among others there is "a Treatise on Simeon's Song; or Instructions advertising how to live holily and dye happily:" (Lond. 1659), composed for his use, when weakness and old age confined him to his chamber, by Timothy Woodroffe.[b] Woodroffe had been tutor to Hobbs of Malmesbury, and had suffered himself much in the beginning of the civil wars, from both parties; through Sir Robert's kindness he had been preferred to the rectory of Kingsland, in his own gift, and through his influence made one of the parliamentary preachers in the cathedral of Hereford.

[b] Wood's Athenæ. vol. iii. p. 1113.

Sir Robert died at Brampton Bryan 6th Nov. 1656, and was there buried 10th Dec.[c] on which occasion the church at Brampton,

[c] B. Bryan, Reg.

events, both domestic and foreign, of the momentous years in which she lived.

The letters are printed in the order of their dates, some few undated are so placed by authority of internal evidence. Upon a more careful examination of the contents, No. 106 appears to be misdated in the year (not an uncommon mistake, when, as in these letters, the old style is used, and the new year commenced 25th March), and misplaced, and the undated letter No. 134, misplaced.

All the letters except the first, dated Ragley, the seat of her father in Warwickshire, are from Bromton or Brompton, now Brampton Bryan Castle. They are written in a bold and legible hand, with few contractions, and scarcely an erasure; but the use of capitals, and the spelling, not only of the names of persons and places, but of everyday words, are varied and irregular. A few of the letters are written by an amanuensis, in seasons of sickness, but signed by herself as usual, or with her initials. They were generally sent by an express messenger or the carrier, occasionally by a friend, or the tradesmen, but most rarely by the post of Hereford, Leominster, Shrewsbury, or Ludlow, then recently established, and not much to be depended upon: the insecurity of letters at this time gave rise to a variety of secret correspondence, one of which, very simple, is exemplified by Letters 188, 189, &c.

The earlier letters (1625—1633) are addressed to her husband; and the remainder (1638—1643), with the exception of a Letter to Sir Robert and two letters written to her friend Mrs. Wallcote of Wallcote, during her troubles at Brampton, to her son Edward, commencing in Oct. 1638, his residence in Oxford.

The letters are written with the greatest fondness of maternal affection, and abound with excellent remarks and advice on his studies, health and conduct in the University, with frequent allusions to affairs home and foreign. A deeply religious tone pervades the whole of them; it is scarcely possible to find a single letter without the evidences of practical piety. It is unnecessary to notice any particular passages. It is clear, that her mind was imbued with the doctrines and discipline of Calvin, which were at this time working powerfully in many of the most learned, pious and patriotic people, lay and clerical, of this country. Numerous allusions attest the accuracy of her information, and the interest she took in public affairs, and in the proceedings of the Parliament. She deeply sympathized in the feelings of her husband in his varied employments, and entered fully into his interests and pursuits. They agreed in regarding Episcopacy as Anti-Christ, and nothing short of "down with it, down with it, even to the ground," would satisfy their zeal.

The ministrations of Brampton Bryan under two successive rectors, accorded with their views, and afforded them ample opportunities of religious exercises, in the observance of public and private fasts; how strictly they were there observed, appears by the memorandum now in the register of that parish, a copy of which will be found in the Notes.

The rectors here alluded to, were Thomas Pierson and Stanley Gower. The Rev: Thos. Peacock, Fellow of Brazennose college, had preceded Pierson, but appears from Froysell's sermon, already mentioned, never to have resided at Brampton. Sir Robert had no doubt been acquainted with him in Oxford, and not improbably derived benefit from his advice and instruction, as he was "highly esteemed for his great learning, great sanctity of life, and counsel," and was known as the convertor of Robert Bolton, a well-known puritan divine; by whom "an account of the last visitation, conflict, and death of Mr. Peacock was published, 1646."[a] Pierson had been brought up in Emmanuel college,[b] where he resided for several years, and was the friend of the learned Calvinist William Perkins, whose works he had been engaged in editing, and also in the publication of Brightman's work on the Apocalypse, and was known as a profound scholar and theologian. Instituted in 1612, he continued to reside at Brampton

[a] Wood's Athenæ, vol. ii. p. 514.
[b] MS. Notice of Rectors of Brampton Bryan, in Brit. Museum.

xvi INTRODUCTION.

until his death, 1633. In the early years of Pierson's residence, his ministrations had not been acceptable to Thomas Harley, the father of Sir Robert, who made frequent complaints of him to Bennett, Bishop of Hereford, who used to declare, with truth, "that he received letters from the father against Mr. Pierson, and from his son in his behalf." John Harley, the grandfather of Sir Robert, never adopted the reformed doctrines, and was a zealous Romanist, and was said to have given some protection at Brampton Castle to Parsons and Champion, the Jesuits. It may be inferred, therefore, that these differences arose out of the religious views now probably first put forth at Brampton; for it is said, "that a solemn day of prayer was observed at Stanage Lodge,[a] where Sir Robert and his most pious and virtuous lady (sister of Sir Richard Newport), Mr. Pierson and his godly family, and some few neighbours, presented supplications to the Lord, to turn the heart of Mr. Harley to express kindness to his son, and friendship towards Mr. Pierson; to which it pleased the Lord to give a most gracious answer of peace; for, within a very short time, Mr. Harley, by a trusty servant, sent to Sir Robert,—'Tell my son, I will take care of the concerns of the estate, and pay his debts; and tell him, I will be friends with Mr. Pierson, and then you will be a welcome messenger;' and, accordingly, he began and continued all expressions of high esteem and real friendship for him, and gave a copyhold estate to him and his wife for their joint lives, and in his enfeebled old age received his continual ministrations," and "to his dying day, no man, except in nearest relation to him, was more in his esteem, more dear unto him, or in whom he put more confidence, than Mr. Pierson."

In Brampton, Pierson set up the strict observance of the Ember weeks and public and private fasts, frequently alluded to in these letters, "the resort to which of many godly persons from remote places was as the flight of doves to the windows of holy light;"[b] and,

1602—1617.

[a] MS. Notes on the Rectors of Brampton Bryan, in the Brit. Museum.

[b] MS. Notes of Rectors, &c.

INTRODUCTION.

under authority from the Bishop of Hereford, a monthly lecture, in the adjoining parish of Leintwardine, in the manner of "the prophecyings" which had given so great offence to Queen Elizabeth, occasioning her displeasure with Archbishop Grindall, and calling forth his noble letter to her majesty;[a] after which model many other lectures were established in the neighbourhood. He was also one of the London feoffees for buying in impropriations,[b] and to maintain a constant preaching ministry where it was wanting; a design which was much applauded by the religious party in England, but which soon giving offence to the High Church party, was interrupted by the Star Chamber, when the tithes which had been purchased were seized for the King's use. He received young men into his house, to prepare for the Universities and holy orders; and in all these ways exercised a very great influence, not only in his own parish, but far and wide in that district, which is represented as having been in great religious darkness. A minister of this time, Mr. Gwalter Stephens, of Bishop's Castle, "who had lighted his candle at famous Mr. Pierson's,[b] of Brampton Bryan," used to say, that "when he preached, in his younger days, for a great space, there was never a preacher between him and the sea one way, and none near him the other, but one in Shrewsbury." Pierson objected not to the Liturgy or the gesture of kneeling in the receiving of the Lord's Supper, but scrupled the use of the surplice, and the cross in baptism; yet is said to have been liberal enough, to allow the use of both to his own curate. A Mr. Brice, of Henley upon Thames, was nominated on Pierson's death, but his old parishioners expressing their sense of the great loss they should sustain by his removal from them, he was allowed to relinquish it, and returned to his old charge, when Stanley Gower became rector, and a great blessing to the place, following the steps of Mr. Pierson.

Gower was a man of piety and learning, and had been brought up

[a] Grindall's Remains, Park. Soc. p 376.

[b] MS. Rectors of Brampton Bryan, Brit. Mus.

by Dr. Hoye, probably at Dublin, as he had been chaplain to Archbishop Usher for some time. His last ministration recorded in the register of Brampton is dated 1 May, 1642. He had been nominated and approved as one of the Assembly of Divines,[a] and removed at once to London, and became a constant attendant and active member in that assembly, being employed in the compilation of the Assembly's Confession of Faith and the larger and smaller Catechisms. He was one of the committee appointed by ordinance of Parliament for the examination and approval of such clergymen as petitioned for sequestered livings,[b] and himself in possession of one near Ludgate. He was also a select preacher before the House of Commons at St. Margaret's, and one of the presbyters and members of the Assembly to examine and ordain by imposition of hands all those whom they should judge qualified to be admitted to the sacred ministry.[c] No doubt he agreed with Sir Robert Harley in all such matters, and disapproving, like his patron, of the wicked designs upon the King, he was one of the ministers who assembled at Zion College,[d] and published " a serious and faithful representation of their judgment, in a letter to the General and his Council;" and also, "A Vindication of the London Ministers from the unjust aspersions cast upon their former actings for the Parliament, as if they had promoted the bringing the King to capital punishment."

But to return to the Lady Brilliana. Moving but little from home, her time was much given to her children and domestic matters—and, in the absence of Sir Robert, to the management of his estate, on which several judicious remarks will be found in these letters. The affairs of the country, in these sad times, afforded too great cause of anxiety to allow her to be a quiet observer of what was passing. It was but to be expected, on the breaking out of the Civil Wars, in a county which was generally devoted to the King's cause, that Brampton Bryan, the seat of one so influential on the other side, would soon

[a] Journals of the House of Commons, 23 April, 1642. MS. Notes on the Rectors of B. Bryan.

[b] Neal's History of the Puritans, by Toulmin, vol. iii. p. 89.

[c] Neal, vol. iii. p. 140.

[d] Neal, vol. iii. p. 491. 18 Jan. 1648-9.

INTRODUCTION. xix

attract a more than agreeable notice. Whilst Sir Robert was engaged in Parliament, she became an object of suspicion to her loyal neighbours, and after repeated minor provocations and threatenings, the plundering of his park of deer and game, and the withholding of his rents, the castle was surrounded by the soldiers of the royalists or "malignants," under Sir William Vavasour and Colonel Lingen.[a] Shut up now in Brampton Castle with her children, and neighbours "who resorted thither to keep themselves from the plunder and villanous usage then the practice of the Cavaliers,"[b] with the advice of Dr. Nathaniel Wright, a physician of Hereford, frequently in attendance upon her, and who now, with his wife, took up his quarters there, and devoted himself and his money to the cause, and that of a veteran, sent to her by Colonel Massey from Gloucester, and her own servants, she defended it with a prudence and valour worthy of her distinguished family. The siege commenced 25 July, 1643, "on a day on which she and her young children were engaged in prayer and humiliation for the mercy of God to avert the dreadful judgment then justly feared," and continued for six weeks; when the besiegers, alarmed by the operations in and about the Forest of Dean, were hurried off to the neighbourhood of Gloucester. "The first stroke of the Cavaliers in the siege was upon a poor aged blind man, who was without any provocation killed in the street."[c] During the siege, "the cook was shot by a poisoned bullet, and a running stream that furnished the village was poisoned." The church, parsonage house, and dwelling houses, together with the mill about a quarter of a mile off, with the buildings belonging to the castle, were all destroyed: and early in the following year, Sir Michael Woodhouse, governor of Ludlow (having been successful in his brutal attack on Hopton Castle,[d] which in its distress had received assistance from Brampton Castle,) came before it again, when, after a gallant defence made by the servants, under Dr. Wright's

[a] Letter CCIII.

[b] MS. Notice of Rectors.

[c] MS. Notice of Rectors.

[d] See the Journal of the Siege of Hopton Castle, by S. More, Esq. in Blakeway's Hist. of Sheriffs of Shropsh., p. 216—220.

xx INTRODUCTION.

direction, it surrendered at mercy only, and the inmates, including three of Sir Robert's younger children, were taken prisoners, after a siege of three weeks. There were taken 67 men, 100 arms, two barrels of powder, and a whole year's provisions.[a]

17 April, 1644.
[a] Mercurius Belgicus.

Lady Brilliana was of a delicate constitution; and, enfeebled by repeated attacks of illness and continued anxieties during her troubles, and the long absence of her husband and son, whom she fondly loved, she took a cold, alluded to in her last letter, and after a few days' illness died, soon after the raising of the first siege, in Oct. 1643, leaving three sons and four daughters, all baptised at Brampton, as follows:—Edward, 24 Oct. 1624; Robert, 16 April, 1626; Thomas, 13 Jan. 1627-8; Brilliana, 26 April, 1629; Dorothie, 12 Sept. 1630; Margaret, 25 Dec. 1631; and Elizabeth, 26 Oct. 1634.[b]

[b] Brampton Register.

Edward Harley, born at Brampton, 21 Oct. 1624, and baptised as above, three days afterwards, was as his mother, in his infancy, of a delicate constitution. Having passed some period at school, first in Shrewsbury and then at Gloucester, he was sent to Magdalen hall, at that time under the principal Dr. Wilkinson, and the tutorage of Edward Perkins, described by Calamy[c] "as a great man, a very ready and well studied divine, especially in school divinity, a great tutor, and particularly famous for his giving Mr. John Corbet (the historian of Gloucester, and a good divine) his education and the direction of his studies." Magdalen hall at this time was in Oxford what Emmanuel College was at Cambridge, a famous puritanical school, and several remarkable men had been there educated, on which account, no doubt, it was selected by Sir Robert for his son. Dr. Ingram, in his Memorials of Oxford, states, "as a house of learning, it could have been inferior to none in the university in eminence at that period, since in the year 1624, under the elder Wilkinson, it reckoned 300 students on the books, forty of whom

1605—1643.
[c] Baxter's Life by Calamy.

were Masters of Arts." He resided there for two academical years, until July 1640, but, on account of the unhealthy state of the place, his residence was broken in the following October term, when he joined his father in London, where he was at the opening of the Long Parliament, 3 Nov: of that year. He was present too, at the trial of Lord Strafford, in April of the following year, and at that time gave himself much to the proceedings of the Parliament. His mother was eagerly bent upon his entering public employment, and though only eighteen years of age, she exercised her interest among her friends, to secure his return as burgess for the city of Hereford, on the death of Mr. Weaver; in which, however, she failed. Remaining in London, he had a lodging in Lincoln's Inn, and was probably a member of that society; but in 1642 he became a captain of a troop of horse in the parliamentary army, which he joined under the command of Sir William Waller, and in a few weeks had himself the command of a regiment of foot. In one of Sir William Waller's skirmishes about this time,[a] probably at Lansdown, his horse was shot, "and on another occasion a musket-ball,[b] levelled at his heart, was bent flat against his armour, (not reckoned of such proof,) without harm." He distinguished himself particularly in the conflict at Red Marley, near Ledbury, where "at the head of his troop, he gallantly and in good order gave the charge, beat the enemy from their ambuscadoes, put their horse to flight, and in an instant of time got into the van of their foot, cutting some down, and taking others prisoners, so that few escaped."[c] He there received a severe wound in the arm, which obliged him to seek surgical assistance in London; but he was again in the field early in the following year, and in the conflict between Prince Rupert and Colonel Massie,[d] near Ledbury, in which it is said "Massie was in great peril, as the Prince sought a personal encounter with him, and shot his horse." Edward Harley was here again hurt, and he is said to have

Letters cvi., cx., cxxxiv.

Letters cxcix., cc.

Letter ccii.
[a] 11 July, 1643.
[b] Sir Edward's retrospect of his life in App.

27 July, 1644.

[c] Corbet's Hist. Rel. of Mil. Gov. of Glouc. 1645, p. 111.

[d] 22 April, 1645. Webb's Historical Introduction to the Bibliotheca Gloucestrensis, p. ciii.

carried a bullet in his body to his death. He was ordered with his men to Plymouth in Nov: 1643,[a] made Governor of Monmouth 1644, and of Canon Frome, a garrison near Hereford, in 1645, and quartered with the Major-General at Marston, near Oxford, in May 1646.

On the disabling of Humphrey Coningsby, member for the county of Hereford, he was chosen member.[b] He was at this time warmly affected to the Presbyterian cause, which his father had so zealously espoused; but notwithstanding his devotion to that party, and the spirit with which his family was regarded by the Royalists, when the faction in the army began to form the scheme of a military government, he was among the first to perceive the intrigues of Cromwell and Fairfax, and afterwards openly to oppose them in the House of Commons, for which, with Denzell Holles and others, he was impeached by the army of high treason, "for that by their power the ordinance for disbanding the army did pass." He was now disabled by an order of the House[c] which was afterwards revoked,[d] and joining with his father in December following,[e] as before noticed, in favour of the King, they were by the army made prisoners. Henceforth he was an object of suspicion to Cromwell, and in 1650, on grounds of disaffection to the government, was summoned by letter from Major Winthrop at Leominster,[f] to appear at Hereford before the Commissioners of the Militia. This summons was followed by a visit from soldiers, who searched and read his papers, and carried him and Mr. Clogie, the minister of Wigmore, to Hereford; both his brother Robert then M.P. for Radnor, and his brother Thomas, being at this time prisoners at Bristol. Refusing a bond urged upon him at Hereford for his appearance in London, he gave a promise to be there at his father's house from 18 Aug: to 1st of Sept: following, which, under authority of a pass from Wroth Rogers,[g] of the city of Hereford, he was enabled to keep. What proceedings were then taken do not appear, but he was not permitted a residence in Herefordshire for ten years.

[a] J. C. H. 13 Nov. 1643. Whitelocke.
[b] 11 Sept. 1646. Cobbett's Parliamentary History, vol. ii. p. 609.
Ibid.
[c] 29 Jan. 1647-8.
[d] 8 June, 1648.
[e] 7 Dec. 1648.
[f] Letter in Appendix, pp. 233-236.
[g] Appendix, p. 235.

In a memorandum which will be found in the Appendix,[a] he records, "that he was preserved from the cruelty of that power which put to death holy Mr. Love." Love was a Presbyterian minister;[b] the martyr of the cause; he was charged with treason, tried, and condemned, as implicated in the plot with the Scots, for bringing in Charles II., and was executed on Tower Hill.[c] When on the scaffold, attended by Manton, Calamy and other Presbyterian ministers, he exulted in the cause for which he was about to suffer; declaring in a calm and manly manner his dislike of the Commonwealth, and his detestation of the Engagement, saying, "I am for a regulated mixed monarchy, which I judge to be one of the best governments in the world. I opposed the late King and his forces, because I am against screwing up monarchy into tyranny, as much as against those who would pull it down into anarchy. I was never for putting the King to death, whose person I did promise in my covenant to preserve, and I judge it an ill way to cure the body politic, by cutting off the political head."

In the Parliament of 1656 he was again chosen for the county of Hereford, and being again secluded with other members, he was one who signed and published the Remonstrance,[d] "that they would not be frightened or flattered to betray their country, and give up their religion, lives, and estates, to be at the will, to serve the Protector's lawless intentions;" setting forth his depredations, and the power he had assumed; protesting "that the assembly at Westminster was not the representative body of England, and that all such members as shall take on them to approve the forcible exclusion of other chosen members, or shall sit and vote, or act by the name of the Parliament of England, while to their knowledge many of the chosen members are so by force shut out, ought to be reputed betrayers of the liberties of England and adherents to the capital enemy of the Commonwealth." It was the lot of himself and family still to lie under suspicion in the

[a] P. 247.
[b] Marsden's History of the Later Puritans, p. 347. Neal's History of the Puritans. Wood's Athenæ, vol. iii. p. 278.
[c] 22 Aug. 1661.
[d] Whitelocke's Memorials, p. 643, ed. Lond. 1682.

time of Richard Cromwell, when his brother Robert was arrested at Kynsham Court, in Herefordshire, not without grounds of disaffection to the Government.

At the Restoration, Edward Harley was a zealous asserter of the royal cause, and met the King at Dover, and was shortly afterwards made Governor of Dunkirke, of which garrison he took immediate possession. During the short time he held that charge, he much improved and strengthened it; and it is a fact which Marshal Schomberg owned to Sir Edward, when he came over with the Prince of Orange in 1688, "that the French had often during his time attempted to take it by surprise."[a] Lord Lansdown, in his Vindication of General Monk, gives this account of Harley:[b]—
"General Monk foresaw early what might happen to be the fate of Dunkirk, and took his precaution in the very beginning to preserve it, by placing Sir Edward Harley in the command, a man of public spirit, firm to the interests of his country, and not to be biassed, tempted, or deluded to be assistant in any thing contrary to it; which appeared clearly afterwards, for the first step taken, as soon as the treaty was projected, was to remove that gallant man, and place another General there." Nor was he deceived in the estimate of Sir Edward, for he strenuously opposed the sale of it to the French, and persevered so far with the House of Commons, to pass a resolution to prepare an Act, that it should never be alienated, but be part of the King's hereditary dominions. Neither threats or promises could prevail with him to be a party to its surrender. It being known that he would refuse to deliver it up to the French, he was removed, but received a most honourable discharge of the trust from the King.* "When he took leave of the King before the

[a] The Auditor's notes.
[b] Quoted by Collins.

* Collins gives the commission for his appointment (14 July, 1660), and the order for his giving up the town to Lord Retorfort or Rutherford (22 May, 1661), Lord R's discharge (28 May, 1661), and also King Charles's release (3 Dec. 1663).

INTRODUCTION. XXV

Lord General,[a] the Duke of Albemarle, he told him that the guns, [a] Collins, p. 204.
stores, and ammunition he left them were worth more than the
French were to give for the place (500,000*l.*), and that he had left
him one thing more, that his Majesty might not think of, and that
was 10,000*l.* in an iron chest, which he had saved, against a siege or
any other exigency that might happen." By a fragment of a letter
given in the Appendix,[b] it will be seen that the Earl of Montague was [b] Appendix, p. 245.
told by the King "that he would not have parted with Dunkirk if he
could have been permitted to retain Colonel Harley in that post,
which he would have preserved for his Majesty; but, said the
King, I am continually disturbed, because he is represented to be
a notorious Presbyterian." The King was clearly not insensible to
the worth of the man who had declined a viscountcy, lest his zeal and
his services for the restoration of the ancient Government should be
reproached as proceeding from ambition and not conscience; and
his being made a Knight of the Bath was done without his knowledge: when employed at Dunkirk, the King inserted his name in
the list, with his own hand.

Sir Edward Harley was a member in all the Parliaments of Charles
the Second, after the Restoration, either for the town of Radnor or the
county of Hereford; and, as he complied not with the corrupt measures
of the Court, so he never entered into the plans of others, who, under
pretence of serving the public, pursued their own interest or revenge.
He vigorously opposed all the acts for persecuting the Dissenters, and
the act which made the holy sacrament of the Lord's Supper a civil test;
and, when King James II. came to the throne, and set up a dispensing
power, under cloak of which, he intended to bring in Popery, he endeavoured, without success, to prevail with Croft, bishop of Hereford, and
with the Dissenters of that county, with whom he had justly a great
influence, not to read the King's declaration, nor make any address upon
it: and neither he nor any of his family ever took any oath to that King.

Though he was a favourer of such as dissented from the Church of England for conscience sake, and sometimes went to hear Mr. Baxter and others in London,[a] which brought him under suspicion of being still a favourer of the Presbyterian cause, yet he constantly attended church; and having, as his son Edward says, "by the grace of God, and a constant reading of the scriptures, attained a very Christian temper, he never engaged in the narrow principles with which several parties in the Church had embroiled themselves and the country:" a confirmation of which will be seen in his letter to Lord Clarendon, in the Appendix.[b] Sir Edward was a good and religious man, untainted by the evils of that most licentious age, and during the reign of King James "he weekly spent the greater part of one day, either alone or with some of his family, in imploring the mercy of God, that the storm which seemed then to be falling on the nation might be averted."

At the commencement of the Revolution he exerted himself with his sons on behalf of the Prince of Orange, and was at once made Governor of Worcester by the gentry there assembled; which city, by his great prudence, was kept in absolute quiet, whilst most others felt the shock of that great change. He was unanimously elected in the first Parliament of King William for the county of Hereford, and, consistently with the high principles which had ever actuated him, avoided all place and recompence, but devoted himself to the obtaining of such laws as might be of real service to his country; and by his means the act for abolishing the arbitrary court of the Marches of Wales was passed. To the second Parliament his return was factiously opposed, under the cry of his being an enemy to the Church; but, the successful candidate dying within a few months, he was again unanimously elected, and continued, in that and the succeeding Parliaments, constantly to oppose the extravagant ways that were taken for running the nation in debt, by raising funds

[a] Auditor Harley's Notes.

[b] P. 240-241.

under great discounts, whereby a dependence was created on the minister, and vast estates obtained . . He was much regarded in the House of Commons for his sound reasoning, and frequently closed the debates. He was well acquainted with the character of men, yet in public avoided saying anything that might the least prejudice the reputation of any person. His conversation was very entertaining; having read much of history and retained what he read, and having himself been engaged in many of the most stirring events of his own times. The Auditor records:—"Our father, Sir Edward Harley, may be truly said to have had all the accomplishments of a gentleman. His features were very exact, and (he) had great quickness in his eyes, which commanded respect. His temper was naturally very passionate, though mixed with the greatest tenderness and humanity. His passion he kept under a strict restraint, and had a manner totally subdued; but his generosity and tender compassion to all objects of charity continued to his last." He was not less generous than brave. Sir Henry Lingen having been engaged in the siege of Brampton castle, his estate was laid under sequestration, and the profits thereof ordered to be applied to make satisfaction to Sir Edward. After an inventory of all his goods and personal estate was taken, Sir Edward waited upon the Lady Lingen, and having asked whether that was a perfect inventory, he presented it to her, with all his right to the same. His cousin Smyth having cut off the entail of his estate, left it to Sir Edward; but this he gave up at once to the next of kin. As a testimony of his unfeigned love for religion, and its public maintenance, he not only rebuilt the church at Brampton Bryan in his father's life-time, but augmented the livings of Brampton Bryan, Leintwardine, Wigmore, Lyngen, Kington and Stow:" and on the death of his mother-in-law, becoming interested in the lease of the impropriate tithes of Folden in Norfolk, the property of Caius College, he proposed surrendering the same, on condition of its perpetual annexation to the vicarage;

Auditor Harley's Notes—

xxviii INTRODUCTION.

which was effected, thereby augmenting the value of it to 100*l.* a-year: and when the College offered him the nomination to the living, then void, he only so far availed himself of it, as to request the person to be nominated should be first approved by his father's friend, Dr. Tuckney, the Master of St. John's College, and at that time Professor of Divinity in Cambridge. His letters to the Master and Fellows, and also to Dr. Tuckney, will be found in the Appendix, together with a memorandum of the Master and Fellows relative to the business.

<small>Appendix, page 237.</small>

<small>Appendix XI. p. 245.</small>

The Appendix contains a letter of Sir William Gregory, which, bidding Sir Edward to the funeral of John, Lord Scudamore, records the friendship which existed between these two worthies of Herefordshire, who had taken opposite parts in the Civil Wars. Truly, they were among the excellent of the earth. They loved and feared God, and left substantial proof of their devotion to His cause, in the restoration to the Church of tithes, of which she had been despoiled.

For the two or three last years of his life he wisely retired from public, and, as his father and grandfather before him, died in peace at Brampton Bryan, 8 Dec. 1700. So exemplary was his virtue, and love to his country, that he was called by discerning persons, "ultimus Anglorum."

<small>Auditor's notes.</small>

<small>Collins.</small>

Sir Edward was twice married: firstly, 26 June, 1654, to Mary, daughter of Sir William Button, of Parkgate, in co. Devon, by whom he had issue:—

<small>Letter in Appendix, p. 218.</small>

Brilliana, wife of William Popham, of Tewkesbury:
Martha, wife of Samuel Hutchins, of London, merchant:
And two Maries, who died young.

Secondly, to Abigail, daughter of Nathaniel Stephens, of Essington, in co. of Gloucester, (by whom his children were allied to Sir Francis Walsingham, Sir Philip Sydney, and the Earl of Essex,) and by her had four sons and one daughter: viz.—

Robert, the Earl of Oxford:
Edward, the Auditor of the Imprest:
Nathaniel, a merchant, who died at Aleppo:
Brian, who died young:
And Abigail, who died unmarried 1726.

Lady Frances Vernon Harcourt's collections contain many letters of Sir Edward, but none written to his Mother, or during her life-time. They were, no doubt, all preserved and treasured up by one who loved him so fondly, and must have perished, with many valuables, in the ruin of the castle, when a considerable library of MSS. and printed books was destroyed. Portraits remain of Thomas Harley, Esq., Sir Robert Harley by Oliver, and Sir Edward by Cooper, all engraved by Vertue, and published in Collins's Historical Collection; and there is a portrait of the Lady Brilliana Harley still in the possession of her descendant, Lord Rodney, and now at his seat at Berrington, in the county of Hereford.

In addition to the originals, the Editor has had the use of a complete transcript of them, made by the Lady Frances Vernon Harcourt, and illustrated by her own notes; and it would be unjust to his friend and neighbour, the Rev. John Webb, of Tretire, whose accurate knowledge of the history of the times to which these letters refer is well known, if he did not here gratefully acknowledge the ready and valuable advice he has at all times received from him in the preparation of this Introduction and the notes which accompany the Letters.

Bridstow Vicarage, near Ross,
   2 *Dec.* 1853.

THE CHARACTER OF SIR ROBERT HARLEY, TAKEN FROM A SERMON PREACHED AT HIS FUNERAL, ENTITLED, "THE BELOVED DISCIPLE," BY THOMAS FROYSELL, MINISTER OF CLUN, IN SHROPSHIRE. LOND. 1658.

We have marched all this day in sable posture: I pray we may all walk in white one day with Jesus Christ. This present scene of sorrow becomes us. As the aire receives severall impressions from the superiour bodies, she looks lightsome when the heavens shine, and sad again, when they look black again upon her; so, when the celestiall providence shall change her countenance upon us, 'tis our duty to change our aspects.

Our losse is very great. We have lost a chiefe man, one that was a common and publick good. The sun of this country is set. Sir Robert Harley gave a great light to these parts. We are wont to say of fair weather, "'tis pitty it should doe any hurt," because we are loth it should ever leave us. I am sure, I may say, 'tis pitty that good men should dye and leave us—that brave Sir Robert Harley should ever be missed among us; he was as choyce a piece as our age hath known; a man that was the rariety of men; a man whom his descent had elevated above the rate of ordinary men; and a man whose veins free grace had filled with nobler blood; a man of whom I may say, in the words of my text, "Thou art greatly beloved." (Page 1—3.)

(Page 97 to the end.) And this leads me now into the discourse of this great man and great saint, whose funeralls we at this time celebrate. He was a great man by birth; he was a great saint by grace; and therefore greatly beloved. I shall not speak the greatnesse and antiquity of his honourable family, although these shining adjuncts set him out in brightnesse and splendour to the eye of the world; yet, because they make not a man greatly beloved in the eye of God, I shall rather speak of those titles of honour that are not written in dust—those things that did greaten his greatnesse.

I know he had his humanities, for we are all but men till we are glorified saints, and then our infirmities as well as sorrows shall be done away; as all tears shall be wiped from our eyes, so all stains shall be washed from our natures.

My language is not a match for his excellent vertues. His spirituall lineaments and beauties are above my pencill. I want art to draw his picture. And though little grace seems much (nay, more than it is,) in a great person, yet I think I may safely say that his gracious greatnesse did transcend his outward greatnesse. If other saints are candles, he was a torch. If others are starres, he was a starre of greater magnitude. He made his outward greatnesse but a servant to the exercise of his graces. He was a copy for all great men to transcribe in all descending ages. He was a man of desires: a saint in great letters: famous (I think) throughout the land, one where or other, for his graces. To my knowledge eminent ministers did most eminently prize him. Sir Robert Harley was a sweet name upon their lips. When they spake of him, they would speak with honour and delight in him.

(1). I have heard himself say, that God (in His great mercy) had kept him unstained from grosse sins: a great priviledge and favour of Heaven! More than many a worthy saint can say, that his life (like a fair sheet of paper) should be preserved pure and white from foul blots, and then written upon with golden letters of grace. I must tell you, this is a lovely manuscript.

(2). He was the first that brought the Gospell into these parts. This country lay under a vaile of darknesse till he began to shine. He set his first choyce upon that transcendent holy man, Mr. Peacock, in Oxford, but God took him to Heaven, which prevented his coming to Brampton. Then Providence led him to the knowledge of that now blessed servant of God, Mr. Peirson, whose exemplary graces and ministery shed a rich influence abroad the country.

And as God removed godly ministers by death, he continued still a succession of them to you. Not onely Brampton Brian, but ye also of Wigmore, and ye of Leyntwardine, owe your very souls to Sir Robert Harley, who maintained your ministers upon his own cost, that they might feed you with the Gospell of Jesus Christ.

(3). He was the pillar of religion among us. How would he countenance godlinesse? His greatnesse professing Christ brought profession into credit, and cast a lustre on it Profession began to grow and spread itselfe under his shade

(4). His planting of godly ministers, and then backing them with his authority, made religion famous in this little corner of the world. Oh! what comfortable times had we (through Gods mercy) before the wars! How did our publick meetings shine with his exemplary presence in the midst of them!

(5). He would feed heartily upon the ordinances. He came with hunger to them, and did afterward digest them into reall nutriment. How would his heart melt under the word, and dissolve into liquid tears! I have seen him thaw and distill as the weeping trees under the winter sun-beams.

(6). He did deal much in prayer. He would embark no undertaking till he had sought God. He would frait his vessell, hoyse up the mast, and spread the sailes: (he would not neglect the meanes) yet he would, by prayer, beg the winds, and wait the gales of Providence to set his ship a-going.

(7). His house was an house of prayer: 'twas the center where the saints met to seek God.

(8). He was noble in his liberality to the saints in their wants: their necessity was his opportunity.

(9). He was spirited with a keen hatred of sin and prophanenesse. He would not, I may say, he could not brook it, in any under his roof. He would often say, he cared not for the service of one that feared not God.

(10). He was a friend to Gods friends. They that did love God had his love. Gods people were his darlings: they had the cream of his affections. If any poor Christian were crush'd by malice or wrong, whither would they fly, but to Sir Robert Harley?

(11). Againe, if at any time he had been angry, he would quickly desire to be reconciled; saying, "We must take heed least the devill come between."

(12). He loved his children most tenderly; I think no man in the world carried more of a fathers dearnesse in him than he did, yet he would never bear with any evill in any of his children; he would often say to them, I desire nothing of you but your love, and that you keep from sin.

(13) The soule of his religion was sincerity; he knew no end but to serve God and to be saved. I shall, in this place, bring in a notable speech of his about a year and a halfe since: when a most eminent minister of the land came to visit him, and ask't him what comfortable evidences he had of his salvation? he answered, "he had nothing to rely upon but Jesus Christ, and he knew no religion but sincerity."

(14). He was a great honourer of Godly ministers; he carried them in his bosome; of all men in the world they sat next his heart, he did hug them in his dearest embraces; I must tell you he was their sanctuary in evill times. How oft hath he interposed between them and dangers! when sinfull greatnesse did frown upon them, this great man would show himselfe upon the stage for them. When Mr. Pierson was questioned before the Bishop, Sir Robert Harley was not afraid to appear constantly in his defence; I could tell you that he felt the frowns and displeasures of a near relation rather than he would desert that servant of Jesus Christ. When Dr. Stoughton and Mr. Workman were in trouble, Sir Robert Harley accompanied them to the High Commission, which made the Archbishop dart frowns upon him.

(15). He was also a magistrate; and herein (I must tell you) he was animated with a most nimble soul of zeal against sin. He was full of spirits against all dishonours done to God; he was a terrour to evill works; he knew no respect of persons in a businesse, wherein God was wronged. Among other things, how would he vindicate the Sabbath from contempt! Prophannesse durst not appear upon the face of it. By this means the congregations were frequented on the Lords dayes, and many thousand soules, prevented from their sinfull sports, sate under the droppings of the word.

(16). He paid a dear devotion of love to the Lords day (that pearle of the week). When the licentious sinfulnesse of times cryed it down, how often have I heard him plead it up! with excellency of arguments! and in his own practice he rose alwayes earlier upon the Lords day (and dayes of humiliation), even to the times of his extreme weaknesse. He rejoyced still when the Sabbath came, and was usually more chearfull that day than others, even in his sicknesse. He wept much when his servants suffered him to sleep on the Lords day later than he used, although he had not rested all that night.

(17). He was one that did swim deep in the tide of fasting and humiliation. I have seldom seen an heart broken upon such a day as his was wont to be. He was one that did stand in the gap, that did sigh and cry for the abominations done in the land, and for it God set a mark upon his forehead. Though his castle was ruined, yet God set a mark upon him, when the naked sword, that messenger of death, walkt the land, and lookt keen upon you; and God set His seal of safety upon his dear Lady. That noble Lady and Phœnix of Women dyed in peace; though surrounded with drums and noyse of war, yet she took her leave in peace. The sword had no force against her, as long as God preserved her, He preserved the place where she was. And the Man cloath'd with linnen set a mark also upon the forehead of his children; for when they with the castle were surrendered up, God made their enemies to treat them gently; he had his jewells sent safely to him by the hand of Providence.

(18). He was (I know not how oft) chosen by his country to the High Senate and Court of Parliament, and there (that I may speak within my knowledge) he was a bright and glorious star in that shining constellation; as some stars are more excellent than others, so was he there. He was a man of fixed principles; religion and solid reformation was all the white he shot at. He appeared all along for a setled ministery, and the liberall maintenance thereof. He procured the ordinance for settling the ministers at Hereford; his compasse, without trepidation or variation, stood constantly right to that pole, the good of his country and gospell, which he kept ever in his eye. And though his losse were vast in those destroying times, yet he laboured not for recompence of his private losses, nor receiv'd any in the world.

He was very zealous against Superstition and Heresie, and for Church Government. When one of the Parliament said to him, "Sir Robert Harley, why are you thus earnest for Presbytery? you see it is so opposed that it is in vain to seek to settle it." He replyed, "Let us so much rather be earnest for it, though we gain it by inches; what we obtain now with much difficulty and opposition shall be of use one day, when there shall not be heard so much as the sound of a hammer."

(19). He could (when he was put to it) live by faith. In the wars, when the stream of his estate (which should have maintain'd and watred him and his family) was diverted wholly from them, he would say often, "Dear children, it may be, God will bring us to want bread; some say it is base to live from hand to mouth, but I am of another mind; I finde it the best way of living, and (which was an high expression) who can be afraid of God's providence? welcome what the Lord sends, if it go well with the Church, it is no matter."

(20). His soul was paved with humble submission to God in hardest dispensations. When after the wars he returned into the country and came to see with what face Brampton look't, he rode toward his castle gate, and seeing the ruines, put off his hat, and said, "God hath brought great desolation upon this place since I saw it; I desire to say 'the Lord hath given and the Lord hath taken, and blessed be the name of the Lord;' in His good time He will raise it up again; when His house is built, God (I trust) will build mine;" and observe, that he took care to build this house a place of worship, and let his own lie buried still in its woefull ruines.

You have had the fair and sumptuous prospect of his life, which stood aloft like a beauteous city upon an hill.

Let us now follow him to his sicknesse, which (you know) confined him some years to his chamber; and here I see the seaven stars, or seaven celestiall signs, appear in the night of his sicknesse.

First. The greatest trouble of his sicknesse to him was, that it disabled him from enjoying the publick ordinances; he dearly loved the solemn assemblies; one day in Gods court was better to him than a thousand. The want of the publick ordinances was the sicknesse of his sicknesse.

Secondly. His divine employment. Most of his time (both day and night), whilst he was detained in his chamber, was spent in hearing some good book, or the Scriptures, read to him; he used very often to hear the 17 chapter of St. John and the 8 to the Romans read to him; and those two golden texts in the 8 to the Romans, "all things work together for good to them that love God," and "He that spared not His own Son, but delivered Him up for us all, how shall He not with Him also freely give us all things?" he would repeat often, saying, "he knew no such cordialls."

Thirdly. His victory over Sathan. It pleased God, about two years since, to permit Satan to buffet him severall times. Once he lay all night and slept not, and he was heard to say often, "Lord, rebuke the tempter!

Lord, give victory! Lord, be gracious!" With these expressions he spent five or six hours; in the morning he spake very chearfully, and said he would be laid to sleep; and having taken quiet rest, he awaked, and said that all the sins of his life had been laid before him that night, and those things (he said) that he had long forgotten, he then remembered. He said, the tempter had been very busie, " But, blessed be God, I did not sleep untill I had made my peace with God, through Jesus Christ." Then he chearfully said, a little while after, " God may let Satan buffet us for a time, but he shall never prevaile." After this his chearfulnesse continued without interruption.

Fourthly. His willingnesse to die. He was wont to say, many wish to live over their lives againe, that they might mend what had been amisse. " I would not be to live over my life again, least I should make it worse; I would not for all the world be young again, because I would not be so far from Heaven." And he would say to his children, when he had them about him, " I have taught you how to live, and I hope I shall teach you how to die."

Fifthly. His patience under his sharp sufferings. His disease was stone and palsie, and they that know these must look for tortures; yet in his sharpest pains and torments he would mollifie them with this consideration, —that is best which God doth. He would often say, the will of the Lord be done, above all and in all, for that is best of all; and he would support himselfe under his sharp pains with this meditation,—Heaven will make amends for all; and sometimes, when asked how he did, he would answer, " poor, but going to Heaven, as fast as I can." His lips (like an honeycombe) would drop such sweet expressions as these, " if the Lord see it best for me, that the stone in the bladder should be the way to bring me to Heaven, His will be done: it is better to die of the stone in the bladder, than of the stone in the heart." Thus (if you observe) he fed his patience under the divine hand, with divine arguments. That place of Scripture, 1 Cor. 10, 13, " there hath no temptation taken you, but such as is common to man; but God is faithful, who will not suffer you to be tempted above that you are able," he did often mention with joy; saying, it was the first place whereby God gave him comfort; and some few days before his death, when he was in much pain, he said, " blessed be God, who brings this place with comfort to me, whereby I had received first joy;" and so repeated those words, "there is no temptation," &c.; adding further, "blessed be God, blessed be what comes in the name of the Lord; Lord, be gracious." Thus you see his admirable patience.

Sixthly. His love to the Glory of God, and the Church of God. To joy under great afflictions is a hard matter; water quencheth fire, yet his joy in that which concern'd God his affliction could not extinguish. He was wont to pray constantly since the ruines and desolations of Brampton, that God would restore the Gospel hither: and two days before his death he rejoiced exceedingly, when he was told that this place of publick worship was finished. About three days before his death, when he arose and went to prayer (as he constantly used to do), though not able to enlarge in prayer, because of weaknesse, he prayed for the ruine of Antichrist, for the Churches of God beyond sea, naming Savoy, Switzerland, Germany. Upon the fifth of November, though very weak, and under great pains, yet he blessed God, for the great mercy of that day to the Church, and the nation, and to himself, who was of the Parliament when the Powder Plot was intended, and for the many mercies God had vouchsafed him to see since that time in the Church and in his own family; for his lady, the mother of his children, who (he said) was gone to Heaven before him, and for his childrens children; and for his hearing, which being lost, God restored him perfectly. Thus, the day before he dyed, he kept a day of thanksgiving to God, for all His former mercies. Oh, what spiritual and angelical elevation of heart was this! His soul was musical, like the swan; he sang before his death: which leads me to another branch.

Seventhly. His faith and assurance. A godly minister speaking to him concerning his dissolution; he said, "What matter is it if my poor cottage be falling here below! I am sure of a fair house upon the top of yonder hill." A day or two before his death, the 5 of Job being read to him in course, he said, "He that hath been with me in six troubles will not leave me in the seventh." And, lastly, having (like good old Jacob) given his blessing to all his children that were then at home, and to his grandchildren; desiring the Lord to blesse and sanctifie them particularly; I say, having done this about an hour before his death, though under extream pain, he said, "Blessed be God for this quiet peace." Thus his peace with

God shined like a candle in his heart, till his lamp of life went out with these last words, " I die, Lord be gracious!" In the flame of these words his soule (like the angell of God that appeared to Manoah) ascended, and went up to Heaven Thus this glorious saint went up to glory.

In the best times there were few or none better; in these declining times he hath left almost none like him among us. I pray God to double the spirit of deceased Elijah upon his surviving Elisha. The Lord repair the ruines of this castle, and build up this great family for the glory of His name in these parts.

Before I leave, I cannot but tell you, how God hath taken three brave men of late from us. The first upon whom the lot fell was Mr. Richard More of Linley, the next was Mr. Humphrey Walcot of Walcot, and now it hath fallen upon renowned Sir Robert Harley. I mention them here together, because these three were the triangles of our country; and whilst they lived were special friends, and of one heart for God in the concernments of His Gospell. And now I have done: onely to put you in mind a little of yourselves. You see, you are dying creatures: oh, then! consider your later end! the consideration of our last end should be the exercise of our first thoughts : to consider our end, would be the end of our sins, and the resurrection of our repentance; ashes keep fire alive; so this consideration, that we are dust and ashes, will keep our graces alive.

FINIS.

NOTES TO INTRODUCTION.

Page v. *Harley, family of.*—The family of Harley is of very ancient descent; it is still a question whether it be Roman, Saxon, or Norman, but certainly it was settled in Shropshire before the Norman Conquest, at which time Sir John de Harley was Lord of Harley Castle. In the obit or leger book of Pershore abbey there is a commemoration of one of the Harleys who defeated the Danes at Goodluck Hill, near that place, about the year 1013. Sir John de Harley, of Harley Castle, married Alice, daughter of Sir Titus de Leighton (by Letitia his wife, daughter of Hugh le Brune), and left issue Sir William de Harley, who accompanied Godfrey de Bulloigne to the Holy Land, 1098, and in honour of which he was made a Knight of St. Sepulchre. He married Katharine, daughter of Sir Jasper Croft, a knight of that order. He was buried in the abbey at Pershore, where there is a monument to him, of which it is to be observed, " that the shield on his effigies is plain, without any arms, according to the custom of most ancient times."—Collins. In the seventh descent from Sir William (24 Edw. I.) the King granted to Malcolm de Harley, his chaplain and beloved clerk, the marriage of his ward, Margaret, daughter and co-heir of Bryan de Brampton, for his nephew, Robert de Harleigh. The descent of the Bryans is traced from and beyond Maud, daughter of Sir William de Breos, Lord of Brecon, and widow of Roger Mortimer, Lord of Wigmore. The issue of this marriage was Robert, Bryan, Walter, and Joan. Robert and Bryan married two sisters, Joan and Eleanor, daughters of Sir Roger Corbet, of Morton, knight, and dividing the inheritance, the only daughter of Robert carried the Castle of Harley and other Shropshire property into the family of Grendon. Joan married Gilbert de Lacy, Lord of Castle Frome, co. Hereford. Brampton, Bucton, Byton, and other lands in Wiggesmoreland, fell to the lot of the second son, Bryan, who distinguished himself in the French wars, and was there knighted, and was recommended by the Black Prince to his father to be one of the Knights of the Garter, but died before the election. By his marriage he left *a son Bryan*, and a daughter Eleanor, married to Sir John Bromwich, of Bromwich Castle. This Bryan (2) was governor of Montgomery and Dolveren Castles, which he successfully defended against Owen Glendower; in memory of which his crest was changed from a buck's head proper to a lion rampant gules, issuing out of a tower triple-towered proper. He married Isolda, daughter of Sir Ralph Lyngen, of Stoke Edith, in the county of Hereford, knight, and left two sons, Richard and Jeffery: the former died unmarried, but Jeffery, by his first marriage with Johan ap Harry, had a daughter, Margaret, who married Hugh Wolley, and by his

Abridged from Collins's Peerage of England, vol. iv. p. 231, Lond. Ed. 1768: and MS. Pedigree in Lady F. V. Harley's collections.

Sir William de Harley.

Malcolm de Harley.

Bryan de Brampton—Robert de Harleigh—William de Breos—Roger Mortimer—Robert.

Bryan (1).

Bryan (2).

Richard, ob. s. p. —Jeffery.

CAMD. SOC.   *f*

second marriage with Joce or Juliana, daughter of Sir John Burleigh or Burley, two sons, John and Bryan, and a daughter, Joan. Bryan (3) was killed in Brampton Bryan, on Palm Sunday, by Radnorshire felons; and John, engaged in the cause of the House of York, was knighted on the field at Gaston, near Tewkesbury: he married Joan, daughter of Sir Richard Hackluit, of Yetton, by whom he left Richard, and Alice, married first to Richard Monington, and secondly to William Tomkins, of Monington. Richard Harley married Catharine, daughter of Sir Thomas Vaughan, of Tretower Castle, in the county of Brecknock (whose descent is traced from the ancient British princes of Hereford, Brecknock, and Radnor, previous to the Norman Conquest, and from the noble families of Clares and Mortimers, as also from all the Princes of Wales), and had issue John, William, and Thomas, and a daughter, Catharine, married to Robert Hopwood.

This John Harley signalized himself as a Commander at Flodden Field (1513), and married, 11 Henry VIII. (1519-20), Anne, daughter of Sir Edward Croft, of Croft Castle, knight, by whom he had issue: John, Thomas, Rector of Brampton Bryan, William, Edward, and Margaret married to Thomas Adams, also Joyce and Elizabeth, who died unmarried; and by his second marriage, with Anne, daughter of Sir Ed. Rouse, of co. Worcester, a daughter Alice, who married Simon Macklew.

On the 30 March, 1541, John Harley covenanted for the marriage of his son John, then a minor, with Maud, daughter of Richard Warncomb, of Hereford, esquire, and afterwards co-heiress (with her sister Alice who had married, first, William Wigmore of Shobdon, and secondly, Sir James Croft,* of Croft Castle, by whom she had three sons, Edward, John, and George; and three daughters, Eleanor, married to Sir John Scudamore, of Holm Lacy, Gentleman Usher to Queen Elizabeth; Margaret, married to William Rudhall of Rudhall, esquire, and Jane, who died unmarried,) of James Warncomb, who died possessed of the manor of Lugdwardine, and divers other manors and lands in the co. of Hereford. She had for her share the manors of Aylton, Picksley, and lands at Bodenham, Webton, Gothermet, Leyntall Starkes, Elton, and several houses in Leominster and Hereford. Of this marriage came John, slain in the French wars, Thomas, William, and Richard; and three daughters, Catharine, married first to John Cresset, of Upton Cresset, and secondly to John Cornwall the Baron of Burford; Elizabeth, married to Giles Nanfan, of Birch (now Birts) Morton, co. Worcester; and Jane, married to Roger Minors, of Treago, in the county of Hereford.

This Thomas was the father of Sir Robert.

The following circumstance gave occasion to Sir Robert being born at Wigmore Castle:

"Thomas Harley, when married, resided with his father at Brampton Bryan, who, being a zealous Romanist, prevailed with his son to attend a secret mass in the castle, of which his good wife having intimation, came to the chapel door and ask't to have her husband away, with threats, if it were denyed, to acquaint Queen Elizabeth. Thereupon the doors were opened and he let go to his wife, who prevailed upon him to remove to Wigmore Castle, where Robert was soon afterwards born."

Sir Robert had expressed a wish (1621) to go and see the army in the Netherlands; which his father refused in the following letter:—

THOS. HARLEY TO SIR ROB. HARLEY.

"Good Son—As c'cerning y^r lett^r to my dau't^r of y^r desyr too goe into ye Lowe Countries too see ye noble army there, iff I wold grāte you leave, wherwith my daut^r acqu'ted me, my answer was, that you s'old never haue my c'sent, and if there were a neccasytye of goinge, I wold be ye man. Alsoe I receaved from my dau'ter vpon Thursday ye letter tendinge to that purpose, wch I dyd reade that day, and the nyght following did consider therof, not too sende a bare letter, but my servant Ihon Hopkins, whom I sent to Mr Pierson that I myght acq'nte hym wth y^r letter, and to knowe whether he wold have any thinge to you, who verye frealye offered to be the messenger hymselfe, w^h I doe take most kindlye att his hands, whom I have instructed to deale with you very ffreely. Human' est errare, but no wysdom to p'severe; therefore, good sonne, lette me p'vayle soe ffarre w^h you, that no further sppeches maye growe hereof, lest there thence maye cō a ryppynge upe of them and other occasions, but rather a ———; wherin I know Mr Pierson, who loveth and honoreth you in his heart, will advise you. Therefore for once agayne intreatinge you will come to vs wth speed, w^h wylbe noe small c'forting to us all, and especially to my dau'ter. The God bless you.

"Y^r lovinge and naturall Ffather,
"T. HARLEY.

"Brōpt. Castel, 23 June, 1621."

In Sir Robert's time, Harley was occasionally spelt Harlow, Harlowe, and Harloe.
Lord Conway writes Harlow, Appendix, p. 214.
Major Winthrop writes Harlowe, Appendix, p. 233.
Whitelocke, in Memorials, writes Harlow, Harloe, and Harley.

Page vi. *Provost of Oriel.*—"John Tolson, Procter 15 April, 1607; D.D. 21 March, 1621; was Provost (1621-44); and pro-Vice-Chancellor 1642. In his time the new Chapel and Hall were built, between 1637-1642, himself contributing 1,150*l.*"—Ingram's Memorials of Oxford.

Page vii. *He represented in Parliament.*—Among Sir Robert's papers is the following in his own hand-writing:—

"COPPIES OF GENERALE LETTRES VPON NEWS OF A PARLAM^t.

"Sr T. C.

"Honorable knight and my worthy friend,—I heare that wee shall shortlie hav a parlament, wch it may bee is no newes to you. To answere yor many noble respects to mee, I desire to impart it to you, beeing newes to mee, beseeching you to bee pleased to reserve your voyces for the knights of the parlament for this county, till we all meet to deliberate of the fittest persons for that attendance, that ye choyce may not be made by affection but discretion. So in hast."

"S^r Jo. Sc.

"S^r,—I understand wee shall shortly have a parlament, the immediate consequence of wch truth amongst vs will bee the choyce of knights of the shire. I beseech you, sir, therefore acquaint yo' grandfather with it, beseeching him from mee, that he will reserve his voyces till we all meete to consult of ye fittest men for that service, that affection possesse not the place of discretion in o^r election. So in haste p'esenting you wth my newes, wch it may be is none to you, I commend you to o^r good God, and rest."

"Sr R. Hop:

"S^r,—I understand for newes y^t wee shall shortly have a parliament, wch I desire to impart to you, as to my frend and loving kinsman, wth all intreating you to reserve yor voyces for the election of the knights of this shire till we shall meete to deliberate and resolve of the fittest for that service, wherin I desire that neither faction nor affection, but discretion and true understanding, may poynt us out the men. So in hast."

"M^r Ja. Fo:

"S^r,—I have newes that ye parliament will shortly be summoned, and I pray that my love may so fare prevayle wth you to entreate you to reserve yor voyces for electing ye knights of this shire till wee all meet to advise of such as shall be thought fitest for that service. So, etc."

Page ix. *The suppression of the surplice, &c. &c.*—"The House of Commons made an order, and Sir Robert Harlow had the execution of it, to take away all scandalous pictures, crosses, and figures within churches and without. And the zealous knight took down the cross in Cheapside, Charing Cross, and other the like monuments impartially."—Whitelocke, 5 July, 1641, p. 45.

This is certainly incorrect as to time, for in the Jour. H. Commons we find (1 March, 1641-2,) it "*Ordered*, That the Com^e on Cheapside Cross shall be revived." Again, "Cheapside Cross and other crosses were voted down."—Whitelocke, 3 May, 1643.

Evelyn says, 2 May, 1643, "I went from Wotton to London, where I saw the furious and zealous people demolish that stately cross in Cheapside."

In the Supplement to the Gent. Mag. 1764, a plate and notice is given of the demolishing of Cheapside Cross. "2 May, 1643, the crosse in Cheapside was pulled down: a troope of hors and two companies of foote wayted to garde, and, at the fall of the top crosse, dromes beat, trumpets blew, and multitudes of capes were thrown in the ayre, and a greate shoute of people with joy. The 2 May, the Almanake sayeth, was the Invention of the Crosse, and 6 day at night was the leaden popes burnt in the place where it stood, with ringing of bells and a great acclamation; and no hurt done in all these actions."

Lilly, in his Observations on the Life of Charles I. (quoted by Percy in his Reliques of Ancient Poetry, in illustration of the ballad "On the Downfall of Charing Cross") says, "Charing Cross, we know, was pulled down 1647, June, July, and August. Part of the stones were converted to pave before Whitehall. I have seen knife-hafts made of some of the stones, which, being well polished, looked like marble."

Jour. H. Com. 24 Ap. 1643. "Sir Robert Harley, Mr. White, Mr. Corbett, and others, a Committee to receive information from time to time of any monuments of superstitious idolatry in the abbey church of Westminster, or the windows thereof, or in any church or chapel in and about London. And they have power to demolish the same, where any such superstitious or idolatrous monuments are informed to be. And the churchwardens and other officers are hereby required to be aiding and assisting in the execution of this order."

Ibid. 5 Feb. 1643-4. "*Ordered*, That it be referred to the Comᵉ for superstitious pictures, where Sir Rob. Harley has the chair, to take into their custody the copes and surplices and other chapel stuff at Whitehall, and to view the superstitious pictures about Whitehall, and to report what they are. They are likewise to search and view all the plate in Sir H. Mildmay's custody, and search and view such other things in Whitehall as they shall think fit. *Ordered*, That the product of goods, copes, and surplices seized at Whitehall, and also the plate in Sir H. Mildmay's custody belonging to his Majesty, be employed and disposed of to the Lady Essex, for payment of arrears to Sir W. Essex, her husband, who died at Oxford, and the remainder to Col. Ven, for payment of arrears due to the garrison of Windsor."

Ibid. 17 April, 1644. "*Resolved*, That the chest or silver vessel in St. Paul's shall be sold for the best advantage, and employed towards providing necessaries for the artillery by the Comᵉ at Grocers' Hall."

23 April, 1644. "*Ordered*, That the materials informed of by Sir Rob. Harley be forthwith sold by Sir Rob. Harley, viz. the mitre and crosier-staff found in St. Paul's Church, London, and the brass and iron in Hen. VII. Chapel, Westminster, and the proceeds thereof, the necessary charges deducted, be employed according to the direction of the House."

Ibid. 25 April, 1644. "That Sir Rob. Harley do report on Saturday the ordinance for defacing copes, &c. &c."

"The ordinance for taking away altars, levelling chancel-floors recently raised, tapers, candlesticks, basins, crucifixes, crosses, images, and pictures of the Holy Trinity or Virgin Mary, and all other images and pictures of saints and superstitious inscriptions *excepted*, images, pictures, coats of arms in glass, stone, or otherwise, in any church, chapel, or a churchyard, set up or engraven for a monument of any king, prince, nobleman, or other dead person, who had not commonly been reported or taken for a saint."—Neal's Hist. of the Puritans, by Toulmin, vol. iii. p. 644.

Page x. *Master of the Mint, &c.*—Journ. H. Com. 6 March, 1642-3. "*Ordered*, that Sir Rob. Harley shall have power to give a privy mark for the pixe money in the Mint, and that he bring in an ordinance for the restoring of himself to his place in the Mint." See other notices in Journ. H. Com. 3 and 5 May, 1643.

Self-denying Ordinance.—The self-denying ordinance concludes thus: "Provided always, and it is hereby declared that those members of either house who had offices by grant from his Majesty before the parliament, and were by his Majesty displaced sitting this parliament, and have since by authority of both houses been restored, shall not by this ordinance be discharged from the said offices or profits thereof, but shall enjoy the same, any thing in this ordinance to the contrary thereof notwithstanding."—Parl. Hist. vol. iii. p. 355.

The Mastership at the Mint, worth 4,000*l.* a-year in Sir Robert's time: in the time of £4,000 a-year. Sir Isaac Newton it was considered to be worth from 1,200*l.* to 1,400*l.* a year.

NOTES TO INTRODUCTION.

Page xi. *Piedmont collection, &c.*—The collection for the persecuted Protestants in Piedmont, &c. is said to have amounted to 37,097*l.* 7*s.* 3*d.* ; about 30,000*l.* was remitted in 1655 and the following year: the confusion following the Protector's death prevented the clearing of the whole amount till the Convention Parliament at the Restoration, when the remainder, 7,000*l.*, was ordered to be paid."—Neal's Hist. of the Puritans, by Toulmin, vol. iv. p. 141.

Page xii. *Thos. Froysell.*—Journ. H. Com. 17 March, 1642-3. " An ordinance for sequestering the rents and profits of the parish-church of St. Margaret's, New Fish Street, London, into the hands of certain sequestrators, to the use of Thos. Froysell, M.A., a godly, learned, and orthodox divine, who is hereby required and appointed to take care for the discharge of the cure of the said place in all the duties thereof, until both houses of parliament shall take further order, was read, and by vote upon the question assented to, &c."

Ibid. 25 March, 1643. " It was ordered, upon the petition of the common councilmen and others of y⁰ parish of St. Dunstan's in the West, that Mr. Thos. Froizell shall preach the lecture every Thursday forenoon."

" Mr. Froysell of Clun, an ancient divine of extraordinary worth, for judgement, moderation, godliness, blameless life, and excellent preaching, who with many others, in poverty and sickness, and great suffering, continued to preserve the peace of his conscience."—Calamy's Abridgment of the Life and Times of Baxter, p. 355.

Recent generations of the Harleys since the time of Henry VII.—In the curious old mansion of Birt's Morton in county Worcester, formerly the seat of Giles Nanfan, who married Elizabeth, the sister of Thomas Harley, and first cousin of Sir John Scudamore and William Rudhall, as stated above, there is, along the cornice of a fine old panelled room, the arms and names of the following gentlemen, among whom, no doubt, an extensive cousinship was recognized:

    William Rudhall, of Rudhall, Esq.
    Jhon Blount, of Eye, Esq.
    Y⁰ Lord Copley.
    Sr Henry Polle, Knight.
    Sr John Scudamore, Knight.
    Sr Thos. Throgmorton, Knight.
    Sr James Croft, Knight.
    Thomas Cornwall, Esq.
    Baskerville of Erdesley, Esq.
    Thomas Harley, Esq.
    Walter Vaughan of Hergest, Esq.
    Roger Minors, Esq.
    Jhon Bridges, Esq.
    Bromwich of Bromsberro, Esq.
    John Hyett, Gent.

NOTES TO INTRODUCTION. xlvii

Hackluyt of Yetton.—Richard Hackluyt, the author of English Voyages, Navigation, and Discoveries. Lond. 1598-99, 1600, 3 vols. folio, and other geographical works, according to Wood, was of the family of Hackluyt of Yetton.—Wood's Athenæ, vol. ii. p. 186.

Page xiv. *Post of Hereford, Leominster, Shrewsbury, or Ludlow, then recently established, &c.*—See an interesting notice of the early history of the Post-office in the Gentleman's Magazine, Aug. 1853, p. 153.

In a table appended to the Description and Use of two Arithmetical Instruments, &c. by S. Morland (Sir Samuel), Lond. 1673, is a notice "concerning letters which may be sent from London."

Page xvi. *A solemn day of prayer, &c.*—Numerous allusions to fasts occur in these letters in Ember weeks, private days, &c. Sir Robert keeps a solemn day of prayer at Stanage Lodge, also a day preparatory to his entering on his parliamentary duties. The Ember days and monthly parliamentary fasts, the last Wednesday in the month, and special days, were strictly observed at Brampton. Instead of the last Wednesday the King, 5 Oct. 1643, ordered the second Friday in each month, to be so observed. The last Wednesday in December, 1644, falling on Christmas Day, and doubt having arisen with the divines whether that day should be observed as a fast—on the 19th Dec. it was ordered by the House of Commons so to be kept. The Royalists made a clamour against this as a great impiety and profaneness. The parliament—now to a man Presbyterian—taking the views of the Kirk, approved of it. Mr. Edmund Calamy, in his sermon before the House of Lords, on that day, says, "This day is commonly called Christmas Day, a day that has hitherto been much abused to superstition and profaneness. It is not easy to say whether the superstition has been greater or the profaneness. I have known some that have preferred Christmas Day before the Lord's Day—some that would be sure to receive the Sacrament on Christmas Day, though they did not receive it all the year after—some thought, though they did not play at cards all the year, yet they must play at Christmas; thereby, it seems, to keep in memory the birth of Christ. This and much more had been the profaneness of this feast—and truly I think the superstition and profaneness of the day is so rooted into it—that there is no way to reform it, but by dealing with it as Hezekiah did with the Brazen serpent. This year, God, by His providence, has buried this *feast* in a *fast*, and I hope it will never rise again. You have sent out, right honorable, a strict order for keeping this day, and you are here to-day to observe your own order, and I hope you will do it strictly. The necessities of the times are great—never more need of prayer and fasting—the Lord give us grace to be humbled in this day of humiliation for all our own and England's sins, and especially for the old superstition and profaneness of this feast."—Neal's Hist. of the Puritans, by Toulmin, vol. iii. p. 156.

In the letter from Lord Westmorland to Edward Harley in the Appendix, p. 215, there is, in a Latin Epigram, an allusion to this keeping of Christmas Day as a fast—fixing the year of that undated letter to be 1644.

On the monthly fast days, the business of the House of Commons was usually voting thanks to the preachers for the great pains taken in their sermons, requesting the preachers to print the same, and nominating two other preachers for the next fast day. After the calling of the Assembly of Divines, they were usually, if not always, selected from that body.

Soon after the death of the King, the ordinance for keeping the monthly fast was repealed and occasional ones substituted; for which this reason is assigned: "That such times of extraordinary duties of worship are apt to degenerate into mere formality and customary observances."

In the Register of Brampton Bryan is the following:—

"*Memorandum*, That whereas Dame Brilliana Harley is lycenset by Thomas Pierson, Rector of this parish of Brampton Bryan, to eate flesh on fast days, in reason of her greate weakness, wch licence was made the first day of the month, and for that her greate weakness does yet continue, the continuance of the seyd licence   according to the statute of Elizabeth, till it shall please God to render her ....

"March 14, 1632."

"THOMAS × PIERSON.
the mark of

A similar notice occurs in the Register of Sellack, in the county of Hereford:—

"1632, ye 16th Nov. Mem. That upon the day and year above written, a license was granted by Richard Prichard, Vicar of Sellack, unto John Viscount Scudamore, his Lady, and their sonne, in respect of manifest sickness and infirmityes, to eat flesh upon dayes prohibited, during the time of their sickness and infirmityes. Registered in the sight of Walter Holland, one of the churchwardens, 22 Nov. 1632."

Page xvii. *Pierson objected not to the Liturgy, but scrupled the use of the surplice, &c.*— "Mr. Pierson's scruples, expressed in his own hand, as follow:—

"GROUNDS OF REASONS AGAINST THE CEREMONIES.

"1. I desire to see good warrant for a proper ministering garment under the Gospell.

"2. How a proper massing garment can be decent for Christ's members of the Gospel, or his service.

"3. Good warrant for ye use of significant ceremonies in God's service such as ours be.

"4. Whether these, being idolatries in Rome, should not be rejected as *idolathytes* out of God's service."—MS. Acct. of Rectors of Brampton Bryan in Harl. MSS. Brit. Mus.

Page xviii. *Stanley Gower.*—Jour. H. C. (1 Nov. 1643) directs that Stanley Gower do preach on the next Lord's Day at St. Margaret's, Westminster—being Gunpowder Treason-day.

Page xix. *Plunder and villanous usage then the practice of the Cavaliers, &c.*— "Divers of Worcestershire, under Mr. Dingley, declared for the Parliament, and complained of the insolencies and injuries by the garrison of Worcester." Whitelocke gives a specimen of this, but of a later date, 25 Nov. 1645: A copy of a warrant from Col. Bard, the Governor of Worcester, to the constables for contributions was sent up, wherein were these expressions: "Know that unless you bring unto me, at a day and houre, in Worcester, the monthly contribution for six months, you are to expect an unsanctifyed troop of horse among you, from whence if you hide yourselves they shall fire your houses without mercy, hang up your bodies wherever they find them, and scare your ghosts," &c.—P. 188.

Dr. Nathaniel Wright.—Nathaniel Wright, M.A. of Cambridge, took the degree of Doctor of Physic at Bourges, in France, and was incorporated at Oxford, 30 May, 1638. Wood says he was afterwards "Physician to O. Cromwell, when he was sick in Scotland."—Wood's Fasti, vol. i. p. 503.

The siege commenced on the 25 Sept. 1643.—This happening on a Tuesday, the day before the monthly fast, was kept as a special day of prayer and supplication at Brampton.

Page xx. *Lady Brilliana's children.*—The issue of Sir Robert and Lady Brilliana Harley:—

1. Edward, afterwards noticed, page xxviii.
2. Robert, knighted, married 8 Feb. 1670, Edith, daughter of —— Pembrugge, esquire, widow of Major Hinton, but left no issue; buried at Brampton Bryan, 18 Nov. 1673.
3. Thomas, of Kinsham Court, by Abigail, daughter of Sir Richard Saltinstall, knight, had four sons, who died issueless.
4. Brilliana, wife of James Stanley, second son of Sir Robert Stanley, knight, who was second son of the Earl of Derby.
5. Dorothy, wife of William Mitchell, of co. Norfolk.
6. and 7. Margaret and Elizabeth, who died unmarried.—Collins, vol. iv. 252.

Dr. Wilkinson.—John Wilkinson was Principal of Magdalene Hall from 1605 to 1644, when he fled from Oxford—to which he was restored 1646—and became President of Magdalene College in 1648; he took his D.D. in 1613. The Hall flourished under his government, and that of his nephew Henry Wilkinson, to the Restoration; and was the chief school of Puritanism in Oxford. Wood speaks disparagingly of him, and says, "he published nothing."—Fasti, vol. i. p. 354; and again "contrasts the liberal conduct of John Oliver, President of Magdalene College, who had been displaced 1648, but restored 1660, with that of Drs. Wilkinson and Goodwyn, who had been thrust into his office by the Parliament and Oliver, for their saintship, and zeal to the blessed cause, and gave not a farthing, but raked and scraped up all that they could get thence, as the rest of the saints did in the university."—Wood's Athenæ, vol. iv. p. 300.

"SIR ROBERT HARLEY TO ED. H.

"Ned Harley,—I thank you for y^r letters, and desier so to carry ye buisiness with you y^t you may alwaies thanke mee for mine, and now y^t ye Lord hath in His good providence disposed you in ye university, and with so worthy a tutor as is Mr Perkins, and under ye vigilent government of ye Principall Do^r Wilkinson, whose holy example lett every day make impression in you of ye good in wch he moves. You must consider y^t ye end is to gett inlargement of knowledg in y⁰ understandinge chiefly of God in Christ, wᶜʰ is life eternall, then of morrall science, wᶜʰ will not only enriche y' mind but sett of yoʳ conversation amongst men, as shaddowes do some pictures, to y⁰ workeman's greater com'endation. Fyrst then take y⁰ wise man's counsell to remember y' Creator in y⁰ dayes of y' youth, to love Hym yᵗ made you when you were not, and redeemed you with y⁰ preciouse blood of His deare Sonne when you were lost, wᶜʰ you must finde to be from a vaine conversation, and love will teach you y⁰ feare of y⁰ Lord, and yᵗˢ y⁰ beginninge of wisdome, wᶜʰ not only makes one man differ from another, as reason doth man from a beast, but giveth life to hym yᵗ hath it; and it will give you an elevation above y⁰ base wayes wherein many young men wallow; and I feare y⁰ universities do too much abound with such pigges, from wᶜʰ y⁰ preservative must be daily prayer for God's blessinge on y' owne and y⁰ endevours of y' loving and graciouse tutor, whose care and counsells if you answer with diligence and obedience you will allsoe my expectation, with no little comforte; so, with my constant prayers for y⁰ blessings of our heavenly Father upon you, I send you y⁰ blessing of y' loving father, Ro. HARLEY.

"Brampton Castle, 19° 9bris, 1638."

Page xxi. *Edward Harley, Captain of a troop of horse, &c.*—Jour. H. Com. 13 Nov. 1643. "*Ordered*, That the men raised under the command of Col. Harley shall be forthwith sent to Plymouth by sea, part raised by imprest. The Committee of the West to take care for the raising of these men."

21 Aug. 1648. "Letter from Salop, that Sir Henry Lyngen, with a party of horse, took 60 of Col. Harley's men; and, about two days after, a party of Col. Harley and Col. Horton's men met with Sir Hen. Lyngen's men about Radnor, regained all the men, horse, and prisoners, took Sir Hen. Lyngen and Col. Croft and many others of the King's commanders prisoners, slew divers of the party, and routed the rest."—Whitelocke, p. 325.

In the Auditor's notes there is an allusion to the barbarous treatment Colonel Edward Harley received from Sir Herbert Croft and other deputy lieutenants, in sending part of a troop of horse to seize a pair of pistols given him by Lord Vere as a memorial, these being the pistols with which he charged at the battle of Newport.

Page xxii. *Mr. Clogie.*—Alexander Clogie was buried in the chancel of Wigmore church, where there is a slab in the floor under the communion table with this inscription:—

"Here lyeth, in hope of a glorious resurrection unto life eternall, the body of that holy, reverend, and learned divine, Mr. Alexander Clogie, who departed this life 24 Oct. 1698, aged 84. Minister of Wigmore 51 years."

He was the author of a Sermon, "Vox Corvi; or, The Voice of a Raven that thrice spoke these Words distinctly: 'Look into Colossians the 3rd, 15th.' The Text itself looked into and opened in a Sermon preached at Wigmore, in the County of Hereford; to which is added, 'Serious Addresses to the People of this Kingdom,' shewing the use we ought to make of this Voice from Heaven. Lond. 1694."

NOTES TO INTRODUCTION.

There is a MS. Life of Bishop Bedell in the Harl. MSS. in the Brit. Mus. supposed by Archdeacon Hone to be the MS. which Bishop Burnet made use of in the compilation of his Life of Bedell, which was published in 1685; for this reason, the writer appears to identify himself with A.C. minister of Cavan, and Burnet's authority (see Preface, page *b*) was Mr. Clogy, minister of Cavan, "a worthy and learned divine," and as having lived in the bishop's house, and shared his troubles up to the time of his death, 1642. In a letter of the Bishop of Meath, dated Dec. 14, 1685, found amongst Mr. Boyle's Correspondence, "a Life of Bedell is mentioned lately published by one Clogy, who is somewhere beneficed in England, if he be alive, and as having married the bishop's daughter." May not this Mr. Clogy,—A. C. (Minister of Cavan) be Alexander Clogie, Minister of Wigmore from 1647 to 1698? Stanley Gower, the Rector of Brampton Bryan, had been chaplain to Archbishop Usher, and to him Mr. Clogy or his family might have been known; and it is not at all improbable that, seeking an asylum in England, as he did, he might have found a friend in Mr. Gower, which may have led to his being fixed at Wigmore. There appears to be an inaccuracy in the Bishop of Meath's letter not noticed by Archdeacon Hone, for it is there said that Clogy had married the bishop's daughter; but in the Life of the Bishop it is said, "of his four children, two died in infancy, the other two, being sons, grew up to man's estate, and survived their parents."—Archdeacon Hone's Lives—Bishop Bedell, vol. ii. pp. 211, 248—257.

Mr. Clogie's marriage with Susannah Nelmes at Ludlow, 11 Dec. 1665, is noted in the Register of Wigmore. Among his children was a daughter named Brilliana, after the Lady Brilliana Harley.

Page xxiv. *Dr. Herbert Croft, Bishop of Hereford.*—See an interesting account of him in Wood's Athenæ, vol. iv. p. 309—318. In 1688, he published a short discourse concerning the reading his Majesty's late Declaration in churches. This pamphlet coming into the hands of a certain courtier, he communicated it to the King, who, upon perusal, commanded so much as concerned the reading of the Declaration (which was for the indulging of consciences,) to be printed, but suppressed all that he said against taking off the Test and penal law.

Page xxvi. *Sir Edward Harley, Governor of Worcester.*—When Governor of Worcester, "A party having brought into the city the plunder of horses and other things, Sir Edward ordered all that could be seized to be restored, except a blasphemous image of the Holy Trinity, which (having been first shewn to the Bishop,) he ordered to be broken in pieces in the open street."—Auditor's Notes.

Page xxvii. *John Lord Viscount Scudamore.*—See a view of the ancient and present state of the churches of Dore, Home-Lacy, and Hempsted, endowed by him; with remains of that ancient family, by Matth. Gibson, M.A. Rector of Dore.—Lond. 1727.

Page xxviii. *Dr. Tuckney.*—Anthony Tuckney was originally of Emmanuel College, of which he became a fellow, and thence removed to the vicarage of Boston, from which place he was selected as one of the Assembly of Divines: he is said to have assisted in composing the Westminster Confession and Catechism, and, in particular, to have drawn up the exposition of the Commandments in the larger catechism, but to have voted against subscribing to swearing to the confession, &c. set out by authority—a conduct the more deserving of notice and commendation as the instances of a consistent adherence to the principles of religious liberty were so few and rare in that age. In 1645 he became Master of his College; and in 1653 Master of St. John's, Cambridge, in which year he was named one of "the Tryers;" and on the death of Dr. Arrowsmith became Regius Professor of Divinity. He was one of the Presbyterian Divines in attendance at the Savoy conference, where he received a Royal letter from Secretary Nicholas, giving him a supersedeas from his public employments, with the promise of 100*l*. a-year for life out of his successor's income, which was punctually paid. Calamy says, "he left behind him the character of an eminently pious and learned man, a true friend, an indefatigable student, a candid disputant, and an earnest promoter of truth and godliness." His modesty was as distinguished as his learning, and he is said to have shewn more courage in maintaining the rights and privileges of the university in those lawless times than any of the heads at Cambridge. He presided over St. John's with great prudence and ability, and that college had never flourished more than under his rule. In the elections, when the president, according to the language and spirit of the times, would call upon him to have regard to the godly, his answer was, "no one should have a greater regard to the truly godly than himself, but he was determined to choose none but scholars; adding, very truly, "they may deceive me in their godliness, but they cannot in their scholarship." He published in his lifetime some small pieces, as "Death disarmed, or the Grave swallowed up in Victory, 1654;" "Balm of Gilead for the Wounds of England, applyed in a Sermon, 1654;" "A good day well improved, in 5 Sermons, 1656." After his death, were published Forty Sermons of his, preached on several occasions; also his "Prælectiones Theologicæ," containing all his theological lectures and exercises while he continued in his public employments in the university: and in 1753, Dr. Samuel Salter, Prebendary of Norwich, published a correspondence between Dr. Tuckney and Dr. Benjamin Whichcote, on moral and interesting subjects.—Neal's Hist. of the Puritans, vol. iii. p. 115, vol. iv. p. 556; Dyer's Hist. of Cambridge; and Baxter's Life, by Calamy.

LETTERS

OF

THE LADY BRILLIANA HARLEY.

1625—1643.

I.

To my deare husband Sʳ Robart Harley, Kinght of the Bathe.

Sʳ—Docter Barker has put my sister into a cours of ientell fisek, which I hope by God's bllsing will doo her much good. My sister giues you thankes for seending him to her. I pray you remember that I recken the days you are away; and I hope you are nowe well at Heariford, wheare it may be, this letter will put you in minde of me, and let you knowe, all your frinds heare are well; and all the nwes I can seend you is, that my Lo. Brooke is nowe at Beaethams Court. My hope is to see you heare this day senet, or to-morrowe senet, and I pray God giue vs a happy meeting, and presarfe you safe; which will be the great comfort of

Your most true affectionat wife,   BRILLIANA HARLEY.

Ragly: the 30 of Sep. 1625.

II.

To my deare housband Sʳ Robart Harley, Knight, in Blackfriers,
at my Lo. Lewsons howes.

Deare Sʳ—I thanke you for your letter which you sent me from Tuddington: which gaue me satisfaction of your being well, so farc on your journey: which ascurance of your health is the beest nwes

I can heare, except that of your comeing home. I ernestly desire to heare howe you came to Loundon; and doo thinke your men stay longe: but I hope they will bringe me good nwes of you, and then I shall be well pleased. Ned, I thanke God, is very well, and you will beleeve me, if I say he looses non of his grandfather loue, whoo is better than you leeft him. And no more to you at this time; but I beceache the Allmighty presarue you, and giue you happy meeting with

    Your most faithfull affectionat wife,   BRILLIANA HARLEY.

Brompton, the 10th of Phe. 1625.

III.

To my deare housband S[r] Robart Harley, Knight.

S[r]—I thanke you for sending me word, I may hope to see you at Easter, which time will be much longed for by me. I hope the parlament has spent as much time as will satisfy them in dooing nothing: so that nowe some good frute of theare meeting will be brought to ripnes, which is the effect of our prayers. This day I deleverd the £100 to my father: which he has payed to Mr. Davis: that mony that was wanting of it, was made vp with the £50 pounde Mr. Lacy payed for wood. The payling of the nwe parke is made an end of. Yesterday your company only was at Heariford, to shewe what they had lerned, whear Sr. Jhon Skidemore and Mr. Vahan weare judges; and so they meane to be of the reest of the companis, and they haue apointed teen of your company to learne the vse of theiare armes and so to teache the reest. This last night I not being very well, made me seend this day for the midwife, which I thinke I should haue defered to longe. I asure myself I haue your prayers, becaus you haue so great a part of mine: and I blls God that you injoy your health, which I beeg of you to take care of. I thanke God, Ned is well, and I beeg your bllsing for him: and I pray God preserue you well and giue you a happy and speedy meeting with

    Your most faithful affectionat wife,   BRILLIANA HARLEY.

I pray you present my humbell duty to my father, and my lady. My cosen Thomkins remembers her loue to you.

Brompton, the 17 *of Mar.* 1625.

IV.

To my deare husband Sr Robert Harley.

Deare S^r—Your two leters, on from Hearifort and the other from Gloster, weare uery wellcome to me: and if you knwe howe gladly I reseaue your leters, I beleeue you would neeuer let any opertunity pase. I hope your cloche did you saruis betwne Gloster and my brother Brays, for with vs it was a very rainy day, but this day has bine very dry and warme, and so I hope it was with you; and to-morowe I hope you will be well at your journis end, wheare I wisch my self to bide you wellcome home. You see howe my thoughts goo with you: and as you haue many of mine, so let me haue some of yours. Beleeue me, I thinke I neuer miste you more then nowe I doo, or ells I haue forgoot what is past. I thanke God, Ned and Robin are well; and Ned askes every day wheare you are, and he says you will come to-morowe. My father is well, but goos not abrode, becaus of his fiseke. I haue sent you vp a litell hamper, in which is the box with the ryteings and boouckes you bide me send vp, with the other things, sowed up in a clothe, in the botome of the hamper. I haue sent you a partriche pye, which has the two pea chikeins in it, and a litell runlet of meathe, that which I toold you I made for my father. I thinke within this muthe, it will be very good drinke. I sende it vp nowe becaus I thinke carage when it is ready to drincke dous it hurt; thearefore, and please you to let it rest and then taste it; if it be good, I pray you let my father haue it, because he spake to me for such meathe. I will nowe bide you god night, for it is past a leauen a cloke. I pray God presarue you and giue you good sugsess in all your biusnes, and a speady and happy meeting.

Your most faithfull affectinat wife, BRILLIANA HARLEY.

I must beeg your bllsing for Ned and Rob. and present you with Neds humbell duty.

Bromton, the 5 of October, 1627.

V.

To my deare husband S[r] Robert Harley, Knight.

My deare S[r]—I ame glad of this opertuenity to present you with the remembranc of my deare loue. I hope you came well to Bristo; and I much longe to heare from you, but more a thousand times to see you, which I presume you will not beleeue, becaus you cannot poscibilly measure my loue. I thanke God your father is well, and so are your three soons. Ned presents his humbell duty to you, and I beeg your bllsing for them all; and I pray God giue you a happy and speady meeting with

    Your most affectinat wife,   BRILL. HARLEY.

If I thought it would hasten your comeing home, I would intreat you to doo soo.

I pray you remember me to Mr. Pirson. I thanke God all at his howes are well.

Bromton, the 7th, 1628.

VI.

To my deare husband S[r] Robert Harley, Knight.

My deare S[r]—I thanke you for your letter, which I reseaued this weake by the carrier, and I thanke God for my father's health. I trust in our good God, in his owne good time, he will giue a happy end to your biusness. I haue rwitten a letter to my father, which I send you heare inclosed. If you thinke it will not displeas him, and it may any thinge at all seet forward your biusnes, I pray you deleuer it to him. If you do deleuer it to my father, I pray you seale it first. Allas! my deare S[r], I knowe you doo not to the on halfe of my desires, desire to see me, that loues you more then any earthly thinge. I should be glad if you would but rwite me word, when I should hope to see you. Need has bine euer sence Sunday trubled with the rume in his fase very much. * * * * * * The swelling of his face made him very dull; but nowe, I thanke God, he is better, and begins to be merry. He inquires for Jhon Walls comeing downe: for he thinkes he will bringe him a letter. I must desire you to send me downe a littell Bibell for him. He would not let me be in peace, tell I promised him to send for on. He begings nowe to delight in reading: and that is the booke I would haue him place his delight in. Tom has still a greate coold; but he is not, I thanke God, sike with it. Brill and Robin, I thanke God, are well; and Brill has two teethe. Ned presents his humble duty to you, and I beeg your bllsing for them all: and I beceach the Allmighty to prosper you in all you doo, and to giue you a happy meeting with

Your most faithfull affectinat wife,   BRILLIANA HARLEY.

I pray you, S^r, send downe no silke grogram. I hope you haue reseuefed the siluer candell-stike.

Your father, I thanke God, is much better than he was. I pray you, S^r, present my beest loue to my sister Wacke.

Desem 4, 1629.

VII.

To my deare husband Sr Robert Harley, Knight, at his howes in Alldermanbery.

My dearest S^r—Your men came to Bromton on thursday last. I thanke God that you haue your halth. I hope the Lord will giue vs bothe faith to waite vpon him; and I trust that in his mercy he will give a good end to your biusnes. It pleases God that I continue ill with my coold, but it is, as they say, a nwe disceas: it trubelles me much, more becaus of my being with childe; but I hope the Lord will deale in mercy with me; and, deare S^r, let me haue your prayers, for I haue need of them. Docter Barker is nowe with me. I thanke God the childeren are all well, and Need and Robine are very glad of theire boose, and Ned is much discontented that you come not downe. I beeg your bllssing for them all, beceaching the Allmighty to presarue you, and to giue you a joyefull and happy meeting with your

Most faithfull affectinat wife, BRIL. HARLEY.

I pray present my humbell duty to my father. This day theare came a man from Ragley to feetche my cosen Hunkes to her mother, whoo is very sike.

Bromton, the 8 of May, 1630.

VIII.

For my deare husband Sr Robert Harley, Knight.

My deare S^r—I pray you reseaue my thankes for your letter by my cosen Pris, and by the carrier; they weare both very wellcome to me, which I thinke you beleeue, for in part you know howe deare you are to me. I ame very glad that my brother Raphe is come to Loundoun; I hope he is nowe well. I pray you to giue him counsell what to doo. I desire from my hoole hart that he may grow in the feare of God, and then he will be happy. Pinner shall send some woole to Lemster. I haue heare inclosed sent you the aquittance of the pursevant, by which you may knowe his name. I doo blles my good God, that you haue had so a good an end about the presentation of Bromton. I thinke you haue doun a very good worke, in recommending Mary Wood to my Lady Veere, to home I hope shee will doo acceptabele sarvis. I am toold of a gentell-woman by Docter Barker. She was bread with my old Lady Manering. She, they say, is religious and discreet, and very ham-some in dooing of any thinge; her name is Buckle, a Sharpsheare woman: if you like of it, I would thinke of haueing of her; for I haue no body aboute me, of any judgment, to doo any thinge. My heate continueing, I sent to Docter Barker to come and see me let bloud; he came on thursday night, and yesterday morning I sent fore a curgen at Bischops Castell, that let Mrs. Wallcot blud, and he pricke my arme twis, but it would not blled; and I would not try the third time. I hope the Lord will derect me what to doo: and for gooing abrode I will endeuor to doo it as soune as it shall pleas

God to inabell me. It is a word of comfort which you rwit me, that you hope shortly to send for your horsess. I beceache the Lord to giue you a good and happy end to all your biusness. I thanke God all the chillderen are well, and so is Ned Smith. Ned and his brother present theaire humbell dutis to you; and I begg your bllesing for them all, and your loue and prayers for my self. I beceach the Lord to giue you a speady and happy meeting with

Your most affectinat wife for ever,   BRILLIANA HARLEY.

Mr. Littell, I thanke God, is well, and abell to goo a littell abrode.

I thanke you for my very fine wascott: by this carrier is sent vp the clocke and dublet and houses you sent for.

May the 18, 1633.

IX.

To my deare sonne Mr Edward Harley.

Good Ned—I hope thease lines will finde you well at Oxford. I longe to reseaue the ashurance of your comeing well to your iournyes end. We haue had faire weather sence you went, and I hope it was so with you, which made it more pleaseing to me. You are now in a place of more varietyes then when you weare at home; thearefore take heede it take not vp your thoughtes so much as to neglect that constant saruis you owe to your God. When I liued abroode, I tasted something of thos willes: thearefore I may the more experimentally giue you warneing. Remember me to your tutor, in home I hope you will finde dayly more and more cause to love and respect. I thanke God my coolde is something better then when you left me. I pray God blles you, and giue you of those saueing grasess which will make you happy heare and for ever heareafter.

Your most affectinat mother,   BRILLIANA HARLEY.

Oct. 25, 1638.

X.

To my deare sonne Mr Edward Harley.

Good Need—I was dublly glad to reseaue your letter, bothe for the asshureanc of your comeing weell to Oxford, and that I reseued it by your fathers hand, whoo, I thanke God, came well home yesterday, aboute foore a cloke. I am glad you like Oxford; it is true it is to be liked, and happy are we, when we like both places and condistions that we must be in. If we could be so wise, we should finde much more swetness in our lifes then we do: for sartainely theare is some good in all condistions (but that of sinn), if we had the arte to distract the sweet and leaue the rest. Nowe I ernestly desire you may haue that wisdome, that from all the flowers of learneing you may drawe the hunny and leaufe the rest. I am glad you finde any that are good, wheare you are. I belleue that theare are but feawe nobellmens sonne in Oxford; for now, for the most part, they send theaire sonnes into France, when they are very yonge, theaire to be breed. Send me word wheather my brother Bray doo send to you, and wheather Sr Robert Tracy did come to see you, for he toold your father he would; and let me knowe howe sheawes you any kindenes, when you haue a fitte opertueniy. Comend my saruis to Mrs. Willkeson and tell her I thanke her, for her fauor to you. I may well say, you are my well-beloved chilld; thearefore I cane not but tell you I mise you. I thanke God I am somethinge better with my coold then I was; your brother Robine has had no fite sence the Munday before you went away; the rest of your sisters and brother, I thanke God, are well. Remember me to your tutor. If you would haue any thinge, let me knowe it. Bee not forgetfull to rwit to me; and the Lord in mercy blles you, both with grase in your soule and the good things of this life.

Your most affectinat mother till death, BRILLIANA HARLEY.

Be carefull to keepe the Sabath.

Nov. 2, 1638.

XI.

To my deare sonne Mr. Edward Harley, in Magdeline Halle in Oxford.

Good Ned—I beceach the Lord to blles you with those choys bllesings of his Spirit, which none but his deare ellect are partakers of; that so you may taste that sweetness in Gods saruis which indeed is in it: but the men of this world can not perseaue it. Thinke it not strange, if I tell you, I think it longe sence I hard from you; but my hope is that you are well, and my prayers are that you may be so. As you say you haue founde your tutor kinde and carefull of you, so I hope he will be still. If you wante any thinge, let me knowe it. On Saterday last I hard from your aunte Pelham: shee and all hers are well. I beleeue you haue all the inteligence of the Quene mothers arriuall and entertainement, thearefore I will omite it. Your father, I thanke God, is well; and for meself, I haue not yet shaked off my coold. Your brother Roberd by Gods mercy to him has bine yet free from his fitts, and goos to scoule carefully; and I hope he is now so wise to see his stubborneness was not the way to gaine any thinge but reproufe. I purpos, if pleas God, to send the next weeke to see you. Your father prays God to blles you. Remember me to your tutor, and I beceach the Lord to keepe you from all euil. I haue sent you some juce of licorich, which you may keepe to make vse of, if you should haue a coold. So I rest,

Your most affectinat mother,   BRILLIANA HARLEY.

Bromton, Nove. 13, 1638.

XII.

To my deare sonne Mr. Edward Harley.

Good Ned—This day I reseued a letter from you, in which you rwite me, that you had rwit to me the weake before; which letter I haue not reseued, so that I thought it longe sence I hard from you. It is my ioye that you are well, and I beceach the Lord to continue your health, and aboue all to giue you that grase in your soule which may make you haue a healthfull soule, sounde without erors, actiue in all that is good, industrious in all the ways in which good is to be gained. I am glad you finde a wante of that ministry you did inioye: labor to keepe a fresch desire affter the sincere milke of the word, and then in good time you shall inioye that bllesing againe. The Lord has promised to giue his Spirit to his chilldeten, which shall leade them in the truth. Begge that bllesed Spirit, and then errors will but make the truth more bright, as the foile dous a dioment. My deare Ned, as you haue bine carefull to chuse your company, be so still, for piche will not easely be tuched without leaufeing some spot. I had not hard of Duke Roberts and my Lord Crauens being taken. I hope the nwes of the Sweeds is not true; but in all theas things we must remember the warneing, which our Sauiour has giuen us, when he had toold his decipels that theare must be wars and rumers of wars; (but he saith, let not your harts be trubled; in my aprehention, as if Christ had saide) greate trubells and wars must be, both to purg his chruch of ipocrits, and that his enimies at the last may be vtterly distroyed, but you my saruants be not carefull for your selfs, you are my jewells, and the days of trubbell are the days when I take care of jewells: and, my deare Ned, tho I fermely beleeue theare will be great trubells, yet I looke with ioy beyond those days of trubell, considering the glory that the Lord will bring his chruch to; and happy are they that shall liue to see it, which I hope you will doo. I hard that theare was a cardenalls cape brought to the Custome Howes, valued at a high rate, but none would owne it; and, to requete your inteligence, I let you knowe what I heare. The Scoch buisness is not yet ended. Theare is lately come to the court a frech duke with two or three other gentellmen or nobell men, being fleed from the French king's army, for some vnfiting words they vsed of the French kinge. The Quene mother was so transported with joy, as they say, at the sight of the quene, that shee was in a trance. This day I hard it confermed from Lounddoun that the Palsgrave in besceachgeing a towne in WestPhalia was raised and most of his army defeated, and his brother taken prisner, but this is our comfort, that the rod of the wicked shall not allways rest on Gods peopell. I haue sent Hall purposly to see you; for, sence I can not speake with you, nor see you so offten as I desire, I am willing to make make theas paper mesengers my depuety. I hope I shall heare from you by this mesenger; I thanke God your father is well, and your brother Robert has had no fitte sence you went. He goos to scoule and eates his meate well; and I hope the Lord will spare him. You must rwit to him; you know he is apte to aprehend vnkindness. When you rwite by the carrier, rwite nothing but what any may see, for many times the letters miscarry. My deare Ned, you may see how willing I am to discourse with you, that have spoune out my letter to this lentghe. I thanke God my coold is goon. I beceach the Lord to blles you, as I desire my owne soule should be bllesed:

Your most affectinat mother, BRILLIANA HARLEY.

I haue sent you a cake, which I hope you will eate in mory of Bromton.

Bromton, Nove. 17, 1638.

XIII.

To my deare sonne Mr. Edward Harley, in Magdeline Hall, in Oxford.

Good Ned—I reseued a letter from you this weake, by the carrier; it was very wellcome to me, for sence I can not see you, I am glad to haue the contentment of a paper conuersing with you, for still you are most deare to me, and I hope euer will be. When I rwit to Gorge that I had not hard from you (as I thought a longe time) I had then reseued no letter sence I did that sent by Looker, but now I haue reseued all you haue rwit to me, but that by my brother Brays man. As I much reioyce to be asshured of your health,

...uch as I inioye my owne, so much more dous it reioyce me that the Lord dous so in mercy incline your hart to seeke him, and that you finde sweetnes in his ways. The Lord, whoo only has the harts of men in his hands, keep your 'art cloose to his feare; that you may remember your Creator now, in the days of your youth; that in youth and old agge you may haue that joye which surpases the joy of the world, that so in your old agg you may say, Lord, remember thy sarvant whoo has allways desired to sarue thee. I did always thinke Mr. Longly would not stay long with my Lord of Middelsexcess; I whisth my Lord my brother had him. I haue not time to rwite you the nwes I heare from a shure hand; thearefore I haue sent you my brothers letter, that you my knowe the truth and particulars of it. Keepe my letter safe, and send it me againe. Another letter I send you with it, that you may knowe what I heare, and I hope, you will vse the knoweledg of things in this kinde wisely. The Scoth biusnes I hope is well composed. I would willingly haue sent you the booke, but as yet I could not geet on; but I hard it read, a booke printed by aughterity from the kinge, in which he has forbide ther booke of Common Prayer, which they weare offended at, and grated them a publick fast, which they heeld the 10 of this month, as I take it; and now they haue a publicke assembely and a parlament in May or March, I haue forgot which. I take this to be good nwes. Your father, I thanke God, is well. Your brother Robert has no fitte sence you went, and yet he has bine crost, when he desarued it; but he left of some of his cloths, and tooke a greate coold, and yesterday was exceeding ill, feauerisch, his throate sore. I had not bine so fare has his chamber sence you went, but yesterday went to see him; when I was glad I did, for vpon my giueing him somethinge, he was much better. They that weare with him did not perseauefe his illness: I thanke God, to day he is vp, and I hope it will be no ague, tho I feare it. All the rest are well, and I thanke God I am reasnabell well. The Lord in mercy blles you, and take this assurance, that I am

Your most affectinat mother till death, BRILLIANA HARLEY.

Remember my saruis to your worthy tutor. I did rescaue a letter from him by Looker, and I thanke him for it.

I haue no time to rwite to Gorge.

In hast.

Nou. 24, 1638.

XIV.
To my deare sonne Mr. Edward Harley.

Good Ned—I haue now reseued your letter by my brother Brays man. I giue God thankes that you are recouered from that indispotion you fellt, and thanke you that you did send me word of it; for I desire to knowe howe it is with you in all condistions. If you are ill, my knoweing of it stire me vp more ernestly to pray for you. I beleeue that indispotion you feelt was caused by some violent exersise: if you vse to swinge, let it not be violently; for exersise should be rather to refresch then tyer nature. You did well to take some bolsome; it is a most sufferen thinge, and I purpos, if pleas God, to rwite you the vertues of it. Deare Ned, if I could as easely conuae meself to you as my letters, I would not be so longe absent from you; but, sence I must waite for that comfort, I joy in this, that I asshure meself, your prayers and mine meete dayly at the throne of grase. I must nowe tell you, your letter, by the carrier this weake, was wellcome to me; and your father has reseued his from you, and one from your tutor. I take it for a greate bllesing, that your worthy tutor giues so good a testimony of you, and that you esteme him so highely. I blles the Lord, that has giuen you fauor in his eyes, to seet his good will vpon you. It is found experimentally true that conquerores must be as carefull to keepe what they haue gained as they were to obtained it. It is alike true, we must be, as carefull and stuedious to keepe good opinions and affections towords vs as we weare to gaine them; and I hope you will be a good practicinor of that leesson. Deare Ned, if you would haue any thinge, send me word; or if I thought a coold pye, or such a thinge, would be of any plesure to you, I would send it you. But your father says you care not for it, and Mrs. Pirson tells me, when her sonne was at Oxford, and shee sent him such thinges, he prayed her that shee would not. I thanke you for the Man in the Moune. I had hard of the booke, but not seene it; by as much as I have looke vpon, I find it is some kine to Donqueshot. I would willingly haue the French booke you rwite me word of; but if it can be had, I desire it in French, for I had rather reade any thinge in that tounge then in Inglisch. I know not sartainely wheather I haue it, tell I see it. Take it vpon likeing; if I haue it not, I will not return it backe. Your father was yesterday at Loudlow, wheare the caus was hard betwne Sr Gillberd Cornewell and his sisters, and it went against Sr Gilberd Cornewell, to his shame. I thanke God, your father is well, and so is your brother Roberd, and all the rest. Smaleman has beueried his wife; and Mrs. Steuenson remaines very ill. Deare Ned, the Lord in heauen blles you, and giue you that principell of gras, which may neuer dye in you, but that you may growe in gras, and so haue the fauor of your God, which is better then life, and the fauor of good men, which small number is worth all the millions of men besides. So, asshureing you that I will still reioyce to sheawe meself

Your most affectinat mother tel death, BRILLIANA HARLEY.

I rwit to the last weake; send me word wheather you had my letter; I would not haue it loost.

In hast.

Noue. 30, 1638.

XV.

To my deare sonne, Mr. Edward Harley.

Good Need—This night Hall brought me your letter; but he is so perplexed aboute the horses that he seems not to be Hall. He was apointed by your father and meself to come downe by Oxford, and to haue rested theare the Seboth; but the spoileing of the horses did so distract him, that he can not say any thinge of Oxford or Loundoun. I rwite you worde by the carrier that your father did purpos to send to you this weake: my cosen Prisc sending for his horsess, your father takes that opertunity to send to your tutor. I take it for a great mercy of God, that you haue your health; the Lord in mercy continue it to you, and be you carefull of your selfe: the meanes to presarufe health, is a good diet and exersise: and, as I hope you are not wanteing in your care for your health, so I hope you are much more carefull for your soule, that that better part of yours may growe in the wayes of knowledg. And in some proportion it is, with the soule as with the body; theare must be a good dyet; we must feede vpon the worde of God, which when we haue doun we must not let it lye idell, but we must be diligent in excrsiseing of what we knowe, and the more we practes the more we shall knowe. Deare Ned, let nothinge hinder you from performeing constant priuet duties of prayeing and redeing. Experimentally, I may say that priuet prayer is one of the beest meanes to keepe the hart cloos with God. O it is a sweet thinge to open our harts to our God, as to a frinde. If it had not bine for that I had recours to my God sheure I should haue fainted before this. I heare no nwes at this time from Loundoun, only Mr. Wallker is still in prison; all my frinds theare are well, and I thanke God all your frindes are well heare. Your father is cheerefully well, and your brother Robert has had no fitte sence you went. Your brother Tomas cried very much the other day, becaus he thought howe he was vsed to fight with you at Sheareswesbury. The Ember weake nowe drawes on a pase. I wisch you and your tutor weare heare then; howesoeuer I hope, you will in desires be with vs: and so our prayers, I hope, shall meete in heauen, before the Lord. I thanke God, I am much better then when I rwite last to you. I beceach the Lord to blles you, and that you may be still the beloued childe of

  Your most affectinat mother, BRILLIANA HARLEY.

I haue sent a token to Mrs. Wilkinson: it is a box. Doo not you vndoo the boxe; but deleuer it to her, eather yourself, or send it by Gorge Griffits. It is two cruets of chinna, with silluer and gilt couers, and bars and feete. Doo not let the boxe be opened before she has it.

I haue giuen my cosen Prisis man a great charge of the box. If it come safe, I will giue him a reward.

Send me word how he bringes the box.

In hast affter sauper.

Desem. 11, 1638.

XVI.
To her son Edward.

Good Ned—I haue a nwe wellcome for euery letter you send, and a nwe thankes to you for it. I blles God that you are well; the Lord in mercy continue your health, for shure I am, if you be well, I counte it vpon my owne score, and thinke meself so. My deare Ned, be still wacthfull ouer your self, that custome in seeing and heareing of vice doo not abate your distaste of it. I blles my God, for thos good desires you haue, and the comfort you finde in the sarfeing your God. Be confident, he is the beest Master, and will giue the beest waiges, and they weare the beest liuery, the garment of holynes, a clotheing which neuer shall weare out, but is renwed euery day. I remember you in my prayers, as I doo my owne soule, for you are as deare to me as my life. I hope in a speciall maner, we shall remember you at the fast; and, deare Ned, thinke vpon that day, howe your father is vsed to spend it, that so you may haue like affections to ioyne with vs. Let your desire be offtner presented before your God that day; and the Lord, whoo only heares prayers, heare vs all.

Deare Ned, be carefull to vse exersise; and for that paine in your backe, it may be caused by some indispocion of the kidnes. I would haue you drinke in the morning beare boyled with licorisch; it is a most excelent thinge for the kidnes. For the booke, if you can not have it in French, send it me in Inglisch: and I will, if pleas God, send you mony for it. Deare Ned, it is very well doun, that you submite to your fathers desire in your clothes; and that is a happy temper, both to be contented with plaine clothes, and in the weareing of better clothes, not to thinke one selfe the better for them, nor to be trubelled if you be in plane clothes, and see others of your rancke in better. Seneque had not goot that victory ouer himselfe; for in his cuntry howes he liued priuetly, yet he complaines that when he came to the courte, he founde a tickeling desire to like them at court. I am so vnwilling that you should goo to any place without your worthy tutor, that I send this mesenger expresly to your tutor, with a letter to intreate him, you may haue the happines of his company, wheather souer you goo; and your father by no means would haue you goo any wheather, without him. If you should goo to my brothers, I heare theare is a dangerous passage; I desire you may not goo that way, but aboute. The Lord in much mercy blles you, and presarue you from all euell, especially that of sinn: and so I rest

Your most affectinat mother, BRILLIANA HARLEY.

Your father dous not knowe I send. Thearefore take no notis of it, to him, nor to any.

Desem. 14, 1638.

Nobody in the howes knowes I send to you.

XVII.

To her son Edward.

My good Ned—I was very glad to reseaufe by Marten, the asshurance of your being well, at Barington. Your letter was wellcome, for Marten could tell me nothinge of you, but that you weare well, and that was wellcome to me. Sence I could not haue you with me, I was glad you weare with my brother, wheare I doute not, but that you weare made much of. I can not but be glad to haue you make some aquantance with my frindes. I doute not, but that you are of my beleefe, that my Lady Bray is of a very kinde and sweet dispotion. I beleeue you found my brother very kinde, tho not very full of expressions; but if theare weare caus to try a frinde, I beleeue he would truely aproufe himself one: but that is the euill in melencoly; it actes most, inwardly; full of thoughts they are, but not actiue in expressions. Many times they are so longe in studeing, what is fite for them to doo, that the oportuenity is past. My deare Ned, nothing heare belowe on the earth is more deare to me, than your being well. It is that, I pray for, and reioyce when I am ashured of it; but, my deare Ned, aboue all, the well being of your soule is most deare to me, next to my owne. I reioyce, that you keepe that aquantance with your self, as to take notice of the pasages in your hart; keepe that wacth still, and the more you knowe of your self, the lees you will trust in yourself, and then you will desire to be seet in that Rocke, which is higher then yourselfe, and so you will be safe. I hope theare will no such things be imposed vpon your howes, as is in some others; and I hope, if it should be, you will keep to the truth in euery thinge; and, in my opinion, he whoo stands for the truth in a smale thinge (as we thinke, for none of Gods truths in his saruis is smale), is of a more coragious spirit, then on that will only sheaw themselfes in greate matters. I hope this letter will meete you returned safe to the vniuercity, which I should be glad to be ashured of. My deare Ned, rwite to me as soune as you cane; for I longe to heare from you, and the Lord in mercy let me heare well from you. Your father is nowe at Heriford; he went theather on wensday to the musters; he returnes not tell to morrow. I thanke God, he has his health well. Your brother Robert has had no fitte this fortnight; he is not much changed. Your brother Tomas and cosen Smith are very well, and I beleeue, they begine nowe to looke to theaire recknings; they thinke theas days haue bine short. Your sisters are, I thanke God, well; and so is all your frindes in theas parts; only my cosin Pris brought a greate coold with him, and has it still. The Lord in mercy blles you, and giue you a hart to vnderstand thos things which belonge to your peace, both in this life and your euerlasting peace; and the Lord in mercy presarue your health, and prosper your indeuors in the ways of knowledg; and still beleeue, that I take comfort in expresing meself

   Your most affectinat mother,   BRILLIANA HARLEY.

Janr. 4, 1638.

Remember my saruis to your worthy tutor. Mr. Gowor telles me, he rwit to you, and so did I, by the carrier of Lemster, when your father rwit to your tutor; for your father rwit by both the carriers, feareing the one of them might faile the deliuery of his

XVIII.
To her son Edward.

My good Ned—I thinke it longe sence I hard from you, but my hope is that you are well. My thoughtes are as much vpon you now, as when you weare with me, and thearfore I must conclude, that absence abates no loue, but that which is but a shawdow of loue. I send this mesenger (whoo makes me beleeue he goos with a good will) purposly to see you, and I hope, he will bringe me the ashurance of your being well returned to Oxford. The carrier sent me word you weare not returned on Tusday last. Your father came well home from Heariford, on Saterday last; he was a littell ill at Heriford, but I thanke God, he is very well nowe. Your brother Robert has some times a fite; all the rest are well, and I beleeue they will tell theaire owne mindes to you themselfes. I hard of no other thinge they did at Heariford; but, by order from the Lords, they haue made two prouesmarchalls, to home they give £20 pound a peace, euery yeare, to ride well armed, and each of them a man, and to let noe roges or idell persons wonder aboute the country; and the depuetie liftenantes haue entertained two shoulders to discipline all the bandes: on is taken out in your fathers company, to be his sargent; his name is Weare; he has bine in all theas wars in Jermany, and sarued vnder your ouncell Sr Tomas Conway; the others name I knowe not; and this I rwite you word of, that you may not be ignorant of what is doune in your owne cuntry. Your cosen Scriuen, they say, is to be a curenall, if any troups goo vpon any saruis. He is called Curenall Scriuen. For forane nwes, I beleeue, you haue hard that Briscake is taken; and nowe the Curantes are lisened againe, you will wekely see theare relations. Now, my deare Ned, howe much doo I longe to see you, and the Lord in mercy still giue me that comfort, that I may acounte you my beloued child, and the Lord in mercy fille you with his gras, that so you may be louely in His sight; and if you are beloued by the Lord, it is happines enoufgh. None are partakers of his loue but his childeren; and he so loued them, that he gaue his sonne to dye for them. O that we could but see the depthe of that loue of God in Chirst to vs: then shure, loue would constraine vs to serue the Lord, with all our harts most willingly. And this loue of the Lord is not commen to all. Others may partake of his mercy, as Ahab, who the Lord spared vpon his humeliation; and they may partake of his power, as the Kinge in Samaria did, when the Lord made plenty to flowe in the citty, affter so greate a famine. And all his creaturs partake of his liberallity in feeding them, and his most wise gouerning of the things heare belowe; but none tastes of his loue but his chosen ones; and if we be loued of the Lord, what need we care what the men of the world thinke of vs? We in that respect, should be like a good wife, whoo cares not, howe ill fauored all men ells thinke her, if her husband loue her. And, my deare Ned, as this loue of the Lord is his peculier gifte, only to his deare onse, let it be your cheefe care to geet ashurance of that loue of God in Christ; and, sence he has loued you, sheawe your loue to him, by hateing that which he hates, which is sinn; and it was sin that crucified our Lord, that so loued us that he gaue himself for vs. My deare Ned, the eye, which I put vpon my owne soule, I put you in minde of. Be constant in holy dutys; let publicke and priuet goo to geather. Let not the on shoulder out the other. I beleeue, before this, you haue reed some part of Mr. Caluin; send me word how you like him. I haue sent you a littell purs with some smale mony in it, all the pence I had, that you may haue a penny to giue a power body, and a pare of gloufs; not that I thinke you haue not better in Oxford, but that you may some times remember her, that seldome as you out of my thoughts: the Lord blles you.

 Your most affectinat mother,   BRILLIANA HARLEY.
Janu: 14, 1638.

 I haue sent your tutor a smale token. I can not but desire to sheawe thankes to him, who sheawes so much loue to you. I heare in closed send you the bookebinedrs letter from Woster, that you may see bookes are not so cheep theare as in Oxford.

XIX.
To her son Edward.

Deare Ned—I pray God blles you, first with thos rich grasess of his Spirit, and then with the good things of this life. I haue thought it longe sence I hard from you; and I can not be very mery, tell it pleases God, to giue me that comfort; my hope is that you are well, tho I haue bine in a greate deale of feare of it. I haue thought theas three weakes a longe time; but I hope the Lord will in mercy refresch me, with good asshurance of your being well. I may well say, that my life is bounde with yours, and I hope I shall neuer haue caus to recall or repent of my loue, with which I loue you. I rwite to you by the carrier, and to Gorge Griffets. I rwit the last weake: but I heare from none of you. I thanke God, your father is well. Yesterday he came from my Lady Cornewells, wheare he was, about the shute which shee and her daughters haue with Sr Gillberd Cornewell. Theare, he meet with Mr. Penell and his sonne, whoo is of Oxford. Your father sayes, he is a very pretty jentellman; he toold your father he would goo to see you; if he doo, vse him kindely. His mother was Sr Edwarde Griuell's daughter, and so shee was my cosen, and you haue caus to esteme your, my kindered, which I beleeue you doo. Mr Scidamore, that dwells hard by Heariford, whoo maried my Lord Scidamores sister, toold your father the other day at Heriford, that he would see you at Oxford; he has bine a brood in France and Italy: if he doo come to you, be carefull to vse him with all respect. But ˙˙ the etertaineing of any such, be not put out of your self; speeke freely, and all ways remember, that they are but men; and for being gentellmen, it puts no distance betwne you; for you haue part in nobellness of bearth: tho some have place before you, yet you may be in theare company. And this I say to you, not to make you proude or consaited of your self, but that you should knowe yourself, and so not to be put out of your self, when you are in better company then ordineray: for I haue seene many, when they come in to good company, loose themselfes. Shurely they haue to highe esteme of man; for they can goo booldly to God, and loose themselfes before men. Remember, thearefore, when you are with them, that you are but with thos whoo are such as yourself; tho some, wiser and more honnerabell. Your brothers and sisters, with Ned Smith, are well. Mrs. Pirson is still ill. I pray God spare her, if it be his will. I had a letter from my Lord, the last night; I thanke God he is well. I heare that Duke Robard is brought to a castell with in 20 miles of Vienna, wheare he is keep clos prisinor; a senternall standing at his chamber doore with a drawne sword. My Lord Crauen is in the same place, but they come not to on another. My Lord Crauens ramson is 50 thousand pounds. My paper will giue me leaufe to say no more, but to conclud as I begane; the Lord blles you.

Your most affectinat mother,   BRILLIANA HARLEY.
Janu: 19, 1638.

Remember my saruis to your worthy tutor. I had but a littell time to rwite in; yet I have scribelled ouer a longe letter.

XX.

For my deare sonne Mr Edward Harley.

Good Ned—I reseued your letter by the carrier, and by the mesenger on frieday last. Your father was very vnwilling you should goo to any place without your worthy tutors company; and I douted the carriers comeing so soune as to preuent your tutors gooing to some other place, and that made me hasten a letter to you. I desire to be thankefull that the fier in Oxford fell not out in your howes. I like it well that your tutor has made you hamsome cloths, and I desire you should goo hamsomely. Dear Ned, I am exceeding glad that you did seet Wensday a part; I hope the Lord did hear vs all; and nowe our duty is, when we haue so prayed, and so promised, to be more wacthfull and obedient to our God, that we doo not turne againe to foolly, and like brokens bowes that start a side, for so we shall loose our paines, and the sweet frute of our prayers, and bringe more sorrow vpon our soules. Deare Ned, I thanke you for ioyneing with me in desireing, I might be abell to goo to the congregation and the beauty of holynes. It is true, my sweet Ned, I may truely say, on thing haue I desired, and that I will seeke affter, that I might inioye thos sweet preueleges in Gods howes; but sence you went I haue not had that happines. The sharpnes of the weather is such as I can not beare it so longe togeather. I must waite vnder the gratious hand of my God. Your father and I, haue sent Marten, hopeing he will finde you at my brother Brayes. I desire to heare howe you doo, and I hope, I shall heare well from you, and I beceach the Lord in mercy, to continue that comfort to me. And nowe, my dear Ned, in company and in inioyeing the recreations of this life, looke to your hart, that you may resarufe a higher meashure of joye and delight for the saruis of your God; and to doo so, labor to finde out the vanity in all the things heare belowe: the vanity is this, they last not; and theare is a wearines in them, if they be still inioyed. The Lord bless you.

Your most affectinat mother, BRILLIANA HARLEY.

(No date.)

Your brother Robert has had three or foore fits within this weake, to my great greefe; all the rest, I thanke God, are well.

On the Envelope:—

Mune knwe he should be quite out of countenance if he brought no letter, thearefore, to make vp the matter, he tells me that Mr Tomes came home the last night, and sends me word that he left you well. I hope Mune does not make it, but that it is true that you are well, which is all ways a joy to me.

XXI.

To my deare sonne Mr Edward Harley.

Good Ned—The last night the gardener brought me your letter, which was a greate frescheing to me, for I had not bine well satisfied, neuer sence Martaine was with you, for he toold me, you said you weare sleeppy that morneing he came away, and that you spake very littell to him; and not heareing, as I thought, so longe from you, made me afraide; but nowe, I thanke God for his mercy to me, that I haue hard with comfort from you. The Lord in mercy continue your health, and, aboue, the Lord in his rich mercy giue you such life in Christ, that you may haue a stronge and liuely soule, allways actife in the ways of gras. My deare Ned, be carefull of yourself, and forget not. Doo exersise; for health can no more be had without it, then without a good diet. I much reioyce, and giue the Lord thankes, that Mr Pirkins was an instruement to bringe two in my deare brothers famerly out of darkenes into light, and from the power of sin, vnder the sweet regement of our Lord Christ Jesus. I am confident, your worthy tutor reioyces in it, that he did so shine as to bringe glory to his Lord and Master; and as the worke is begonne, and we reioyce in it, so I desire from my soule, that the Lord would perfect it. I begone with this, becaus I most reioyce in it; and nowe I must tell you, I am glad my brothers howes, is so well gouered, and that his daughter and sonne are of so good dispocions. I pray God, add gras to it, and then it will be a sweet harmmony. I am not sorry that euery one tells you, you are like my lord. I haue not bine very well theas three days, and so enforsed me to keepe my beed, as I haue doune many times, when you weare with me. I hope, I shall be able to rise to day. My letter should haue bine longer, had not I bine in beed. I heare my Lord Conway is goone suddainely into Ireland, and that he has a troup of hoors, but more of that, a nother time. Your father, I hope, is well. He purposed to be with Mr Vahans at Mockes, and to be at home this night. The Lord blles you, and beleeue that I am neuer weary in expresing meself to be,

 Your most affectinat mother, Brilliana Harley.
Janu: 26, 1638.

 Deare Ned,—My agge is no secret; tho my brother Bray is something mistaken in it. When I was maried to your father, your father would haue bine asked in the chruch, but my lord would be no means consent; what his reson was, I know not. Then they haue a custome, that, when they fetch out the liscens, the agg of the woman, must be knowne; so that, if I would haue hide my agg, then it must be knowne, and then I was betwne two or three and twenty. I was not full three and twenty, but in the liscens they rwit me three and twenty, and you knowe how longe I haue bine maried, for you know how old you are, and you weare borne when I had bine maried a yeare and 3 months.

My brother Bray has bine a maried man ever since I can remember, and I neuer had much aquentance with him, but I knwe he was my brother, and so I could not be a stranger to him, and he is a very good man.

XXII.

To my deare sonne Mr Edward Harley.

Good Ned—This day I reseued your letter by the carrier; it was wellcome to me; and I blles God that you are well, beceaching the Lord in mercy to keepe his feare in your harte, that so you may walke in the ways that leads to life, and avoide all the bye paths that tend to death. I was confident that my lady Cope would vse you courtesely, and I beleeue she keepes her state, as all nobellmens daugtres doo; tho I doo not. Your ouncell Bray sent home Spot the llast weake, and then he writ to your father, howe glad he was of you, and he expreses a large good opinion of you, which I hope you will ansure with respect to him and his. I am sorry his sonne has no better aquantance, or rather I am sorry that he relescheth thos that are of no worth in respect of goodness. My deare Ned, pray ernestley to God, to put such a principell of gras into your hart, from which you may loue thos that are worthy of loue, and then no ill company will be pleaseing to you. I heare as you doo of the displaceing of my lord Anckeram and my lord Morton, that was captaine of the gard, and the leftenant of the Tower; but I did not heare of Mr. Treashurer remoueall. I beleeue you haue hard, that my lord of Arendell eateing of oyesters, the oyesters were bluddy, and affterwards thought he sawe a man runeing at him with a drawne sword; but none ells coued see what he thought he sawe. I am sorry my lord is goone into Ireland. Doctor Deodate was sent for to Mr Roberd Moores wife, whoo is lattely come out of the lowecuntres; shee had a greate feauer. Doctor Deodate being so neere, came to see your father and meself; he did not forget to aske for you, with a greate deale of loue, and expreses a greate deale of desire affter your good; he is very well and merrier than ever I sawe him; his man toold Pheebe, that his mistris was with chillde; if it be so, shure that is the ground of his meerth. Your anchent frinde Mrs Traford is very bigg with child, and doctor Deodate dous somethinge feare her. He tells me he was allmost in loue with her, when shee sarued me, but now he can not fancy her. Mrs Pirson has quited her ague; but good Mr Simons has goot one; he has had three fitts. I beleeue your cosen Smith is not sorry for it; he growes a fine boy, and is more ciuell then he was. Your brother Robert has had no fite this fortnight. I thanke God, he is not alltogeather so stuborne as he was. The gardner would make me beleeue that you are much growne; he likes all well at Oxford, but the capes and littell fiers. It semes it has put him in loue with trauelling, for he would faine be sent againe. I asked him, if Mr Pirkins did not say I was too fond a mother. He ansured me, he said you did very well. Mr Gower toold him, he had learnt no eloquence. Your father came home well on Saterday. Tell my cosen Vahan, that your father sayes they weare all very well at his fathers, wheare he had greate entertainement. I sent this day to see Mrs Wallcott; they sent me word, that theare sonne should goo shortly to Oxford; he is at home to be fitted for it. Mr Cradock is seetled at Clanuer, wheare they say Mr Wallcott means to liue. I thinke it strange that Mr Cradocke should incorage on to preche, by which he puts his frinde vpon such a disaduantage. Mr Cradock is a worthy man, but some times he dous not judg cleerely of things, and when we meet with such men, we must looke through the clowde of theare infirmetyes vpon the suneshine of theare vertues. My paper did deceauefe me, for I thought I had had another side.

Docter Barker was with me lately, and remembered you with much kindenes; he toold me, he would rwit to you, and it semes he is as good as his word; he is a good man. You longe sence riwite for Sr Wallter Rawelys History to your father. I did not forget it, and haue sent it you by this carrier, with a book of nwes. I would haue sent you the relation of the takeing of Brisake, which is of great importance, but your father leaft it at the bischops. I haue sent you another littell booke; you sawe me haue it, when you weare with me. I haue reade it, and it pleases me better then any thinge I haue reade a longe time, and any thing that is good, which I inioye, especiall in the beest thinges, I desire you should haue part with me. Deare Ned, reade it, at your leashure, and well waye it, and then let mee knowe how you like it; for my part I am much in loue with it. Sence the ring I gaue you is broken, and that you esteme a peace of it, becaus I gaue it you, I will, if pleas God, by the next safe bearer send you another, that will not so easely breake: and tell your father keepes his promies, in giueing you a wacth, I will let you haue mine; but I will not venture it by the carrier, and I cannot heare of any that goos to Oxford. My cosen Pelham rwites with a great deale of loue of you, and aproufeing of your carage. The Lord presarue you, that you may still be aproufed of. Vse him kindeley, for I am perswaded, he is of a good nature, and has some morall good in him. My deare Ned, the Lord blles you.

Your most affectinat mother,   BRILLIANA HARLEY.

Pheb: this first, 1638.

You father was not well pleased you did not rwite by the gardner, becaus he was an expres mesenger. Remember my saruis to your worthy tutor. This day Hall brought me " the Holy Court," from Worster. Remember my saruis to Mrs Willkenson.

XXIII.

For my deare sonne Mr Edward Harley, in Magdeline Hall, Oxford.

Good Ned—Sence you keep the brittell ringe tell it brake, I haue sent you on of a more dureing substance, and that you may knowe I haue worne it, I haue left the riben vpon it, which did healp to make it fite for my finger; and keepe this, tell I giue you a better. I beceach the Lord to bless you, with thos choys blessings, with which I desire my owne soule should be bllessed with. My deare Ned, be wacthfull that you grow not slake in keepeing the saboth, and in the performeing of priuet dutyes. O it is a sweet thinge to haue priuet conferance with our God, to hom we may make knowne all our wants, all our foolyes, and discouer all our weakeness, in acurance that he will supply our wants, and will not abrade vs with our infermetys. I thanke God your father is well, and so is your brothers and sisters with your cosen Smith. This opertuenity came vnlooked for, so that the time of the night rather puts me in minde of sleepeing then rwiteing. I can but tell you, I long to see you, and I hope, the Lord will giue me a comfortabell inioyeing of that mercy.

Your most affectinat mother,   BRILLIANA HARLEY.

Pheb: 2. 1638.

I hope, we shall haue a priuet day the next weake, when I trust, we shall remember you.

Remember my saruis to your worthy tutor.

XXIV.

For my deare son, Mr. Edward Harley.

Good Ned—It is my greate comfort, that you inioye your health, which I was assured of this day by your letter. It is my greater ioy that you thirst affter the sweet waters of Gods word in a powerfull menestry. I hope the Lord will grant you, your desire in that kinde. Deare Ned, labor to keepe vp the life of yur soule and be ernest with God, to blles the small means you haue, that by his bllesing, a littell may doo you much good, and that his spirit may heate the cooldness of it. I much reioyce that our hatrs did so neere meet, that you in one weake and we in another sought the Lord. As I rwit to you, I thanke God, we keept wensday last, and I blles God, I ioyned wjth them, and so did your sister Brill and brothers. If euer we had caus to pray, it is nowe. Shure the Lord is about a glorious wofke; He is refineing his Chruch; and happy will thos days be, when shee comes out like goold : and if euer wicked men had caus to feare, it is nowe ; for sartainely the Lord will call them to acounte. Theaire day is at hande. Let vs be found morners, that so we may be marked. I thanke God, I am now out of my chamber againe. Your father is well and so is your brother Robert. I haue not knowne him so well neuer sence he had theas fitts. The rest are well. Mrs Pirson is so well, that shee goos abroode. Mrs Steuenson is still vnder the chrugens hands, and I feare will be. Mr Simons has his ague still; this is all Bromton inteligenc. For that from abrode, I refer you to this inclosed prineted booke. I purpos, if pleas God, to remember you with some of Bromton dyet, against Lent. I wisch you may not eate to much fisch. I know you like it; but I thinke it is not so good for you. I hope you haue something ouer your beeds head. Remember my saruis to Mrs Willkensone. I rwit you a letter by Mr Asson; send me word wheather you reseued it. The Lord blles you and caus you to walke vprightly before him, that so you may be his delight.

Your most affectinat mother,   BRILLIANA HARLEY.

Pheb: 8. 1638.

Mrs Trayford is brought to beed of a daughter this day; shee sent a man a purpos to me, to desire me to be the godmother and that it might be of my name.

Remember my saruis to your worthy tutor, whom I thanke for his loue and care of you, whoo are deare to me.

I beleeue you haue seene the proclamation, which inioynes all barons, knights, and gentellmen, of Linconscheere and the other northern parts, not to be absent from theaire howes, but theair to remaine for the gard of theare cuntrey; which I feare will hinder my sister Pelhams comeing to me.

Deare Ned, rwite againe to my cosen Tomkins and to Mr Simons.

XXV.

To my deare sonne Mr. Edward Harley.

My good Ned—The Lord in mercy blles you, and giue you interest in his sonne Christ, and such a measure of holyness, that you may liue heare like his child. It is my comfort, that you inioye your health, and I beceach the Lord, to continue that mercy to you. I perswade meself you are carefull to improufe your time; this is your time of haruest, and that time being ouer-slipt, it cannot be recalled. I am glad to heare you are cheerefull. Inioy that bllesing, when God giues it you, for cheerefullness of spirit giues more freedome in the performeance of any duety. I hope, as you doo, that the nwes of so many being masacred is not true; the great God of heawen and earth looke in mercy vpon his poore peopell. It is reported, from all parts, the french haue a very great army. I can not thinke yet, that the french would take this time to come into Ingland, when we stand vpon our garde and such preperations for wars. And the report is, that theare goos 30000 foonte and 10000 hoors with the king to Yorke; so that a forieng enimye could not come in a time more disaduantages to him. But if we fight with Scotland, and are ingaged in that ware, then a foren enimy may take his time of aduantage. The caus is the Lords; and He will worke, for his owne glory. Deare Ned, you may remember I haue offten spoke to you aboute theas times; and my deare Ned, would I weare with you one day, to open my minde more largly than I can by rwriteing. They call to super, thearefore I must hasten my letter, but first I must tell you, I haue sent you by the carrier a boxe, derected to you, in which is a turky pye and 6 pyes, such as my lord, your grandfather did loue. I hope to remember you againe in lent. Send me word, wheather you reseaue them, and wheather they be good. Mr. Simons is very ill and very weake. I wisch his wife be not a widowe againe. For Mr. Walcotes sake, I will perswade them to send theare sonne to your tutor: but Mr. Cradock is the only man that preuails with them. I thanke God, your Father is well, and so is your brothers and sisters, with Ned Smith: so in hast, I rest,

Your most affectinat mother, BRILLIANA HARLEY.

Pheb: 15, 1638.

I haue sent your tutor a box of dryed plumes, the box is derected to you; tell him it is a Lenten token. Remember my saruis to him.

XXVI.

For my deare sonne Mr. Edward Harley.

Good Ned—I beceach the Lord to blles you, with thos choyes bllesings, which are only the porcion of his ellect; in which the men of this life, haue no part. They are hide from theaire eyes. Only in the day of trubell and death, then they knowe theare is a happines belongeing to Gods chillderen, which they would then partake of, and howlle, for the wante of that comfort. This day I reseued your letter, and that you are well is so much comfort to me, that when I am ascured of it, it sweetens other trubells, which I goo vnder. Deare Ned, doo not let your dyet be, this Lent, all togeather fisch. I am well pleased, if the pyes fitted your tast, and your frinds. Diuers reports theare be, and it is lightly, the papis will furnisch themselfs, as well as they can. Theare is a booke, which is rwitten by a papis that is conuerted; it discouers much; I would, if I could, haue gained it and haue sent you the booke. I forgot the last time, I rwit to you, to let you knowe the arming, which was seence vpon the seae, were Hollenders; they fought with the Dunckerckes, and had the victory; but what loos the Dunckerckes had, is not yet sartainely knowne. I beleeue you haue hard this, before this letter comes to your hand. For nwes at home, we heare that the lord cheefe justice Finch is sworne a preuy conseller; yonge Mr. Somerseet Fox is sworne on of the presences chamber, and vpon that score he must waite vpon the kinge to Yorke. They say, my lord of Wosters sonne shall be generall of the hors. This day a mesenger, which I sent to my sister Pelham, returned from thence. I thanke God, they are all well theare. My sister rwit me word, that the counsell had sent into Linconscheere 68 shoulders, which weare to be dispersed, and imployed to exersises ther traine bands. My brother Pelham being one of the kings saruants, was sent to by my lord chamberlen, to commade him to waite vpon the kinge at Yorke. We see that honnors are not all ways eassy posestions. I haue sent you a booke of nwes, and on of the weackely corentes. I woould willingly haue your minde keep awake in the knowledg of things abroode. I thanke God, your father is well, and prays God to blles you: your brothers are well. Mr Simons is vpon recouory. My cosen Prise continues ill; what it will proufe, I knowe not. And now I am telling you of thos, whoo are sike, I well tell you of one, that has left this life, and now rest from all sikeness and trubell, Mrs Traford; this day, I hard shee was dead. She dyed aboute 7 dayes affter she was brought to beed. Docter Deodate, when he was with me, told me he feared shee would not liue long affter she was brought to beed. I would haue you rwite a letter to my lady Conway. I have heare inclosed sent you a coppy of the letter I would haue you rwite to her. I beleeue she will take it very kindely. Burgh has bine very sike, which foreslowes your peace of plate. I cane not well tell the waight of it; for I was not by, when your father rwit for it. I haue rwit to Burgh to hasten it. I hope it will be such as it should be. Tell Mr Pirkins rwit to your father that you did wante it, your father said he thought you had no neede of it. It is time nowe to conclude this letter, but it must be in ascuereing you, that I reioyce to aproufe meself,

Your affectinat mother,   BRILLLIANA HARLEY.

Mar: this first, 1638.

Remember my saruis to your worthy tutor. I thinke the carryer goo by Acton, wheare my lady Conway dwells, when they goo to Loundon.

XXVII.

For Sr Robert Harley, Kinght of the Bath.

My deare S^r,—This is only to let you knowe, we are all well, which I had rather tell you, then send the bare message by another. I blless God, that you are well; and hope the Lord, will giue you a safe returne home to morrow, wheare you are longed for. Nowe the Lord in mercy presarue you from all that is euile; desireing still to be beloued by you, as

Your most affectinat wife,   BRILLIANA HARLEY.

Mar: 12, 1638.

Endorsed in Sir Robert's handwriting, "fro' my wife."

XXVIII.

To my deare sonne Mr. Edward Harley, Oxford.

My good Ned—The last weake being not well, I could not inioye this contentment of rwiteing to you. You may remember, that when you weare at home, I was offten enforsed to keepe my beed; it pleases God, it is so with me still, and when I haue thos indispotions, it makes me ill for some time affterwards. It is the hand of my gratious God; and tho it be sharp, yet when I looke at the will of God in it, it is sweetned to me: for to me, theare is nothing can sweeten any condistion to vs, in this life, but as we looke at God in it, and see ourselfs his saruants in that condistion in which we are. Thearefore when I consider my owne afflictions, they are not so bitter, when I looke at the will of my God in it. He is pleased it should be so, and then, should not I be pleased it should be so? And I hope, the Lord will giue me a hart still to waite vpon my God; and I hope the Lord will looke gratiously vpon me.

CAMD. SOC.   F

And my dearest, beleeue this from mee, that theare is no sweetnes in any thinge in this life to be compared to the sweetnes in the saruis of our God, and this I thanke God, I cane say, not only to agree with thos that say so, but experimentally; I haue had health and frinds and company in variety, and theare was a time, that what could I have saide I wanted; yet in all that theare was a trubell, and that which gaue me peace, was sarueing of my God, and not the saruis of the world. And I haue had a time of siknes, and weakenes, and the loose of frinds, and as I may say, the glideing away of all thos things I tooke most comfort in, in this life. If I should now say (which I may booldly) that, in this condistion, O howe sweet did I finde the loue of my God, and the endeuor, to walke in his ways; it may be, some may say, then it must needs be so, becaus all other comforts failed me; but my deare Ned I must lay both my condistions togeather; my time of freedome from afflictions, and my time of afflictions; and in the one, I found a sweetnes in the saruis of God, aboue the sweetnes of the things in this life, and in trubele a sweetnes in the saruis of God, which tooke away the bitternes of the affliction; and this I tell you, that you may beleeue howe good the Lord is, and beleeue it, as a tryed truth, the saruis of the Lord, is more sweet, more peaceabell, more delightful, then the enioyeing of all the vadeing pleashurs of the world. My deare Ned, I thanke you for your letter by the carrier this wake. Howe soeuer trubells may befall me, yet if it be well with you, I reioyce. I thanke God, that you injoy your health. The Lord in mercy continue it to you. My deare Ned, I longe to see you; but I feare it will not be a great whille. I know not well when the Acte is, and I thinke I must not looke to see you tell the Act be past. Whensoeuer it is, I beceach the Lord, giue vs a happy seeing on of another. I am sorry my lady Corbet takes no more care of her chilederen. Sr Andwe Corbet left two thousand pounds a year. Shee has a way that I should not take, by my good will with my chillderen, without it weare to correct some great fallt in them; but my deare Ned, as longe as it pleases God, I haue it, I shall willingly giue what is in my power, for the beest adwantage of you, and your brothers and sisters, as ocation offers itself. Vse your cosen Corbet kindely. I heare his broother goos alonge with the kinge to Yorke, which he dous, becaus he estemes it to be the gallentry of a yonge man. I sent you the last weake a list of thos shoulders, which they say must goo with the kinge. I heare that the Loundoners haue refused to send any of theare trained band, answering, theare weare so many strangers in Loundon, that they feared to let any of theare strentg goo from them. I hard that the kinge caused all the strangers to be numbered in Loundon, and the number of them was two hundred thousand. On wenday last your father had some of his shoulders at Brometon, whean they dyned, and spent the day in trayneing. I wisched you with me, but I did not see them, for then I was not abell to goo out of my chamber: but now I thanke God, I am, and haue some thoughts, if pleas God, to goo to chruch the next Lords day. Good Mr. Gower has an ague. Mr. Simons begins to mend. My cosen Prise is something better. You forget to rwit to Mr. Gower; he has had 4 fitts. Mr. Simons tooke your letter very kindely. I must needs say, I neuer had any maide that profest more respect to you, than Mary Barton, and I beleeue it is in truth; for shee is her fathers daughter and can not desembell. I finde her as good a saruant as euer I had; if I coould but put a littell water in her wine, and make her temper her hastiness! yet I cannot say that euer shee gaue me any ill word, but theare is still the spirit of enuy raingeing amongest some of the saruants, but the humers of my saruants swaye not my affection, and, I hope, shall neuer blinde my judgment: my deare Ned the Lord blles you.

  Your most affectinat mother,   BRILLIANA HARLEY.

in hast, Mar: 22, 1638.

Your brothers and sisters and cosen Smith I thanke God are well.
Tell Gorg Griffets I had not time to rwit to him, which I did desire to haue doun. I haue sent him the mony for Mr Neelham, the

drawer, and I would haue him hasten the sending of the peace of cloth, which he had to drawe. I hope Gorge will bide his countryman wellcome. I had him into my chamber to see him, becaus he went to Oxford. I like it very well, that you goo with your tutor to my brother Brays. I beceach the Lord to goo alonge with you, in all your ways.

Heare inclosed is a booke of nwes. Your father I thanke God is well. He goos and pleas God on Tuesday to the bischops upon a commistion aboute some land that is in question betwne the bischop and another gentellman.

XXIX.

To my deare sonne Mr. Edward Harley.

Dear Ned—Your letter this weak was wellcome to me. It is my joy that you are well, and I blles my God for that mercy to you. I am sorry your eyes haue bine soore, and glad I am that you founde benifite by what Mrs Willkinson gaue you; but feareing your eyes should affter this rume be inclined to a rumeticke humor, I haue sent you a glas of eye watter, which is not only good to cure sore eyes but to presarufe the eyes sight. Drope a litter of the water into your eys, in the morneing and at night; but I hope this watter will come to your hands when your eyes are well. Tho I am not afraide of your eyes, yet I can not but pitty your them; for by experience, I know it to be a great paine; for once I had sore eyes, and when by experience we feele how tender the eye is, we may call to minde, how sencibille God is of all the ronges which are doun his chillderen, when he is pleased to say, that they which touche his chillderen, touch the appell of his eye: thearefore wo be to thos that are so boold; and happy are those that are in that acounte with the Lord.

Your father, I thanke God, came well home from the bichops, the last night, affter I had suped, and this day he was at Wigmore, wheare part of his cumpeny was exersised. On munday last, theare came a letter from the lord leftenants, with commande from the kinge to prees 200 men for soulders, and that they should be at theare randevous the first of Aprill; theare randevous is Assbe, as I take it, neare Yorke; neare Yorke the towne is, if that be not the name. If you weare with me, I could tell you more of my minde; all the ministers are sent to, for mony. Good Mr Steuenson has pleaded a true excuse, his poouerty, haueing 7 chillderen and the sikeness of his wife. Howe it will take, I knowe not, but shure it is true; his wife is still ill, vnder the chrugens hands, but doctor Deodat is not yet come. My deare Ned, I long to see you, and I trust the Lord will giue me that comfort. I thanke God the Lord voutsafed me, that priuelly on the last Lords day, that I was partaker of the comfort in his publike ordinance. Mr Gower did not preach, but on Mr Blineman did, whoo preached very well; he says, he knowes you, and he commends Mr Pirkins very much, which I am very glad to heare so large a commendation as he giues; he is nowe without a place, being lately put out of one. He teaches the scoule tell Mr Simons be abell. I thanke God, I tooke no hurt in gooing to chruch; a littell coold I haue, but I hope it will weare away. I ride one day a broode. I wisched you with me. I beleeue you will be glad to heare, that Mr Gower has mised two fitts. My cosen Pris remains still ill, and I can not but thinke that his drinkeing of so warme beare has doune him hurt.

Your brother Robert had one fite, a weake sence, but sense that he has bine very well, but alas! he cares not to gaine any jentile corage, comes littell to me, but when I exacte it from him; but your brother Thomas is of another minde; your sisters are well. I heare that the kinge begane his journy the 28 of this month. The lord mayor of Loundone has a commistion sealed him by the kinge, to exicute martiall lawe, if theare should be any insorection, when the king is goon. My deare Ned, the Lord in mercy blles you, so in hast I rest,

Your most affectinat mother,   BRILLIANA HARLEY.

Bromton Mar: 29, 1639.

Remember my saruis to your worthy tutor and to Mrs Willkinson, whoo I thanke for her care of your eyes. I am sorry good Mr Pirkins has any thinge to trubell him. But my deare Ned, trubells are multiplyed vpon euery one: many are in douts, and know not what to doo in doutfull cases. Your father prays God to blles you. This night Burgh rwit he had reseued the tancherd, and would make on acording to Mr Pirkins derechon, and send it to Bromton, to be sent to you.

I forgot to rwite you worde that I was very glad you joyned with us in the Ember weake. Mrs Wallcote sent me word she would come to see me the next weake, and then it may be I shall know her minde about her sonne, but my desire is to haue my nephewe Pelham with your tutor.

The greatest * * * I can send you is that an egg was laid by heen of Mr Yats that smels like muske. I haue the egg.

XXX.

To my deare sonne Mr Edward Harley,
at Maudlin Hall in Oxford, these.

Deare Ned—I haue but littell warneing to rwite. Your father hastens the mesinger away; yet in haste, I desire to say somethinge to you, by which you may knowe howe we doo, and howe much I longe affter your good, which I desire next the good of my owne soule. My dayly prayers are for you, and my thoughts are offten with you. Your father has not bine very well theis three days, he has sent for doctor Deodate; but doo not be affraide, for I hope it is but some coold, and I am not affraide of him, tho I am sorry for him, and be you so, and pray for him. He dous not keepe his chamber: his illnes keep him at home, that he was not at Hariford, with depuety leftenants. Your cosen Croft is a lefftnenat, and is come downe for the prest men: he was with me: he came post, and tooke 2 post horsess vp in this towne. All the lusty men are afraide and hide themself. Theare are other letters come from the lord president, to command the depuety lefftenants to haue part of the trained band in rediness, against they are sent for: and the number of them in all countes are acording to that list I sent you. My lord of Arondall is generallisomoe, and my lord of Exexe is lefftenant generall, my lord Nweport a courenell, and S\(^r\) Jacob Aschely another corenell. This bearor will tell you, that my cosen Pris is dead; he dyed yesterday; he has made your father and my cosen Smith his excexotors, which is the ocation of this bearors gooing vp to Loundon. Besides the hast of this bearor, my cosen Foxe and her mother, with other strangers; thearefore I must conclud, but it is with my ernest prayers to the Lord to blles you.

Your most affectinat mother,   BRILLIANA HARLEY.
3 *Aprill*, 1639.

I haue sent you by this bearor a littell box, in which is my wactch, loue it better than you would another wacth; becaus it was yoor good grandfathers. You must not over winde it and it will goo very well.

In very greate haste.

XXXI.

For my deare sonne M\(^r\) Edward Harley,
in Magdeline Halle, Oxford.

Deare Ned—Theare is no earthly thinge that is of more comefort to me than your being well, thearefore you may easely beleeue your letters are sweet comforts to me, and so was your letter this weake. I blles my God that you haue your health, and the Lord in mercy continue that comfort to you and me. My deare Ned, I should be exceeding glad, if your tutor would be willing to let you come home at Whitesuntide: if he will but say the word, I beleeue all partyes would agree; but then I thinke you would desire to goo to the Act, and that would be to much for you; for I desire if pleas the Lord, to haue you at home the longe vacation as they call it. My deare Ned, let me knowe your minde, wheather you are willing, and wheather your tutor be so too, but so that he will be pleased to spend some time with vs at Bromtone. As they doo at Oxford, so they doo in all places, take liberty to inuaye against Puretans. We heare the Scothes haue taken the posestion of the kings howes in Eddenboro. Shure this somer is likely to produce greate matters. The Lord sheawe mercy vpon his poor saruants. I hard the queene as soune as the knige left Loundon to goo towards Yorke, went to her beed with much sorrow.

I rwite to you on wensday last by the gardner, but it was in such hast that I beleue you could hardly reede it. I rwit you word your cosen Prise had made your father and my cosen Smith his excexotors, and thus he has disposed of his estate; they say his land is worth 300 a yare; he owes 2 thousand and 5 hundered pound and some say 3 hunderd pound more. He has giuen to his two sisters chillderen, 12 hundred pounds, and to his brother, 30 pounds a yare anwety; this will he made when he was last at Loundon, and brought it your father, maneing that if any thinge did a rise aboue his deets and leggessess, it should come to his excexetors.

Remember my saruis to worthy Mr Perkins, and let him knowe, the mony shall be sent with all expedition: the sikenes of his scoller is as I aprehinde it, a happy sikenes; for for the most part we are all rather to senceles, then to aprehencif of the condistion of the state of our soules. I thanke God, your father is indiferent well, he dous not keepe his chamber. Doctor Deodate is not yet come, but I beleeue, he will come this night. My deare Ned, I thanke you for hopeing with me, that I should haue my desire in gooing to chruch, which I thanke God, I did two saboths, and I hope the Lord will giue me that mercy this next saboth. I thanke God, your brother Robert has his health well, and so has the rest; some of the sarwants haue agues, but not very violently. Good Mr Simons has his ague euery day and many fairt his life. I haue toold you if you remember of a paper that some statemen make use of, when they would not haue knowne what they riwit of. Rwite me worde wheather you vnderstand what I meane. I pray God blles you and fill you with gras, that sauefeing gras which will neuer leaufe you. I haue not yet reseaufed your letter by Mr. Hackleut, but I hope I shall; so I rest

Your most affectinat mother, BRILLIANA HARLEY.

April 5, 1639.

I thanke you for the booke you sent, but yet I nor your father heau not reed any of it.

Heare incloesed is the key of your box, with a token from your sisters. I should be exceeding glad to see my brother Bray and my sister.

XXXII.

For Mr. Edward Harley, in Magdeline Halle, at Oxford.

Dear Ned—Axcedentally I haue this opertunity to send this letter to the carryer, and haueing forgot some nwes, which it may be you will be glad to heare, I rwit this letter to you; tho this and that which I rwite to you yesterday come by one mesenger.

We heare that the kinge of Spaine begins to deale with the monestries in Spaine, as Harry the 8 did in Ingland. My deare Ned, let me vpon this put you in minde that this year 1639, is the yeare in which maney are of the opinion that Antichrist must begine to falle. The Lord say Amen to it: if this be not the year, yet shure it shall be, in is due time. What nwes I heare conserning Jermany you may see by this inclosed, which I reseued this morneing. I thanke God, your father is reasnabell well. Doctor Deodate is not yet come, nor the mesenger returned. Antony Childe went for him on tuesday last.

The cane for you is come downe to Loudlowe. The boxe was sent for this morning, but yet it is not come: if I can haue my owne minde, it shall be sent to you, if pleas God, the next weake, with the mony that is due for your quarter, and that which is due to Mr Pirkins as your tutor.

The Lord in mercy blles you, and keepe you in his feare and fauor, and giue you fauor with his childeren.

Your most affectinat mother, BRILLIANA HARLEY.
Apr. 6, 1639.

Remember my saruis to your tutor, and tell him I thanke him for his letter.

XXXIII.

To her son Edward.

My deare Ned — I should be glad if I weare in this mesengers place, to see you. Nowe at last I haue reseued your letter, by my cosen Hacklet; it does much reioyce me that you are well, and when I am not well, your being well refresches me, and I blles my God for his mercy to me, that you haue had your health sence you went from me; and I beceach the Lord to blles you, and to fill your soul with thos sweet grases of his spirrit, by which you may both knowe and taste the goodness of the Lord: the Lord is good, and good to his, and his saruis is perfect freedome; and happy are they that are of his famely, whoo serue him dayly, and not as a retainer. My deare Ned, be still wacthfull ouer your hart, that nothing steale away your affections from your God, whoo alone has loued us and whoo alone is to be beloued.

My deare Ned, I thanke you for desireing me to be let blood, shuer if I weare auers to it, yet you might perswade me, but doctor Deodats stay was so short, and I then in a condistion not to take phisek, so that I could not bee let blood, which I did desire and doo still; but I dare not venture vpon Woodowes. I haue not bine well theas 4 days, being extremely trubelled with a beateing at my hart. I thanke God, this day I haue bine something better then I was sence thrusday; I hope the Lord will be mercyfull to me in all condistions. I thanke God, your father is well and cheerefull. Your brother Robert had a littell indispotion, inclineing to a fite the last night, but nowe he is well; your sister Brill is returned from

Lainetarden, wheare shee was to supply my place in being godmother to Mrs. Yates daughter. She was brought to beed on saterday last. I thanke you for the bookes you sent me: the 2 speeches against the Scothes, I red them both; they both sheawe of what spirit they are; Mr Euers was with me yesterday, and your father gaue him the one home with him. You cosen Croft and the other conducter fell out at Loudlowe, and Mr Merek went away with the comistion, but now they are goon. Your father is very willing you should come home the weeke before Whitesentide; it is the Ember weake, but then your tutor must be pleased to come with you. Let me knowe wheather you haue any desire to it. Your father has sent you by this bearer (for yet I knowe not whoo shall goo to you) the mony for your quarter, which Mr Pirkins rwite for, and the mony due to him, and the cane for you; it has bine longe a comeing, and now it is not so good as I would haue it. I haue sent you a purs, which I did promise you, and somethinge in it, only becaus it should not come emty: it has bine all Bleethes worke sence she came to me. Your father purposess to goo to morrow to the bischops about the comistion. My lady Conway rwite me word that shee had reseued a letter from you, which shee takes very kindely. The Lord in mercy blles you, and keepe you from all euell. Strangers are in the parler, and theare I must end this discours, to discours with them, but I am well pleased when I cane expres meself

    Your most affectinat mother,   BRILLIANA HARLEY.
Apr: 16, 1639.

Remember my saruis to your worthy tutor. I hope Piner shall bring this letter to you.

XXXIV.

**To my deare sonne Mr. Edward Harley,
at Magdelin Hall, Oxford.**

My deare Ned—I haue two letters to thanke you for, on by the carrier and on by the gardner; the gardner came not to Bromton tell wensday last; he says he was sike by the way, but I beleeue this has loost his creedet for gooing any more journys. My deare Ned, it is my joy that you are well, and I beceach the Lord in mercy to continue this bllesing of health to you, but aboue all, I desire you may haue that true health in your soule of a sounde minde, that so in theas days of wafereing and douteing you may hoold the truth. I was not well pleased that I did not keepe my woord in sending to you this weake. I hope the next weake your father will send, and thearefore I only rwite theas feawe lines by the carrier to let you knowe I haue sent you a pigon pye; and much good may it doo you when you eate it. Your father returned from the bischops this night. I thanke God he is well: he prays God to bless you, and so dons

    Your affectinat mother,   BRILLIANA HARLEY.
Apr: 19, 1639.

Remember my saruis to your worthy tutor.

XXXV.

To my deare sonne Mr Edward Harley.

My deare Ned—By the date of this inclosed, you will knowe that I had thought to haue sent to you the last weake; but other biusness preuented Piners comeing to you. I thanke God your father came well home from the bischops on fryeday, and I thanke God he is well. Theare are letters come from the lord president, to command all the depetue leftenants not to goo out of the county, and I beleeue it will be the like in Oxfordsheere, and then I must not looke to see my brother Bray. We heare that the Hariford shoulders haue killed on of the conductors, but which of them I doo not yet knowe; they say he was beueried on tusday last at Whitechruch beyond Shrewsbury. The Oxford soulders could not be wors than Harifordsheares weare. Euery on crys out vpon them for theare vilinees which they did. I take it for a mercy that your father had not a hand in it, sence they weare so ill furnished. I hard this day that my lord of Excexes was meet neare Bareke by the treshewe of Scotland, whoo toold him that the Scots had put in many men into Bareke. My lord of Execkes had 150 hundered men with him when he meet him, and vpon his words sent for 3000 more, but when he came to Bareke he found no such thinge, and then he sent the kinge word he should take heed of the tresurerer, vpon which the kinge comemanded him to his chamber; but they say he is broken away. It is confermed by euery on that the Scots haue gained all Scotland without sheeding any blood. I hard that 500 men came out of Irland, and they are put into Carlile. Your father goos to morrow, if pleas God, to Heariford to the sessions, and thinkes not to returne tell saterday. My deare Ned, I did thinke that your tutor would be vnwilling you should come home tell affter the Act; I beleeue he dous it for your benifit, and I must and doo seeke that, beyond all content to meself; but I cannot ynderstand by your letter wheather he be content you should come home as soune as the Act is past, for that I desire you should doo, and I thinke you may well do.

I beleeue my cosen Smith and his wife, and Burgh and his wife, brake theare promis with you, and did not come to you this Ester. Colborne will informe you of all your frinds heare.

I hope your worthy tutor is returned before this. I much reioyce to heare he is so carefull of you. I beceach the Lord more and more to incline his hart to sheawe a loueing care of you, and I hope you will indeuier to ansure his loue, with loue, and his care with all respect.

I am sorry you haue loost so good company as my cosen Vahan.

My deare Ned, be carefull of your health and neglect not exercise. The Lord in mercy blles you and presarue you from all eueill.

I thanke you for the prophesy you sent me.

Remember my saruis to your tutor. So I rest

Your most affectinat mother, BRILLIANA HARLEY.

Apr: 22, 1639.

XXXVI.

For my deare sonne Mr Edward Harley,
in Magdeline Hall, in Oxford.

My deare Ned—I was glad to reseufe your letter, for heatherto you haue bine the great comfort of my life, which I blles my God for; but, my deare Ned, are you willing to hide your being ill from me, whoo only desires to partake with you in all that befalls you? My deare Ned, when you are ill, my prayers are more for you, and the Lord, I hope, will heare me in his Sonne, in home He alone is well pleased. My deare Ned, I hope this is but an ague, which are very much every weare; be carefull of your self, keepe a spare dyet; and, my deare Ned, O that I weare with you; but this is my comfort, my God is with you, and He cane ease you, and vphoold you, and presarue you, and I trust He will doo so. Your father is now at Heareford, and will not returne tell to morrow; but I can not well stay so long from sending to you, thearefore I haue made hast to dispacth this barer to you, and hope he will bringe me wellcome newes of your health, but, if otherways, I hope both you and I shall willingly submit to beare the hand of our God. I thanke you for the kings booke you sent me. Deare Ned, be neuer vnwilling that I should know how it is with you; for none has a more tender aprehention of it then meself. I thanke God, your brothers and sisters are well, and I am reasnabell well, but that I haue bine much trubled with a swelling in my fase and mouth. The Lord in mercy blles you, and restore your health to you againe, and santyfy this sikenes to you, that so, both health and siknes may be aduantage to you, whoo are most deare to

    Your most affectinat mother,   BRILLIANA HARLEY.

Apr: 26. 1639.

I haue sent some bessor stone, which you may take at a night when you goo to beed; and the Lord blles all means to you.

I haue sent you 2 graines of orampotabely, which I would haue you take in 2 spounefulls of cordus watter, when you finde yourself not well.

XXXVII.

To my deare sonne Mr Edward Harley, in Magdeline Hall, in Oxford.

Deare Ned—On saterday last I reseued your letter by Mr. Braughtons man; it was wellcome to me. I hope this day Jones will be with you. My prayers are for your health, and I hope the Lord will be mercyfull to me in you, and as I may so say, to spare my Joseph to me. My deare Ned, nothinge can more pleas me then to haue a simpathy with you, thearefore not to knowe how it is with you would be a torter to me; and when you are not well, sorrow is a thousand times more pleasing to me then to be merry.

My deare Ned, if it pleases the Lord that you are still not well, looke vp to your God; consider why He corrects; it is to better vs, that we may see the euill of our ways, and finde how bitter sinn is, that has brought such bitter thinges vpon us, and has, as we may say, altered Gods dealeing with vs; for the Lord delights to sheawe mercy; and we haue changed His cours, so that we infors the Lord to correct vs for our good; and deare Ned, this comfort we finde in afflictions, that then we tast howe good the Lord is, He then heares our prayers, and giues vs ease, and casts vs not of, howe weake, howe fainte, howe poore or misrabell so euer we are. To the glorry of my God be it spoken, such haue I founde Him to the poorest of all His seruants. My deare Ned, be carefull of yourself for my sake, and I hope your tutor will take care of you, or ells he deceaufs me. I long to heare of you, and I pray God I may heare well of you; but, deare Ned, rwite me the truth, still howe you doo, or ells I can neuer be in any aschurance.

Your father came well home on saterday last. I thanke God, he is very well. I am not sartaine wheather he will rwit to you or no. Your brothers and sisters are well. Mrs. Gower is brought to beed of a daugher, and I am intreted to be the godmother. Mr. Simons is now well. I hard that my lord of Esexkess went from Barek into Scoteland with 500 men, and found none theare that resisted him, or did any thing, and so he returned in peace. To morrow your father, if pleas God, goos to Hariford about prikening the soulders that must be sent out of the trained bands, which makes many of theare wifes to cry.

Mrs Pits sent me word by a saruent of hers that she sawe you at Oxford. I knowe her not, but out of her loue to your ant Wacke shee fauored you with a viset, and sent her man purposely from Rudall to let me knowe you weare well. She married my lady Chokes brother. Mr. Scidmore that I rwit you word of, would see you, was at your chamber to see you the thursday before Easter, but you and your tutor weare not theare. The Lord in mercy blles you, and presarue you in safety, and giue me comfortable seeing of you; so in hast I rest

Your most affectinat mother, BRILLIANA HARLEY.

Apr: 29, 1639.

Remember my saruis to your worthy tutor; to him I would haue rwit, but I heare he is not at Oxford.

XXXVIII.

Ffor my deare sonne Mr. Edward Harley, at Magdalen Hall, in Oxford, deliver these.

Deare Ned—The last night I receaued your l^{tre} by Jones, wch giues me comfortable assurance of yor being well; for which I desire to blesse the Lord; and (deare Ned) as some sharpenes giues a better relish to sweet meats, soe some sence of sickenes makes us tast ye benefit of health. I belieue it was yor comfort, when you were sicke, that you expected health from yor God; and in yor health, that you haue that blessing from Him, with a desire to spinne forth yor health in ye seruice of yor God, wch is perfect freedome; & since you haue soo great priuiledge as to partake of God's mercies in all conditions, labour to see yͤ great and infinite loue of God in Christ, in whom all thinges are made a blessing to us; but without whom, all conditions and all thinges are a curse. Be carefull of yoʳ health for my sake. I belieue yͤ sneezing powder did you noe good, and let it teach you yᵗ wisdome not to take medecines out of a strange hand. Your ffather returned well from Hereford yᵉ last night, where yᵉ deputie lieuetenants met about making choise of some of yᵉ trayned band to be ready against yᵉ king send for them. I hear from London that Mr. Simons (a worthy minister) and three or fower more are gone into yͤ low contreyes to shift for themselues. Dʳ Storton is very sicke. I am exceeding glad to heare that there is some hope of Mʳ Whatlyes recouerie. I thanke you for yᵉ copie of yᵉ oath you sent me. I doubt whether my lord Say & my lord Brooke be set at libertie, but I wish it be true. This morning I receaued yoʳ lᵗʳᵉ by yᵉ carrier, & yᵉ last weake yoʳ l'er sent by Mʳ Braughton's man: they are wellcome to me, & you deserue thankes for them. Some indisposition enforces me to keepe my bed, wᶜʰ is yͤ cause I make vse of another's penne.* I thanke God I am not worser than when I was wont to keepe my bed. Remember my seruice to yoʳ worthy tutor, & tell him I am engadged in yͤ way of thankes to him for his care of you. I desire him, yf he doe not like yͤ piece of plate, that he would returne it to Burghe againe, wᵗʰ directions of what fashion he wold haue it, & the weight of it 28 ounces, as yoʳ ffather wrote to Burghe this should haue been, & write to Burghe that he send it downe to you to Oxford, & not to Brompton. I will, an't please God, send you a draught of yoʳ ffathers armes to put upon it.

I wold haue writ to Mʳ Perkins but that I am so bad. I pray God blesse you.

Send me word how yoʳ watch goes.

Your most affectinat mother, BRILLIANA HARLEY.

* The concluding words, "your most affectinat mother, Brilliana Harley," are alone in the handwriting of the Lady Brilliana.

XXXIX.

For my deare sonne Mr. Edward Harley.

Deare Ned—I willingly take my opertunity both to giue you knowledg howe your father and meself doo, and to inquire affter you, and thearefore I cannot let this bearer goo without a letter, tho I haue but littell time to rwit in, it being affter supper. My deare Ned, when I receued your letter by Jones and by Coolborne I was indisposed, that I could not be out of my beed; but now, I thanke God, I haue more liberty, in which I haue this contentment, that I can tell my minde to you with my owne penn. I acknowledg it Gods great mercy to me that you are well; and I thanke youe for both your letter by Jones and Coolborne; and tho Jones found you well, yet I did not repent my sending to see you. I was afraide you would haue had an ague; but God sheawed both you and me what He could haue brough upon you, and His name be bllesed that He so soone withdrwe His hand. I hope I shall see you affter the Act, which I longe for, and I pray God giue me a joyefull seeing of you. I would by all means, and so would your father, haue the peace of plate changed for a bigger on of 30 ounces; the armes shall be sent you. I like the stufe for your cloths well; but the cullor of thos for euery day I doo not like so well; but the silke chamlet I like very well, both cullor and stuf. Let your stokens be allways of the same culler of your cloths, and I hope you now weare Spanisch leather shouwes. If your tutor dous not intend to bye you silke stokens to weare with your silke shute send me word, and I will, if pleas God, bestow a peare on you. You did well to keepe the beasorstone and orampotabily with you. I thinke I forgot to rwite word that when the orampotabily is taken it must be stired tell it be disolued. Your cosen Fraces thinkes it will doo miracells. I thanke God, your father is well, and on thursday next he goos, if pleas God, to Hariford. For meself, I haue not bine very well; but this day, I thanke God, I haue bine some thinge better. I haue bine a longe time in the scoule of affliction, wheare I desire not to be wary of the correction of my heauenly father, but to learne obedience vnder it.

Heare inclosed I haue sent you some foren nwes, being still desireous to haue your minde keep awake in the consideration of the affairs abroode. I thanke you for the kings booke.

My deare Ned, I comfort meself with the perswation that your cheefe care is to walke before your God in all well pleasinge, and not to deuide His saruis, and so to make a religion to your self, that is, to take so much of Gods saruis as you pleas, and to leaufe the rest, as most men doo; but tho they may passify theare conciences for a time, yet in the end theare comforts will faille theim; which I hope yours will neuer.

I pray God blles you, and presarue you from all euill; so in hast I rest,

  Your most affectinat mother,   BRILLIANA HARLEY.

I reseued the note by Jones, and thanke you for it.

May 7. 1639.

XL.

For my deare sonne Mr. Edward Harley.

Deare Ned—This mornig, with no smale contentment, I reseued your letter by the carrier; it is my joy that you are well, and I beceach the Lord to continue your health to you; and, my deare Ned, be carefull to doo exersis. I did beleue that you did forget to send the letter which you rwite me word of, but now I haue reseued it, and thanke you for it. It is strang to me how fasting and prayer can agree with treacherous weapons, as kinifes and such like; thearefore, for my part, I will vnbeleeue the one of them, eather that they doo not fast and pray, or that they doo not make prouition of such wepons. Theare was a report that the kinge was goone to Loundoun, which came to his eare, at which he was much displeased. I hard that marquise Hamlenton was gone with 7000 men to land them in Scotland. Captaine Brandsheave is gouerner of Barek. My deare Ned, theas things are of the Lord, and as none thought of such a biusnes as this is, so we are as ignorant whate the issue will be: the Lord giue vs harts of depentances vpon him.

Haueing bine offtin not well, and confined to so sollatary a place as my beed, I made choys of an entertainement for meself, which might be eassy and of some benifit to meself; in which I made choys to reade the life of Luther, rwite by Mr. Calluen. I did the more willingly reade it, becaus he is generally branded with ambition, which caused him to doo what he did, and that the papis doo so generally obrade us that we cannot tell wheare our religion was before Luther; and some haue taxt him of an imteperat life. Theas resons made me desire to reade his life, to see vpon what growned theas opinions weare biult; and finding such satisfaction to meself, how fallsly theas weare raised, I put it into Inglisch, and heare in closed haue sent it you; it is not all his life, for I put no more into Inglisch then was not in the booke of Marters.

Theas things of note I finde in it, firstly, what Luther acknowledgs, he was instructed in the truth by an old man, whoo led him to the doctrine of justification by faith in Christ: and Erasmas, when his opinion was asked of Luther, said he was in the right. It is true the truth was much obscured with error; and then it pleased the Lord to rais up Luther as a trumpet to proclame His truth, and as a standered barare to hoold out the ensinge of His truth; which did but make thos to apeare of the Lords side, whoo weare so before. And it is aparent to me, that no ambistious ends moued Luther; for in all the cours of his life he neuer sheawed ambistion: tho he loued lerneing, yet, as fare as I can obsarue, he neuer affected to be estemed more lerned than he was. So that in Luther we see our owne fasess; they that stand for the old truee way they bring vp nwe doctriner, and it is ambistion, vnder the vaile of religion. Another obseruation I finde in Luther, that all his fasting and striknes, in the way of Popery, neuer gaue him peace of concience; for he had greate feares tell he had throughly learned the doctrine of justification by Christ alone; and so it will be with vs all; no peace shall we haue in our owne righteousness. And one thinge more I must tell you, that I am not of theaire minde whoo thinke, if he had bine of a milder temper it had bine better; and so Erasmas says; but I thinke no other spirit could haue sarued his turne. He was to cry aloude, like a trumpet; he was to haue a Jonas spirit. Thus, my deare Ned, you may see how willingly I impart any thinge to you, in which I finde any good. I may truely say, I neuer inioy any thinge that is good but presently my thoughts reflect vpon you; but if any thinge that is euill befall me, I would willing beare it all me self, and so willingly would I beare the ill you should haue, and reioyce that you should inioy what is good. Your father is now at Hariford; I hope he will be at home to morrow. Your brothers are well, and so as your sistwers and cosen Smith. Mr. Simons is recouered, and teaches the scoule againe. Mr. Gowers ague hangs a littell vpon him. My deare Ned, I knowe you doo not loue medicines, yet I would faine haue you drinke, this May, some scuruigras pounded and strained with beare, if theare be any to be had in Oxford; it is a most excelent thinge to purge the blood.

My deare Ned, the Lord in heauen blles you, and giue me a comfortabell seeing of you. So I rest, in hast,

Your most affectinat mother, BRILLIANA HARLEY.

Remember my saruis to your worthy tutor. Tell Gorg his mother is looked for at Bromton to night. His brother is goone to Teuxbery; I beleeue you knowe his biusness.

May 10, 1639.

I haue made a pye to send you; it is a kide pye. I beleeue you haue not that meate ordinaryly at Oxford; on halfe of the pye is seasned with on kinde of seasoning, and the other with another. I thinke to send it by this carrier.

XLI.

To my deare sonne Mr. Edward Harley, in Magdeline Hall, in Oxford.
For your deare self. [Sealed with black wax.]

Deare Ned—Your father haueing some biusnes to send to Loundon giues me an opertuenity to rwite to you, which I willingly doo, tho I rwit to you by the carrier last frieday. When your father went to Heariford, he was not sartaine of his gooing to Bambery; and if he did he meant to send on to let you knowe so much, that you might meet him on saturday at Bambery, wheare I hope by Gods mercy you will see your father; and I pray God you may both haue a comfortable meeting; and tho I cannot haue part in it, yet absent, my desres are with you, and I hope in good time the Lord will giue me the comfort of seeing you.

This morning I reseued your letter by Hollingworth. My deare Ned, I blles the Lord that in mercy he has so shuted you with a tutor, vpon hom your harts desire is so much seet; you might haue had a good man, and not such a shutetabellness in him to your hart. I can not blame you to feare the looseing of him; for when we fined any of like affections to vs we ought to prise them, for they are not to be had euery day. As soune as I hard that Mr Whately was sike, my thoughts weare that if Mr Wheately did dye, Bambery men would desire to haue Mr Pirkins. My poore prayers haue bine euer sense I hard it, and shall be, that the Lord would giued your tutor in the right way, most for his glory; and I hope the Lord will seettell him in the place wheare he now is, for he must as well looke how he leaufs his standing as vpon what ground he would accept of that place which is offred him: it is true his call to Bambery is right and just, but wheather it be as right he should leaufe that standeing in which he is, I knowe not. I feare me that that has bine the spoyleing of the vniuersitys and corrupting of the jentry theare breed, because that as soune as any man is come to any ripeness of judgment and holynes he is taken away, and so they still gleane the garden of the ripe grapes and leaufe sower ons behinde. My deare Ned, my God be bllesed, who has giuen you a hart to looke vp to Him, and a desire to depend on His most holy Prouidence; and the Lord in mercy establisch your hart in waiteing one Him, and then you will neuer be ashamed. It is true that you no souner peeped into the world but you had a taste of the various and changeabellness of the condistions here belowe; for no souner weare you at Glloster but you weare remoued, and from Shearwesbury; but, as you well obsarue, for which I hope both you and I shall endeuer to be thankfull, God still prouied for you; and so I trust He will doo still. My hope is, that you will still inioy your worthy tutor, which will be much contentment to me. I hope your father will be a means to seettell his thoughts. I haue heare sent you a coppy of a sermon preeched in Scotland; you must take care whoo sees it; you neuer read such a peace. I thanke God, I am reasnabell well, and your brothers and sisters, with your cosen Smith, are very well; but to my much trubell I feare your brother Robine learnes but littell.

I purpos to send this weake into Linconschere, for I haue not heard from my sister a longe time. My deare Ned, the Lord in mercy blles you, and fill you with his grase, and giue you a feeleing of his vnspeakebell loue in Christ Jesus, that so you may be tyed by the bonds of loue to all obedience to your God; and so I rest

Your most affectionat mother, BRILLIANA HARLEY.

Your fathers ante Corbet is dead, for which he is very sorry.

Bromton, May 20. 1639.

Your father meet accedentally with on at Hariford by home he rwite to you to meete him.

Your father will bringe his armes with him, if please God, to be set on the plate.

XLII.
For my deare sonne Mr. Edward Harley.

Deare Ned—I pray God blles you, and inriche you with those saueing grasess of His spirit which to inioye is happines, and mesery to be to without them.

Yestrday Lonckford returned from Loundoun, and he aschures me he sawe you well on monday last, but two lines from you would haue giuen me more contentment than all his eloquence has doun. I hope you will haue a comfortabell seeing of your father, which I hope I shall reioyce in the aschurance of, at the safe returne of your father, and I hope it will not be longe before God giue me the comfort of seeing you.

I beleeue you heare that the Scots would none of the proclamation. My lord of Ratesford sonne and one other nobell man is goone to the Couenanters. It is reported thatt the Scots haue sent the kinge the crowne and septer, with most humbell exprestions.

Howe all your frindes doo in theas parts you will heare, I hope, by your fathers man; so recommending you to the protection of the Lord, beceaching Him to keepe you in His feare, which is the begineing of all wisdome; and be aschured I am well pleased when I can expres meself

    Your most affectinat mother,   BRILLIANA HARLEY.

May 23, 1639.

I hope Mr Pirkins resolution continues for his stay in Oxford: send me word how it is.

XLIII.
To her son Edward, endorsed, " for your dere self."

Deare Ned—Most gladely I reseued your letter from Woster, by my cosen Adams. I acounte it as a greate mercy of God that you had so cleere a skiee ouer you, which might make you the better tolerate the ill ways vnder your horsess fooute. I knowe not a greater joy in this world than the aschurance of your being well, thearefore I desire to blles my God, that you past part of your journey so well, and I hope I shall eare longe reseaufe the aschurance of your comeing well to Oxford.

I beleeue you remember wheather your father whent when you parted from him; from whence he brought this inteligence, that the Scots weare intrenched 12 miles of Barek, and that it is a dificulle thinge to knowe what they doo; for if any inglishe man goo to them, thay are vsed kindely, but they returne as wise as they came, for none discouers theaire counsills to them. That they sourrouneded some of my lord of Holluands company, they say is true, by which they did but verify what they had said, that they mente not to take adwntgess to doo ronge, only to defend themselfs. Theare are some Scots taken which weare comeing into Scoteland, who had bine commanders in Jermany: they are put into seuerall prisons; the particulars I beleeue you will heare from other pens, thearefore I omite it. They say, that the Frenche haue had two great ouerthrowes; for which I am sorry. Your father is in some doute wheather he shall goo to Loundone the next weake or noo; if nesescity so constraine him, I can not but be sorry, and I if it be so, I wisch I had you with me that time your father is away. Doo not take notis of this to your father. I hope if he doo goo to Loundoun, it will be by Oxford. Deare Ned, theare is so much discours of wars, that it may well put vs in minde of our spirituall warefare; in both theare is nothing more requisite then to stand vpon the wacth; to be surpirsed is both a shame and greate disaduantage to a soulder, thearefore, deare Ned, stand as it weare senternell, and be shure you be not founde sleepeing; wacth against your enimy, and the Lord of heauen, that neuer comes so neare sleepe as to slomber, keepe you in all saffety. Let me heare from you as offten as you haue opertunity. Your father, I thanke God, is well, and so is your brothers and sisters. I thanke God, your sister Margett as mised her ague theas two days. Mr. Broughton dined heare to day; he proclames a quarell against you and your tutor; but I tell him you are both gillteless. My deare Ned, the Lord blles you, and giue me the comfort of seeing you againe.

Your most affectinat mother,   BRILLIANA HARLEY.

In hast.

June 21, 1639.

Doo with the testament I gaue you as you pleas, and if Asch send one to me for you, it shall be sent you. Remember my saruis to your tutor.

Your brother has sent you your bookes by this carrier.

XLIV.

To her son Edward.—Endorsed, " For your dear self."

Deare Ned—I rwite to you this day, before this, but this night at supper reseaufeing so good nwes of peace, I could not willingly stay tell the next weake before I did impart it to you. This night Tomas Miller came from Loundon, wheare vnexpectedely he founde my lord nwely come to Loundoun from Ireland; his letter to me I send you heare inclosed, and what he rwites to your father, I will relate you as pountually as my memory will giue me leaufe. It is thus, the Scots armey was intrenched within 4 or 6 miles of the kings: they sent comissinars to the kinge, to let the kinge knowe theare griuences, for whous safety they had the lord jenerulls hand; when they weare in his tente treateing with him, the kinge came in vnexpected; the commiscinars offred to kise his hand, which the kinge refused, but affterwards they did. They haue agreed vpon such condistions which is much to the kings honnor; they are to haue a jenerall assembely and a parlament, and bischops; but the bischops must be subect to the assembely and parlament. The armemy in Scotland is vnintrenched; and thus we see a way by which God is pleased to lentghen our peace; for which I pray God, make us thankefull: and for my part I shall be glad if this proufe true: howesower, beleeue this, that I am,

   Your most affectinat mother,   BRILLIANA HARLEY.

(No date.)

  I haue sent my brother Bray a chees; I would haue you carefull to send it him, but not by any expres mesenger. Send my letter to me againe.

XLV.

For my deare sonne Mr Edward Harley,
  in Magdeline Hall, Oxford

  Deare Ned—Your letter by Hullsy, Mr Braughtons man, I reseued yesterday. I reioyce that you are well, and I hope your eyes are so, becaus you say nothing to the contrary; and I hope your minde and tonghe weare in good tune when you ansured in the hall; and if you should not doo as well as you desire, yet let it not discorage you. I wisch I had hard you; and, my deare Ned, I long to see you, for when you weare with me you weare halfe that littell time you stayed, vpon gooing euery day, that it did a littell vnsweeten my contentment; but I hope I shall see you now againe with comfort, which I begg of the Lord.

  My cosen Pelham rwite me word that I made him a seasnabell offer of a buck, for which he thanked me. He did not say he desired on, but for feare least I should be in an eror, I tooke the thankes for my offer, for a willingnes to accept of a buck, which I haue sent him by this bearer, and if it come sweet I shall be pleased; and if it be not the fellowes fallt, I beleeue it will come very sweet: it is a very large deere, and very fat for this time of the yeare, considering your fathers park dous not at any time yeald a very fate deare, but as good a tasted deare as any is: if you see this venson you will say it is a good dare. The place where it was shot I made salt be put, that so that place may not tante the rest. My deare Ned, I would haue you give the mesenger my letter to my cosin Pelham, and direct him to carry the venson to him.

I thanke God your father is well, and so is your brothers and sisters.

I haue not hard of any allterations in publicke affaires sence I rwite last to you. I beleeue you will gees whoo was your sister Dorritys secretary. My deare Ned, the Lord blles you and fill you with thos graseses which may make you shine in the eyes of His chillderen; in hast, I rest

Your most affectinat mother,   BRILLIANA HARLEY.

Bromton: July 4, 1639.

Remember my knife.

Remember my saruis to goode and worthy Mr Pirkins. Let me knowe wheather he be as kinde to you as he was vsed to be.

I would haue you rwit me word by this barrer when your tutor will, and pleas God, let you come home.

XLVI.

For my deare sonne Mr Edward Harley,
in Magdeline Hall, Oxford.

Deare Ned—I rwite to you yesterday, and I beleeue to many others I should haue aleaged that, as an excuse for not rwiteing at this time, yet I cannot give meself leaufe to do so to you, but willingly I vse a kinde of violence to my other ocations, in takeing time to rwite to you, sence I cannot haue the contentment in speaking to you. I reseued your letter by the carrier this morning, so that Moene is now in request againe.

I blles God that you are well, and my deare Ned, be carefull of yourself; be carefull of the health of your body for my sake; and aboue all, be carefull of the health of your soule for your owne and my sake; and as to the body, thos things doo most hart which are of a deadly quallity as poyson, so nothing harts the soule like that deadly poyson of sinn; thearefor, my dearest, be wacthfull against thos great and suttile and vigilent enimys of your presious soule. I beleeue you knowe that one of the best parts of a soulder is to stand vpon his garde, and his greatest shame (next to runeing away) not to be found so; so is it in our spirituall warefare; if Sathen surprise vs, he takes vs at his will, and if we turne our bakes and rune away, O! he will persue tell we be taken. My deare Ned, I beleeue you are confident that you are most deare to me, thearefore thinke it not strange, if I am stuedious and carefull that your peace should be keept with your God, whous fauor is better then life. I longe to see you, and I hope I shall doo it shortly. I hope before this, you haue reseued your hate and stokens, but Burigh is something ngligent. Your father is, I thanke God, well; he is ride abroode. In hast, I giue you this ascurance that I am

  Your most affectinat mother, BRILLIANA HARLEY.

Bromton, July 5, 1639.

Remember my loue to your worthy tutor. I should haue rwit to Gorg, but I haue not time. Your father has diuers times sence you went asked for strawbery butter, and in memory of you this day I made Hacklet make some. I wisch you a disch of it.

XLVII.

To her son Edward.—Endorsed, " For your deare self."

My deare Ned — On tusday last by Tomas Miller I reseued your letter, which was not a littell wellcome to me. I blles God that you are well, most ernestly desireing you may both inioy the fauor of your God, which is better then life, and the fauor of his endeared onsie, which should be more precious to vs than the good will of all the world besides. For the affaires of the Acte, I wisch you hard Miller make the relation: it seemes he meanes not to be a papis, for becaus he vnderstood nothing, he likes it not, and desires rather to be sent to Oxford at any other time then the Act. How biussy soeuer the time was to you, yet it was a vacation to him, for he knwe not what to doo with himself. I beleeue this was his greefe, that he sawe euery one so biussy and he vnderstoode not why.

I much desire to heare from you, now the Act is past, how you did in all that comeboustion: I hard by Miller, but nowe I desire to knowe how you are when it is past. Your father has bine ever sence tusday at Hariford, at the sescions, wheer a strange thinge befell him, for Stiche of Wallford put vp a bille of indictement against him for spoileing the kings highe ways, by the water that he drawes ouer his growndes. You may remember, I thinke, that your father made him pay for his hors that carriede a loade on the saboth: acording to the law he paide, and now against lawe, he seekes to reueng himself: tho it be longe sence, I dout not but your father will cleere himself and forgiue him. Your father had this day senight a falle off his hors which did much hurt him, but I thanke God, he is now much better; this day he is gone to my lord president, whoe has apointed all the depuety leftenants to come to him on tusday next; but they desire a further time, and haue desired your father to procure it; and that is his biusnes to my lord.

My deare Ned, I long to see you, and without your tutor seet doune the day when your father should send horses for you, your father will say the time is not yet this 3 weekes that he and your tutor agreed vpon, but I was not then bye. I hope to see you shortly, and I trust it will be with much comfort. I thanke God, your brothers and sisters are well. This day I reseued many corantes, but I haue reed but one, and that I haue heare inclosed sent you. I hard from Loundon this day, but I doo not heare that the kinge is come theather. All thinges goo one yet well.

I am glad the venson came sweet; if it did not, Miller deceufes me. The questons at the Acte, which weare much longed for, I hard read the last night, tell which time Mr Gower was keep bigg of longeing, becaus I would not open your fathers letter tell he came home.

It is pitty that such yonge men should marry. You knowe home I meane. I doo not say it is pitty that all yonge men should, for some haue need of a nurs or a giude, call them what you pleas. This incke is so bade, that I haue thought I haue had much patience to rwit so large a letter, and you must haue some to reade it.

My deare Ned, the Lord in mercy blles you, and keepe you safe vnder the shawedow of His most holy Prouidence; so I rest,

  Your most affectinat mother,   BRILLIANA HARLEY.

Bromton, July 13, 1639.

Deare Ned, remember my loue to good and worthy Mr Pirkins.

XLVIII.

To her son Edward.—Endorsed, " For your deare self."

My deare Ned—Your letter this weake by the carrier I reseued yesterday, and you may beleeue it was wellcome to me, that reioyces in your being well. I am glad you past all the biusnes of the Act so well, and now I beleeue Oxford is in a calme againe. My deare Ned, I llonge to see you, and thearefore your father has sent horsess for you, which I hope will be with you at the time your tutor desires they should, or ells I mistake your letter. I hope your tutor will come with you; you say he will, but by his letter to me I doute it, for he speakes of some thinge that he will send by you. Upon your word your father has sent a hors for him, and if he come he shall be very wellcome; if he weare only your tutor he should be welcome, but being so good a man, and loueing you and vseing you so kindely as you assure me he dous, I cannot but loue and respect him; and that I cannot doo every one.

My deare Ned, I reioyce with you, and blles my God with you, that you are with one that shuts with your dispocion, for I thinke to liue with a sower nature is a greater paine then to be feed allways with sower and bitter meate, and to have the smoke in ons eyes; for my part, I loue no swernes, and I hope you are of my minde in that; yet it has bine my lot to meete with some of that dispotion.

On munday Mr. Braughton was with me; but his discours was

as short as your letter; yet I thanke you for it; tho it weare short, yet it found a very wellcome.

On tusday your father went to Loudlow, from whence he brought home with him Sr Ihon Kirle, Mr. Vahan, and Mr. Scidmore; it fell out to be at such a time when I was inforsed to keepe my beed, which I did from tusday tell this day, and now I thank God, I am vp againe. Your father purposess to goo on munday to Mrs Bramley, and to come home on tusday, and the weake affter is the assises. My lord schef barron goos no more this sirquite. Your tutor rwit to me to speake to your father, that £10 might be sent to him for your vse, which your father has doune. Remember my loue to your worthy tutor, and tell him I thanke him for his letter, and I doo not rwite to him, becaus I hope to see him at Bromton.

My deare Ned, the Lord in mercy blles you, and giude you in your journy and giue me a comfortabell seeing of you.

Your most affectinat mother,   BRILLIANA HARLEY.

Bromton, July 20, 1639.

I hope to tell you my minde about your brothers. I pray God the nwes you rwit me to true. My lord is at the bathe with my lord of Northumland.

XLIX.

For my deare sonne Mr Edward Harley.

Deare Ned—My cosen Adams returne from Woster was very wellcome to me, becaus he aschured me of your comeing well so fare on your journy, and I trust the same gratious Prouidence brought you to your journis end. Your letter was very wellcome to me, for, my deare Ned, I cannot but say that I inioy meself with more comfort when you are with me, and next seeing you, to heare from you is most pleasing to me. Heare has bine strangers euer since you went, and on Mr Acton came apurpos to see you. He was of the same howes you are of, but left it that yeare you came theather. I like him as well as any yonge jentellman I haue seene a greate while.

I thanke God your father is well, and this day gone ahunting, and your brothers with him, it being procured with much dificullty from Mr Simons.

My deare Ned, the Lord blles you and giue you that heauenly wisdome to remember your Creator in the days of your youth, that you may sarufe your God with an vpright hart, and the Lord in mercy teach you to profet in all the ways of wisdome, and leade you in the way in which you should walke. My deare Ned, omite not priuet dutyes, and stire vp your self to exercise yourself in holy conference, begg of God to giue you a delight in speaking and thinkeing of thos thinges which are your eternall treasure. I many times thinke Godly conference is as much neglected by Gods chillderen, as any duty. I am confident you will noways neglect the opertunity of profeting in the ways of lerning, and I pray God prosper your endeuors. My deare Ned, my thoughts weare filled with other obiects that morning you went away, which made me forget to giue you directions about the stufe I spake to you of; but I gaue Ions a pettren of what kinde of stufe I would haue; but I did not tell him any thinge ells; and I beleue he had not wite to conseafe my meaneing, that you should chus the culler.

Remember my loue to your worthy tutor, and still beleeue that 1 much reioyce when I can expres meself to be

Your most affectinat mother, BRILLIANA HARLEY.

My cosen Dauis presents her saruis to you.

Octo: 18. 1639.

I would have you send this inclosed letter as soune as you can to Sr Gilles Bray, but by a safe hand.

I haue sent you a baskett of Stoken apells; theare are 4 or 5 of another kinde. I hope you will not dispice them, comeing from a frinde, tho they are not to be compared to Oxford appells.

In the basket with the appells is "the Returne of Prayer." I could not find the place I spake of to your tutor, when he was with me; but since, I found it, and haue sent the booke to you, that he may see it, and judg a littell of it; for my part, I am not of that openion, that God will not grant the prayer of others, for the want of our joyeing with the rest, or that God dous stand vpon such a number; but I am not perrentory, but upon good reson I hope I shall yeald: but this I thinke and beleeue, that none joyne in prayer with others but thos that simpathise on with another; for it is not the consenting to, but the ernest desireing of the same.

L.

To her son Edward.—Endorsed, "For your deare selfe."

Deare Ned — Your letter which I receued this day by Lemster carrier was very wellcome to me. I blles God that you inioy your health, and that your eye is now well, which I beleeue has put you to some paine. I thanke Mrs. Willkinson for her care of it, in which shee supplied my place. My deare Ned, I thanke God that the Lord has added the acomplischment of this yeare to the rest you haue lived; and I beceach the Lord whoo has our times in His hand and is the preseruer of man, that He would add many years to your life, that you may be full of dayes and full of gras, that you may liue heare to the glory of your God; to which end you weare made, and that affter this life you may inhearet eternity. I am glad you remembred your birth day; I did, and I blless God that I haue had the comfort in seeing this yeare more added to you. I thanke you for the relation of the seae fight; to requite you, I haue sent you the currances of this weake. Many are of an opinion, the fleet was for Ingland. Bllesed be our God, whoo has wacthed ouer vs when we thought not of such an enimy.

If the gooldsmith dous my wacth well for that prise I shall not think it to much.

Your father is I hope well; he went yesterday to the bischops about the gift of Bucknill; for M'r Griffits is dead, and M'r Morgan has put in a cauit for the kinge, so that M'r Barthy the younger was refused to be admitted by the bischop, but your father did hope to preuale with him. I feare your father will not be at home this night. You may knowe I wisch you with me. I reseued a box from Loundon with your seale, but no letter with it. I purpos and pleas God to send it by M'r Braughton, whoo I heare goos to Oxford on Monday next, becaus it should come by a more shure hand, with a token to M'rs Wilkinson. I thanke God your brothers and sisters are well, and the Lord in mercy blles you and make you still a comfort to

Your most affectinat mother,   BRILLIANA HARLEY.

Bromton, Octo. 24, 1639.

This weake the bischop haue giuen part of a comen to on of his secretaries; his secretary went to sarue on that oposed him with a proses, the mans seruant stroke him downe with a pickeuell, and so they beat out his brains in a cruell maner.

I sent you the last weake a basket of appells. Remember my loue to your worthy tutor.

LI.

For my deare sonne M'r Edward Harley.

My deare Ned—I knwe not of this mesengers gooing to Loundon tell saterday last, sence which time I hawe bine enforced to keep my beed; this day being the first since saterday thatt I haue bine out of my beed to site up out of it, and thearefore, my deare Ned, I can only let you knwe in theas lines howe it is with me; and that still I haue a hart that dous most truly loue and tender you; and I beceach the Lord to presarue you from all euill, especially that only venome of our soules, sinn. My deare Ned, be carefull of your self, and let me heare from you as offten as you can. Your father, I thanke God, is well; he came home on fryeday last, but I fear Mr. Barthy will not haue Bucknill, for a cauite is put in for the kinge.

The greife of it has allmost killed my good cosen Dauis; on saboth day last her husband thought she had bine dead. I hard from your ante Pelham the last weake; they are all well. The Lord blles you.

Your most affectinat mother, BRILLIANA HARLEY.

Oct. 30, 1639. *Bromton.*

I should be glad to heare whether Bleethly be fallty or no.

LII.

For my deare sonne Mr Edward Harley.

Deare Ned—Sr Richard Newport is pleased to doo me the honnor to conuaie this letter to you, and I hope you will haue the aduantag of waiteing vpon him; and I can not but acounte it an aduantage to be in the presence of such a man.

I pray God blles you, and giue you a hart to be in loue with thos ways of wisdome, which will make you for euer happy.

Your brothers and sisters are well.

So in hast I rest

Your most affectinat mother, BRILLIANA HARLEY.

Oct. 31, 1639. *Bromton Castell.*

LIII.

For my deare sonne Mr Edward Harley, in Magdeline Hall, in Oxford.—Endorsed, " For your deare self."

Deare Ned—It is my ioy that you are well, and I blles my God that you haue had your health, which I was aschured of this day by your letter, which is wellcome to me. That the appells came well to your hand I am well pleased, and I hope you haue made vse of them for your descert in your chamber.

What I have hard of the fight with the greate dons, I haue sent you heare inclosed; and if the venter of the Corrantes be in prison, then take your leaufe of them in theas, which I now send you.

My deare Ned, keep my wacth tell you haue a shure hand, and if it like you, I beleeue it will not dislike me, for seldome your fancy differs from what I like; and thearefore besides my owne content I mis you, for when I cannot see what is doun, I rested content when you toold me of the things, I desired to be satisfyed in.

Mr. Braughtone was with me this day and tells me of his intention to goo to Oxford, but he was in hast, so that I could not rwit by him, nor send you the mony to pay for my wacth, which I did desire to doo, but by the next I purpos to send it.

I hope your father is well; he went yesterday to Sr Richard Nweports, whoo intends to goo to Loundon this weake or the next, and in his returne from Loundon he purposes, as he rwit to your father, to see you in Oxford.

I haue not hard of anny yet to supply Mr Simons place in teacheing scoule. I am halfe of an opinion to put your brothers out to scoule. They continue still stife in theare opinions; and in my aprehention vpon samale ground. My feare is least we should falle into the same error as Calluin did, whoo was so ernest in oposeing the popisch hollydays that he intrenched vpon the holy Saboth, so I feare we shall be so ernest in beateing downe theare to much villifyeing of the Common Prayer Booke, that we shall say more for it than euer we intended.

My deare Ned, keepe allways a wacth over your preceous soule; tye yourself to a dayly self exemnation; thinke ouer the company you haue bine in, and what your discours was, and how you found yourself affected, how in the discourses of religion; obsarue what knowledg you weare abell to expres, and with what affection to it, and wheare you finde yourself to come short, labor to repaire that want; if it be in knowledg of any point, reade somethinge that may informe you in what you finde you know not; if the falt be in affections, that you find a wearines in that discours of religion, goo to God, begg of Him nwe affections to loue those things which by nature we can not loue. Affter discours, call to minde wheather you haue bine to appt to take exceptions, or wheather any haue prouocked you, and examin your self how you tooke it. My deare Ned, you are to me next my oune hart; and this is the rule I take with meself, and I thinke it is the best way to be aquanted with our owne harts, for we know not what is in vs, tell ocations and temptation drawes out that matter which layes quiet; and in a due obsaruation, we shall finde at last, in what we are proud, in what fearefull, and what will vexe and eate our harts with care and grefe. I can speake it of meself; theare are many things which I see wise men and women trubell themselfs with, that I blless my gratious God for they neuer tuched my hart; but I will not cleere meself, for theare are some things that of meself I can not beare them: so that if I should haue only obsarued meself in some thinges, should thinke I weare of so setteled a mind I would not be moued; but I knowe theare are blastes that trubell any calme, which is not settled vpon that Rock, which is higher than our selfes. My deare Ned, I will not excus my lentgh of lines, tho it may be you may thinke it to long a letter; but rather thinke vpon the affection with which I rwite it, whoo am

Your most affectinat mother, BRILLIANA HARLEY.

Nour: the first, 1639. *Bromton Castell.*

I haue sent you by this carrier a loyne of veale backed, if the cooke haue doun his part it is well.

Remember my loue to your worthy tutor.

Your father, I thanke God, came well home to night late.

LIV.

For my deare sonne Mr. Edward Harley,
in Magdeline Hall, Oxford.

Deare Ned—It is not many days since I rwit to you, yet I can not let this opertunity pas without inquireing how you doo, and that is biusness sufficient for a letter from me to you. Mr Braughton, I beleeue, has bine with you. I should haue bine glad to have rwit by him, but his stay was short.

He was resouleued to make peace betwne your tutor and Mr Taylor; tho thos that know not Mr Braughton say he is a man that loues quarelling, but I finde him to be no such man. Your father, I thank God, is well; he came home on saterday last, so that he did not resoulfe of sending vp any to Loundon tell this morning.

My deare Ned, I longe to heare from you, and I can not but let you know your letters are most wellcome to me. My deare Ned, I dout not but that you are deligent in the way in which you are to store yourself with knowledg, for this is your haruest in which you must gather the fruts which beare; affter you may bring out to your owne and others profete. It is a sorrowfull repentance to repent for the loos of that which we can not recall; which many men doo in sorroweing over theare loost time. But aboue all, my deare Ned, keepe your hart cloos with your God; O let it be your resolution and practice in your life, rather to dye than sinn against your gratious and holy God. We haue so gratious a God, that nothing can put a distance betwne Him and our soules, but sinn; wacth thearefore against that enimy.

Heare inclosed I haue sent you 33 shilings to pay for the dooing of my wacth. I beleeue you will send it me by the next shure hand. I thanke God this day I haue bine out of my chamber at diner, and am indeferent well. Your brothers and sisters are well. I should be very glad to heare of a scoule master.

Be carefull of your self, and the Lord blles you, that you may be still a comfort to

    Your most affectinat mother,   BRILLIANA HARLEY.

Noue: 4, 1639. *Bromton Castell.*

Remember my loue to your worthy tutor.

LV.

For my deare sonne Mr. Edward Harley.

Deare Ned—On tusday last I reseued your letter by Mr Taylor, and this day yours by the carrier; both weare wellcome to me. Mr Taylor brought your letter to me himself, and toold me you did him the honnor to be at his marrege. He protests he neuer rwite to Oxford in his life, of any thing that might reflect in any ill kinde vpon Mr Pirkins, for he protest he much loues him, and for his wife, he says, he has asked her aboute it, and she says shee neuer hard of Bleethly. I beleeue it did trubell him that you refused to leade his wife to chruch, but I gees you know vpon what ground you denyed such a curtesy to Mrs Willkinson. My deare Ned, I blles my God that that illnes which you found, heald you no longer; I beleeue it was some coold you had taken. Be careful, my deare Ned, of your health, for my sake, and let me still knowe howe it is with you. Mr Taylor toold me he would bringe his wife to me, and that shee would giue me full assurance, that thies reports come not from him nor her, and thearefore he desires them to looke to it who are the aughters of it.

Your father did intend to rwit to your tutor about your comeing home at Christ-tide, and I hope and pleas God he will send for you.

I heare that the prince ellector had good hopes the princes of Jermany would chuse him for theare jenerall, for which employment he was gooing into Jermany, and in his way in France he was taken. Being disguised, haueing a greate train with him; the French king retains him, and he has a great gard seet ouer him. This the French king dous, becaus he would place a jenerall ouer thos troups in Sacxson Waymers place.

The biusnes in Scotland is as bad, if not wors than euer it was; theare is a Duch imbasodor, Mounsire Arttson, come ouer to excuse the fighting of the Duch ships vpon the Inglisch cost.

I thanke God your father is well; it may be he will rwite you himself.

I beceech the Lord to blles you and fill you with His gras, which is only the true riches.

    Your most affectinat mother,   BRILLIANA HARLEY.
Bromton Castell, Noue. 8, 1639.

Remember my loue to your worthy tutor.

LVI.

*For my deare sonne Mr Edward Harley,
in Magdelin Hall, Oxford.*

Deare Ned—I did hope I should haue had this weake a fitte opertunity to rwite to you by a speciall mesenger, but some ocations put by your fathers intention to send to Loundon and so to Oxford.

This day I reseued your letter by the carrier, and on fryeday last I reseued your letter by Hall, which, tho it weare short, yet it a longe wellcome. I thanke God that you haue health, and the Lord in mercy continue it to you and make you growe in all grase, and especially in thos which may make you like to your Sauiour, that you may loue righteousness and hate sinne. My deare Ned, that it has pleased the Lord to imbitter my life with many sorrowes (yet I must say it has bine in mercy and not acording to my desert) has bine caused by my owne sinnes, which has bine the wormwood of my life; and I must say, sweet are my afflictions, if they haue and doo make me finde the bitternes of sinn. My deare Ned, I hope before longe to haue the comfort of seeing you, which I beg of the Lord. I hard from London, from my Lord, that theare is a nwe committy made for the Scote biusnes, but they treate vpon foren afaires. My lord of Holland and my lord admaral are left out with secretary Cooke. My brother goot your father of from beeing sheerife, for which I thanke God.

I thanke God your father is well, but I haue not bine well this therte days, being as I use to be, thearefore I cannot rwit so much as I thought to haue doune; tho I rest

  Your most affectinat mother,   BRILLIANA HARLEY.
Bromton Castell, Noue. 22, 1639.

Remember me to your worthy tutor, to home I would haue rwit, but that I am not very well.

LVII.

For my deare sonne Mr. Edward Harley.

Deare Ned—This bearor stayeing on day longer then I thought he should, which giues me time to rwite theas feawe lines with my owne hand. I haue not bine out of my beed sence saterday, and you may remember howe ill I am when I first doo rise. I beleeue you will pray to the Lord for me; and I hope the Lord will giue me patience to waite in faith for His goodnes to me; for I trust the Lord will deale gratiously with me: and, my deare Ned, I had rather haue the hope of being the Lordes and sarue Him, tho in such a weake and afflicted condistion, then to inioye health and pleashurs and obey my owne harts lusts.

O! sweet is the saruis of our God, that giues sweetness in the midest of bitterness. My deare Ned, it is an ease to me to tell you how I doo; it is a thinge I cannot doo to euery one: but, my deare Ned, as I haue had comfort in you, so I hope the Lord will still giue me comfort in you. I much desire to heare of a good scoulemaster, thearefore, my deare Ned, put your tutor in minde to doo his best for one. Yow know how Mr Simons was before he was maryed, and so may he be, if he be one that is not maried. Mr Simons packes vp his goods apase and sends them away. Mr Cradock is goon from Clanuer, he was sited and would not apeare.

I mistooke in rwiteing you word, it was my lord admarall that was left out of the committy, it is my lord of Arnendell. The Lord blles you and giue us a happy seeing on another.

  Your most affectinat mother,   BRILLIANA HARLEY.
Noue. 25, 1639. *Bromton Castell.*

LVIII.

For my deare sonne Mr Edward Harley,
in Magdeline Hall, Oxford

Deare Ned—With much contentment I haue reseued this weakes letter from you. I acknowledg the Lords mercy to me in the continuance of your health, which is a joy to me in the midest of many ocations of sorrow; and I beceach the Lord I may still haue that refreschment to see it goo well with you, and to see it best with your better part, so that you may euery day more and more aproufe yourself, not only a branch but a member of Christ.

I much reioyce in the hope of seeing you, but I trust I shall haue more joy in seeing you. I am glad your worthy tutor will come with you, by which I see, he is not an obstinate man. A pare of rideing stokens I haue prouided for you, which I purpos, if pleas God, to send you by the horses that shall be sent for you; and knoweing your tutors minde for a hors and saddell, I will endeuor to haue him fitted, that tho the ways may be fooule yet his seate may be eassy. I rwit you word that my lord admarall was spoken to, but that would not doo, but it was my lord depuety of Irland that preuailed to geet your father off from being sherefe. Thinges goo wors in Scotland then euer they did, and it is said theare will be wars; for my part I did allways doute that that buisnes would not so end as many others thought; neaither am I now of theare mindes, that that kingdome will eassely be subdued. The Lord in mercy inabell all His childeren to fixe theare eyes on Him, that so, trusting in the Lord, we may neuer be dismayed. It is thought that such a number of Scote minesters will not be suffred to goo out of Scotland.

The prince elector is put in prison in France; into the same prison wheare princ Casemere is, and Jhon de Wart. It is thought the prince elector will not be seet at liberty; it was fitte he should goo vnknowne; he did disguise himself, but went with such a traine that he could not but be inquired affter. Thus we see, my deare

Ned, all condistions are liabell to misery; and the greater the person is, the greater is the misery; so that honnor dous but enhanse pouerty, or shame or imprisonment: yet man is so forgetfull of his God, that all, and most of all great men, liue in prosperity as if they weare lords of what they had, forgetting that they are but tennants at will.

Your father has promised Mr. Simons £110 for his howes, which is as much as he gaue for it, and now he has had it two years, so that now he is no louser.

Mr. Blineman is goone from Walcot.

I thanke God your father is well, and I am now abell to be out of beed. I haue not bine so well for aboue this weake as I use to be, and with it I haue been trubled with much heauiness at my hart. I thanke God your brothers and sisters and your cosen Smith are well. Deare Ned, if theare be any good lookeing glasses in Oxford, shuse me one aboute the biggnes of that I use to drees me in, if you remember it. I put it to your choys, becaus I thinke you will chuse one, that will make a true ansure to onse face.

All my frute disches are brocken; thearefore, good Ned, if theare be any shuch blwe and white disches as I vse to haue for frute, bye me some; they are not purslane, nor they are not of the ordinary mettell of blwe and white disches. I beleeue you remember what I vse to haue; if you chuse them against the horses come for you, I will take order with the men about the bringeing of them home, and will send mony to pay for them. I see your sister has a nwe hude; it semes shee lost hers and durst not tell, and so, as I gees, rwit to you for one, which I will pay you for. I haue sent you my wacth, and I beleeue it may be mended. I doo willingly giue you the rige of goold that was aboute the agget.

I am hartely sorry for the death of Mr Knightly. I heare my lady Wesmorland is brought to beed of a daughter. My lady Veere was with her, and I thinke shee is so still.

I did thinke your father would haue sent mony by Miller; it

seemes it was forget, but he indends to doo it by the men that goo for you.

Remember my loue to your tutor, to home I wisch the frueition of all happines.

I hope to see him, and thearefore I doo not rwit to him.

My deare Ned, the Lord blles you and giude you in all your thoughts words and actions, that you may still looke vpon them as seeing the ways of an vpright hart. So I rest

Your affectinat mother,   BRILLIANA HARLEY.

Noue: 29, 1639. *Bromton Castell.*

My Lord rwit word this weake that he thought he should not goo this yeare to Louddington.

I would haue 6 frute disches.

LIX.

For my deare sonne Mr. Edward Harley,
in Magdeline Hall, Oxford.

Deare Ned—Tomas Miller came late this nighte, which giues me but a littell time to rwit to you. I blles God that you are well, and I hope by His gratious prouidence I shall see you shortly, which I long to doo. I beceach the Lord to blles you in your journey, and to bring you in safety to the place wheare you are desired.

Dear Ned, be carefull not to ride late, nor to venture through the waters, if they be out, and I beceach the Lord to guide you. Your father will rwit to you, as he tells me, and will send your tutor 20*l.* pound for you, I am hartely sorry for * * * * oughton, I pray God deliuer him, in that intangled trubell. I am very glad that your tutor has lighted vpon on that he judges may be fitt for the scoule. I knowe his father; if he be alike, he is a very worthy man. Mr Simons makes hast away; they growe deeper and deeper in theare opinions, so that he now thinkes it is not fite to ioyne with us in the publicke fast, and so they intend to be goon on the munday before the fast. I heare that Mʳ Cardock is returned to Clanuer, but not to preach. I hope you may bring Mʳ Balham along with you. Your brother Robert has had 2 spisess of his fitts with in this weak. I pray God be merciful to him. Remember my saruis to your worthy tutor. So in haste I rest

Your affectinat mother,   BRILLIANA HARLEY.

Decem: 6, 1639.   *Bromton Castell.*

I haue sent you a paire of rideing stokenens. Deare Ned, bringe Euesebius with you.

I am glad you would not let the agget be filled; that would spoyle it. Good Ned, bring my wacth with you to me.

LX.

For my deare sonne Mr. Edward Harley,
at Magdalen Hall, in Oxford.

Deare Ned—It hath pleased God that I haue beene ill euer since you went; but yet I reioyce in Gods mercy to me, that you enioy your health, wch your letters haue assured me of. I thanke you for them, for they haue beene sweet refreshments to me. Your letter this weeke by the carrier I receiued last night, and I blesse God that I receiue such childlike expressions of loue from you. I hope I receiue the fruit of your praiers, for the Lord hath beene pleased to shew His strength in my weakenesse, to enable me to undergoe such a fit of weakenesse, wch hath made stronger bodies then mine to stoope. This day seuen night it pleased God I did miscarrie, wch I did desire to haue preuented; but the Lord wch brought His owne worke to passe, and I desired to submit to it. Your father out of his tender care ouer me sent for doctor Dayodet, who gaue me some directions, and is now gone. I thanke God I am prity well, and I hope that as the Lord hath strenghened me to beare my weakenesse in my bed, so I trust He will enable me to rise out of my bed. I was so desirous that you should know how I was, that I entreated your father to let you know in what condition I was. My deare Ned, since I canot see you, let me heare from you as often as you can. I thanke God your father is well, and so are your brothers and sisters. Mr. Baalam carries himself very well, who I haue enquired after as much as my illnesse will giue me leaue. Remember me to your tutor, who I desire to remember me in his prayers. I pray God blesse you with those eternall riches of the sauing graces of His spirit. So I rest

Your affectionate mother, *BRILL. HARLEY.

Brompton, January 31, 1639.

My Lady Whitney wrote my father word that she had made choice of one for Whitney.

Here enclosed I haue sent you two letters, by wch you may know Mr. Hibbons tooke a vomit contrary to all counsell, and thereupon died.

Keepe my lords letter to your seal.

LXI.

To her son Edward.

My deare Ned—Tho I rwit to you the last night, yet I cannot let the bearer goo without letting you know how I doo; when you are with me I am best pleased to tell you how I am, and so I am now you are gone.

I thanke God I am pretty well, but haue not yet gone out of my beed. I am confident you pray for me. I waite vpon my gratious God. My great comfort is to heare you are well. The Lord blles you with all bllesinges of gras and thos of this life.

Your most affectinat mother, BRILLIANA HARLEY.

Phe: the first.

* The signature alone is in the handwriting of Lady Brilliana.

I want one to rwit for me,

Remember me to your worthy tutor, whoo I desire to remember me in his prayers.

Your father promised me he would rwit to you.

Directed, in the hand-writing of another,—" To my deare sonne Mr Edward Harley, at his chamber in Magdalen Hall in Oxen. these p^esent."

LXII.

For my deare sonne Mr. Edward Harley,
in Magdalene Hall, Oxford.

My dear Ned—Yesterday I reseued your letter by my cosen Dauis, and this day yours by the carrier, both weare very wellcome to me, and I desire to acknowledg Gods mercy to me, that you inioy your health, which I pray God you long doo, with a hart desirous to spend all your strentgh and health to the glory of your God.

My deare Ned, I thanke you for your ernest desire for my health. I am, I think, better for your prayers. I did not send for doctor to take phisick, for I thanke God I was not sike, but I knwe I had need of cordialls, and thos I toucke of doctor Deodate and not of Doctor Rwit. I thanke God I am now abell to site up a littell. This day I sate vp out of my beed allmost an ower. I should be glad to haue you with me, since I can let your thoughts run with me. I did not thinke I had bine with child when you weare with me. The Lord blles you, and make you still a comfort to

Your most affectinat mother,   BRILLIANA HARLEY.

Pheb. 8. 1639. *Bromton.*

Your father, brothers and sisters are well.

Remember my saruis to y^r worthy tutor, whoo I hope remembers me in his prayers, for I doo him in mine.

LXIII.

For my deare sonne Mr Edward Harley,
in Magdalen Hall, Oxford.

Deare Ned—The last night, by Tho: Millard, I receiued your letter, wch was a sweet refreshment to me. I know your deare loue to me wch makes you desire to heare how I doe: therfore I cannot let this messenger goe without a letter. I thanke God I am indifferent wel, though now constrained to keepe my bed for the same cause as I used to doe heretofore, but now I am a litle worse then I used then to be. I assure myselfe you forget me not in your praiers, which is the best thing that we can doe, one for another. Deare Ned, I long to see you, instead of which I hope the Lord will giue me that comfort of still hearing well of you. The Lord blesse you, and I beseech Him to giue you that holy wisdome, to guide you in all the actions of your life. Your father, I thanke God, is well, and so are your brothers and sisters and your cousen Smith. On saterday I heard from your aunt Pelham; shee and all hers are well: my brother Sir William Pelham hath refused to be knight of the shire. The French pages of newes I did not intend to haue sent you. So I rest,

Your most affectionate mother,   B: H:*

Brompton, Feb. 10, 1639.

Remember my loue to your tutor, and tell him I desire his prayers.

LXIV.

For my deare sonne Mr Edward Harley.

My deare Ned—Miller came home a littell before super; he is wellcome, becaus he bringes me the assurence of your being well,

---

* This letter is in the handwriting of another, and signed simply with the initials, evidently by herself.

which I acknowledg as a greate mercy to me, and is a sweet cordiell to me, in my being ill, for my deare Ned, your being well is much of my being so. I pray God blless you, and make you to grow strong in the feare of the Lord.

I thanke you for your care of my wacth; it is doune very well; I will send you mony, and pleas God, very shortly. My deare Ned, I thanke you for sending me your seale, when you hard it might doo me good. I will take care of it, and I hope to returne it you shortley. I beleeue your loue is such to me, that it makes you glad still to be a comfort to me and your father. Heare inclosed I haue sent you the nwes come in my lords letter to your father.

Your most affectinat mother,   BRILL. HARLEY.

Sr Francis Deuerex elledest sonne and 4 more jentellmen and on kight weare drouned in a bote the last night pasing the water near Worster.

I hope you remember the Ember day.

(No date.)

LXV.

*For my deare sonne Mr. Edward Harley,
in Magdiline Hall, Oxford.*

Deare Ned—This morning I reseued your letter, I thanke you for it, and I much reioyce that you are well. Miller toold me that you did cut your wood for exercise, which I am glad of, but your father would not haue you cut but sawe your wood. I tell him, I thinke you doo saw it. Your father tooke some coold, which made him ill sence Miller went, but now I thanke God, he is well agayne and abroode. For meself, my dear Ned, I am still weake, and, I thinke, allmost as weake as affter lyeing in of any of my chillderen, but your sister Dorrity; yester 1 was vp a littell. I haue sent you a gammon of backen by this carrier, and a Lenten tocken of dried sweetmeats for your tutor, but it is directed to you; if I had bine well I had sent you a larger prouition for Lent. I hard that theare weare 500 men sent to Barwicke. I pray God direct them what to doo. The Lord blless you and presarue you in His feare. Deare Ned, be carefull of your self, and beleeue that I am,

Your most affectinat mother, BRILLIANA HARLEY.

Phe: 20, 1639.

Remember me to worthy Mr Pirkins.

I haue sent the water for Elsabethe Stanton, she may take 2 or 3 spounefulls at a time, shee should take it as soune as shee finds any inclination to a fite; the best way to take it is with 2 or 3 spounfulls of parseley water.

The dried appells are for you.

Sam Pinner waits on your brothers, and I think Blechly goos away; your father dous not like her.

LXVI.

To my deare sonne Mr Edward Harley,
in Magdilen Hall, Oxford.

My deare Ned—Tho your letter by Holingworth and another by Jhon Wall weare long comeing to my hand, and so my thanke may be of an old date, yet reseue it, for them and for your letter this weake by the carrier. I acknowledg it is Gods great mercy to me that you are well, by which I haue much contentment to scheer me in my want of other content, in my owne health. I hope you will find out some way not to keep a strickt Lent, for I am confident it is not good for you. My deare Ned, be carefull of your health; vse exersis and a good diet; goo to beed betimes and rise erlye; yet I desire not that you should put your self in such a frame that you cannot doo otherways, when theare is oction to change your cours; but aboue all, my deare Ned, looke to that precious part of you, your soul; be not you wanting to presarue its health, keep it in a spirituall heate by prayer, and let the loue of your God be the motife of all your obedience. I cannot but prise that care you haue exprest of me, and your ernest desires for my health. Docter Rwit when he went from me did ernestly desire me to haue some about me that would put me in minde to eate; for he toold me, he obsarued I neglected meself. I thanke you for rwiting to your brother to put Hacklet in minde of it, which shee has sence offner remembred then shee did before. I thanke God I am something better then I haue bine; this day and yesterday I sate vp 2 owers a day.

I beleeue you pray for me, and doo still, my deare Ned. Your father is, I thanke God, well, and tells me he will rwit to you; they say, he and S^r Wāter Pye shall be knights for this sheare. Mr. Edwards is inducted into Buckill and theare abides. Mr. Simons is now heare, he is very resolut in his way. Mr. Blineman is goon into NweIngland, and Tabithe is goon. Mr. Balls booke is come forthe about thos opinions, but I haue not yet reed it. You rwit me word you had sent me the book put out by a Jesuet, but I haue not yet reseued it, nor thos thigs Gorg rwit me word he had sent. I purpos, if pleas God, to send shortly to you, if I am well. Mr. Ballam dous well. Your brother Robin had a littell spis of a fite the last weak. I haue sent you by this carrier a turkey pye, but I dout that it is not a very good one, it is so littell. My paper puts me in mind to conclud theas lines.

 Your affectinat mother,   BRILL. HARLEY.

Bromton, Phe. 28, 1639.

Send me word wheather you reseued the band I sent you.
Remember my loue to your worthy tutor.

LXVII.

*For my deare sonne Mr. Edward Harley,
in Magdilen Hall, Oxford.*

My Deare Ned—It is my comfort that I inioy so constant aschurance of your health; in which mercy I hope the Lord will be still gratious to me, and I trust the Lord will croune that mercy in filling you with gras.

I thanke you for your letter by Looker, tho it may be your sister will not thanke you for her token, becaus the expettacon was disapounted, at which I could not but lafe.

Your father, I thanke God, is well, and likly, as they say, to be knight of this scheer; I do not yet heare that the rwit is come into this cuntry, tho it be in diuers others: I thanke God thees 2 days I haue risen betwne a 11 an 12 a cloke, and sate vp tell 6; and I hope I shall doo so this day, I meene, site vp so long, for I rose to day about a 11.

I haue sent you by this carry another turky pye, with 2 turkys in it; I hope the cooke has backed it well. I did thinke the glas of water would not be well stoped up. I take it as a speciall providence of God, that I haue so froward a made aboute me as Mary is, sence I loue peace and quietnes so well; she has bene extremely froward since I haue bine ill; I did not think that any would haue bine so colericke.

I pray God, if euer you have a wife, she may be of a meeke and quiet spirit. My deare Ned, the Lord bless you, and so I rest,

Your most affectinat mother, BRILLIANA HARLEY.

Mar: 6, 1639, from my chare by the fre.

Remember my loue to your worthy tutor.

I haue now resceued the booke you sent me, and thanke you for it.

LXVIII.

For my deare sonne Mr Edward Harley,
at Magdalen Hall, Oxford.

Deare Ned—Yesterday I receiued your letter by the carrier; I much reioyce in Gods mercy to me in continuing your health. I purpose (and please God) to make you some meath, which may be good for the stone, and send it to you, that you may drinke it in a morning. I hope you are carefull not to eat too much fish this lent. I take it for a great expression of my sister Braies loue to me, in the fauour she shewes to you. I am very glad that my neece is to be married into this countrey, where I hope I shall see her. I heare that Mr Francis Newport and Sr Richard Lee are burgesses of Shrewsbury. My cousen Andrew Corbet and Sr John Corbet and Mr Peierpoint contend, who shall be knights for Shropshire. Ludlow haue made choise of Mr Goodwin to be burgesse, hauing refused my lord president his letters for Sr Robert Nepper, his son in law. Mr Harbert is chosen for Mountgomeryshire; he hath a coure of horse giuen him and a thousand pound paid him to furnish him. Your father went yesterday to Hereford: this day being the day for the choise of the knights, if they chuse your father I must be contented, though for my owne particular I haue no cause to be glad. I am in bed, which is the reason I make use of anothers pen.* I thanke God I am not much worse then I used to be when I am enforced to keepe my bed. I promis my selfe part of your praiers. Your brothers and your cousin Smith and your sisters are all well. I pray God blesse you and make you to grow strong in the graces of His spirit, that you may be able to withstand the temptations of the world and of satan. Remember me to your worthy tutor, and tell George Griffithes that I haue received the petticoates wch Mr Nelham did drawe, and the silke and wyre, for which Mr Nelham shall haue money, when I receiue the piece of greene cloth from him. I haue read part of the booke you sent me, and I must needs say, he that wrote it sauours of the spirits from below.

I purpose (and please God) to send you word who are chosen for this countrey. And so I rest,

Your most affectionate mother, BRILLIANA HARLEY.

Brompton Castle, March 14, 1639.

* The signature alone of this letter is in the handwriting of the Lady Brilliana: by the next letter it appears, it was written by her son Thomas. Letter LXIII. is evidently in the same hand.

LXIX.

For my deare sonne Mr. Edward Harley,
in Magdilen Hall, Oxford.

Deare Ned,—A boute sixe a cloke your father returned well from Hariford, wheare this morning aboute 8 a cloke, he and Sr Walter Pye weare chosen with a vanimos consent, to be knights for this cuntry; the Lord fill them with wisdome for that worke.

I thanke God your father is very well. This morning I rwit to you by the heelp of your brother Tomas, but theas lines I send you, becaus I beleeue you will desire to heare whoo is chosen. The Lord blles you.

Your most affectinat mother,   BRILLIANA HARLEY.

Mar: 14, 1639. *Bromton.*

LXX.

For my deare sonne Mr. Edward Harley,
in Magdelin Hall, Oxford.

Deare Ned — This morning I reseued your letter, and I thanke you for it; for sence I cannot see you, I gladly entertaine your letters. I much reioyce that in all places they are so carefull to chues worthy men for so greate a buisnes, as the parlament.

I rwit you word the last weake, that your father and Sr Waltr Pye weare chosen for HerifordScheere, and that your father would not haue you goo out of Oxford, becaus he purposes to goo to Loundon shortly. I thinke he will goo the weake before Ester. On tusday next, if pleas God, your father will keep a day; I beleeue you vnderstand what day I meane. Mr. Moore and Sr Robert Howard are chosen for Bischops Castell. This weake I hard from my sister Pelham; I thanke God shee is well. But I am sorry that they haue made choys of a tutor for theare sonne in Magdeline coledg; it is on Mr. Rogers. As sonne as his ouncell has prouided him a chamber he is to come to Oxford. Your father did not goo this weake to the assises, becaus of his many buisnescess; this day he is gone to Loudlow. I thanke God he is indeferent well. Your brothers and sisters are well. Remember me to your worthy tutor; and I pray God blles you, and make you still a comfort to

Your most affectinat mother, BRILLIANA HARLEY.

Mar: 20, 1639. *Bromton Castel.*

Tell Gorg Griffits that his father and mother are well. I hard from them the last night.

I thanke God I begin to rise agane out of my beed.

LXXI.

To my deare sonne Mr Edward Harley.

Deare Ned—I can not let Mr. Balam goo without a letter, being glad of all opertunitys to let you know I thinke of you.

Your father, I thanke God, is well; but his many buisness and the weather has caused your father to put of his journey for a day or tow; but, and pleas God, he purposes to be at Oxford frieday or saterday next. Your father would haue you, as soune as you can, to rwit to Mr. Smith at Loundon, to let him know that the last weake your father sent vp his trunck, but no letter with it. Heare are many strangers, so that I can but cacthe a littell time to rwit to you; but I haue not keep them much company, only seene them twise. I pray God blles you, and so I rest

Your most affectinat mother, BRILLIANA HARLEY.

Mar. 31, 1640.

I haue sent you some violet cackes.

LXXII.

For my deare sonne Mr Edward Harley,
in Magdeline Hall, Oxford.

Dear Ned—This night I reseued your letter by Jhon Coolborne. I am glad you went vp to Loundon with your father, and I hope this letter will meet you safely returned to Oxford. I acount it a great mercy that your father came so well to Loundon, the weather being so fowele, and that you indured so weet a day so well. I beceach the Lord to inabell you to indure all stormes of this life, being shelltered vnder the sole protection of your gratious God. My deare Ned, I shall longe to heare from you againe; my thoughts are with you. I did thinke theas preparations weare for Scotland. I beceach the Lord to turne all the counsells of men to the aduantag of His chruch. I am now in beed, and so haue bine theas 5 days. Your brothers and sisters are well. My cosen Cornewell is goon to her mother, whoo is very sike. My deare Ned, the Lord blles you, and if it be His will, giue me a comfortabell seeing of you; which I long for.

Your most affectinat mother, BRILLIANA HARLEY.

Bromton Castell, Apr: 11, 1640.

LXXIII.

For my deare sonne Mr Edward Harley,
in Magdeline Hall, Oxford.

My Deare Ned—Sence I can not see you, I am glad of theas opertunitys by which I may let you know my thonghts are offten with you; your father being from me, I haue not much company to take pleashure in, but this is a Chirstians comfort, that God is all ways with them. I should be glad to heare from you a relation how the king went to parlament, and at what ease you hard his speche; for I did feare theare would be a great crowde, which made me desire your father not to be theare. I heare your father had a fitt of the pastion of the hart, the day before yow went from Loundon. I beceach the Lord presaruef him from them. Heare is great presing. Mr Harberd is goon with his trop of hors; on of his soulders killed a man in Shearsbury, but they say he was prouocked to it. They are gallant and merry. The trained band is thought must goo, or ells prouid men to goo in theiare places. I can not yet heare for sartaine wheare theair randeuous is.

I haue sent you by Loocker some violet cakes. Deare Ned, be carefull of your self, especially be wacthfull ouer your hart.

Edward Piners chillderens beed was seet on fier, and it was Gods mercy they had not bine smothered. Piner in puting of it out, haueing none to healp him but Pheebe, whoo is with his wife, tooke coold, for he was in his shirt, and the smoke allmost tooke away his breath, that he is very ill, and I feare has a feauor; it was on firer on wensday night; they rang the bell, which feared all my howes. I pray God to blles you.

Your most affectinat mother,   BRILLIANA HARLEY.

Apri: 25, 164 . Bromton Castell.

LXXIV.

For my deare sonne Mr. Edward Harley,
in Magdalen Hall, Oxford.

Deare Ned—This morning I receiued your letter, which was very welcome to me and since it pleases God that you inioy your health, I do with more ease beare my owne weakenes. I haue not yet this weeke receiued any letter from your father, and it would much trouble me, but that your father wrote me word that he intended to send the cooke downe this weeke. I thanke you for the kings prair, and I pray God to heare all the praiers that are now put up for a happy issue of this parliament. I haue heard of many bold speeches that haue passed there; and that passage betweene the archbishop and my lord Say is diuersly reported; but I beleue that which I receaued from you. The presse of souldiers is now passt; so that the poore fellowes may now appeare, who had hid themeselues for feare. I purpose and please God, to send to you sometime the next weeke with the money your tutor sent for. I haue not beene out of my bed since wednesday, but I thank God I am but as I use to be. I long to see you, I will not say how much, lest your tutor call it fondnesse, and not loue. I thanke God your brothers and sisters with your cousin Smith are well; but your brother Robert had yesterday morning a seice of a fit, which makes me desire he should enter into a course of physicke. Edward Pinner hath beene very sicke. I sent for docter Wright to him, who hath beene here the most part of this weeke, and hath giuen him physicke which hath done him (by the blessing of God) upon that meanes, much good. This morning he was let blood, and bled uery vile blood; and I now hope he will recouer apace, but yet he keepes his bed. I pray God blesse you, and giue me a comfortable seeing of you, which is much desired by

  Your most affectionate mother,   BRILLIANA HARLEY.*

May 1, 1640.

I beleue your cousen —— is not yet come to Oxford.

Mᵣ Walkut was not long since with me. She much reioyced that she had got so excellent a tutor for her son and nephew, and how she had contriued it, that he should haue a seruitor in the house, and so should not need a man to wait upon him. He now feares an ague, and his going to Oxford is put off till he be well.

* The signature alone is in the handwriting of the Lady Brilliana:—the letter in that of her son Thomas.

LXXV.

For my deare sonne Mr. Edward Harley,
in Magdeline Hall, Oxford.

My deare Ned—I am not willing you should be longe without that which you stand in neede of, which makes me send this bearor to you, with £10 and 50 sh: for your tutors quartrege; and haueing this oction to send to you, I send him a littell further to see your father, whom I long to see. Affter I had rwit to you by the carrier, I reseued a letter from your father by the cooke, and on from you; they weare both wellcome to me. I thanke you that you make me partake of what you heare; for your father has not time to rwit many particulars. The state of the parlament which I receued from your father I send you heare inclosed, and that which I had from you. Returne mine againe. I beleeue you haue the lord keepers speach, and the speakers, and thearefore I doo not send them to you. I pray God giue a happy sugsess to this parlement; if not we may feare wors effects then has bine yet. You and meself haue great resen to be ernest with our God for your father.

I beleeue this weake will sheaw what they will doo, as all our expectations are vpon the parlament, so I desire all our prayers may be for it.

My deare Ned, I much long to see you and I hope I shall shortly. I haue not recoured so much strentgh as to goo out of my chamber, and at this time I am in beed. Your brothers and sisters are well, and Edward Piner mends a pace. I thinke doctor Rwite a very good doctor. I like the cooke very well.

My deare Ned, the Lord blles you and make you grow in the strentgh of gras, and that you may dayly grow in the loue of Jesus Christ, that that loue may be all in all in you; that so loueing your God aboue all, you may vse the thinges heare below as if you vsed them not. I thanke you for your care of my candellstike, which I

reseued safe. I heare inclosed send you 20th. out of which, pay for the lookeing glas, and the rest you may dispose of, as pleas yourself. I thinke Hall will bring the glas very well. So in hast I rest
Your most affectinat mother, BRILLIANA HARLEY.
Deare Ned, remember me very kindly to your worthy tutor. The 20th I thought to haue sent in my letter is with the £10; take it out, and giue the £10 to your tutor.

May 4, 1640.

LXXVI.

To her son Edward.—Endorsed, "For your deare selfe."

My deare Ned—I thanke you for your letter this weake by the carrier; beleeue it, your lines are sweetly wellcome to me; it is my joy that you are well; the Lord in mercy presarufe you in health both of body and mind.

I much desire to see you, and thearefore I haue rwit to your father, to desire him to giue you leafe to come home at Whitsontide.

I thanke you for imparting to me what you know of the parlament, and I will requite you with what I knowe. Theas which I send you I had from my cosen Goowdine; you may keepe them, for I had them rwit out for you. Edward Piner begins to goo abroad. Your brothers and sisters are well. I am not yet out of my beed. Remember me to your tutor.

Your most affectinat mother, BRILLIANA HARLEY.

May 8, 1640.

LXXVII.

To her son Edward.—Endorsed, "For your deare selfe."

My deare Ned—I rwit to you but a short letter by the carrier, intending to rwit this day againe to you, but I am not yet sartaine whoo shall carry my letter. I doo so much desire to see you, that I haue rwit ernestly to your father to giue you leaufe to come home at Whitsontide. My deare Ned, I hope it will still be so that you shall be my great comfort. The Lord in mercy make you to grow in the sweet graces of His spirit, and then you will be louely in the eyes of all Gods chillderen.

I am glad you had a day of fast, which is a spirituall feast. I heare that the parlament had granted to them a day of fast, but I cannot tell when it was.

I haue heareinclosed sent you your letter which you sent me, and I thanke you for it, and haue sent you some papers that weare sent me. I had two letters from your father this weake. I thanke God he was well, but he rwit not one word of the parlament; nor Sanky, when he rwits, he says nothing of your father, nor of the parlament. I pray God guie the two howes a happy vnion togeather; for the effects of this parlement will not be indiffrent, neather good nor euell, but eather very good or ells the contrary. The depuety leftenants haue bine at Hariford sence wensday, aboute sending the soulders. Captaine Button is to be captaine of them; he is, as they say, a proper jentellman. Roger Beeb was wilde for his brother being prest, but I could not preuaile with the wise counstablle of Bromton, and was constraind to send Samuell to the deputy leftenants; they thought it much that I could not command that of him, which if I had sent to any jentellman in the cuntry, they would haue doun more, as they said. I heare the soulders are very onruly.

I thanke God your brothers and sisters are well, and Edward Piner is abrood againe.

Good doctor Barker is, as they say, sike to death. Blechly has theas 2 days bin in griuious distres, and is in griuious agony of contience and dispare; shee says shee shall be damned. Desire Mr Pirkins to pray for her, and, deare Ned, pray for her; shee was with me, for her desire was ernest to see me and to speake with me. My deare Ned, long to see me, as I doo, to see you; and the Lord in mercy giue me comfortabell seeing you, which is much desired by

    Your most affectinat mother,   BRILLIANA HARLEY.

Deare Ned, remember me to your worthy tutor.

If you doo not come home at Witsentide, I would haue you send me one of your shirts to take meashure by, and I will, if pleas God, send them you. I like the cooke very well.

May 9, 1640. Bromton Castell.

LXXVIII.

For my deare sonne Mr. Edward Harley, in Magdeline Hall, Oxford.

My deare Ned—I thanke you for your letter by J——rth. It was wellcome to me, and I hope it will not be long before I see you, which comfort I begg of the Lord. On Sunday morning I receued a letter from your father, by which I found the nwes of the disolueing of the parlament to be true. Theare are many rumurs in the cuntry. The prest soulders in Presteene haue fought; and they say, if it had not bine for the trained band they had killed the captaine that is come downe for them, refuseing to goo with him, becaus he is a papis. Mr Haruy and his wife are now heare, comeing to take theaire leafe to goo into Warekschere. My deare Ned, the Lord blles you, and giue your father and you a happy meeting with

Your most affectinat mother,   BRILLIANA HARLEY.

May 13, 1640. Bromton Castell.

I am glade Mr Robert Pye sonn is with your tutor.

Remember me to your worthy tutor, and tell him if he come to Bromton, Mr Gower expects to haue him to preach for him.

LXXIX.

For my deare sonne Mr. Edward Harley.

My deare Ned—I hope theas lines will finde you well at Oxford. I long to heare from you, and I hope I shall, before it be longe.

My deare Ned, be carefull of your self, and especially be wacthfull ouer your precious soule, still to embrace all things that may further thos grasess in you, which may make you like those that liue holy heare, and shall be gloryfyed heareaffter.

I thanke God your father is well, and so is your brothers and sisters; for meself I am as you left me, but that I haue not you, with me.

I heare from Loundon that the Conuocation howes bracke up the 29 of May, and they haue suspended the bis: of Gloster, becaus he would not consent to theare cannons; and they haue sencured doctor Beale for his sermon. The soulders which weare at Heariford are sent to theare seuerall abodes, and theare to abide for a month. I pray God blles you, and make you still a comfort to

    Your most affectinat mother,   BRILLIANA HARLEY.

(No date.)

Remember me to your worthy tutor.

Your father gaue me this packet to send you.

LXXX.

For my deare sonne Mr. Edward Harley.

Deare Ned—On saterday night somethinge late Colborn came home; his late comeing put me in some doutefull thoughts, but I thanke God I reseued by him the aschurance of your comeing well to Oxford. I thanke you for your seale you sent me, I will keepe it safe for you. This day I reseued your letter by the carrier, I thanke you for it, and it dous much reioyce me that you are well, which I beceach the Lord to continue. I am glad my nephewe Pelham is come so well to Oxford; and, my deare Ned, be still kinde to him; tho it may be, his ouncell may make him something strang, but let your loue (if it be so) ouer come it. I beleeue he thinkes all well doun that is nwe to him and that he sees jentellmen to do with a good gras, which he thinkes they doo when they bowe to the allter; but I pray God teach him another leson; but he must be warely dealt with.

I am sorry to heare my sister has bine ill. I doo purpos, if pleas God, to send to her shortly. Your father has not bine well; he sent for doctor Rwit, but tooke nothing. On wensday last, aboute 12 a cloke at night, he was very ill, but, I thanke God, by morning, he was well, and whent into the faire as he was vsed to doo. The faire was reasnabell quiet, only some Shropsheere soulders weare vnruley; but at night they weare all quiet. The deputy leftenants had letters, that they should sertyfy the counsell how the soulders weare, and who did refuse cote and conduck money. This weake I haue hard no nwes. I thinke Mr. Gower will be with you some time the next weake, and then I hope to rwit to you. Your brothers and sisters are well. I thanke God I am as you left me. I pray God blles you, and giue me a comfortabell seeing of you, which is ernestly desired by

Your most affectinat mother,   Brilliana Harley.

Remember my loue to your worthy tutor; and let Gorge know I like the las well.

My cosen Dauis remembers her saruis to you.

Jun: 12, 1640.   *Bromton Castell.*

LXXXI.

To her son Edward.—Endorsed, " For your deare selfe."

Deare Ned—I am glad to take the oportunity to rwite to you, when your father is at dinner; for last night my cosen Vahen and his sister with her husband and Mr. Lawes, with others of theairs, came to Bromton, and I beleeue after diner I shall haue theair company. They are come to make a full agreement with your father. Doct[r] Deodate gaue your father some phisick, and is confident your fathers illness only proseeds from the splene, and is no inclination to a palcy. Woodowes did as Prichards vse to do, and deceaued your father, so that he would not take this which the doctor would haue had him take, while he was with him. I thanke God your father is as well as he usess to be. The doctor let him bloud vnder the tounge, which agreed very well with him. Dr Deodate went away on tuesday last. I thanke you, my deare Ned, for wishing I should take something of him; but my illness comes at sartaine times, and without I should send for him just at that time, I can not haue him then to giue me any thing; for he would haue me take something and be let blood two or three days before I am ill, as I use to be. If pleas God, when you are with me, I will send for docter Rwite and take something. It pleases my gratious God, so to dispose of it, that this illness which I haue, makes me very weake, for as soune as I am pretty well I am ill againe. Doctor Deodate telles me he kowes many so, and he doos much pitty me; but my comfort is, that my God will not cast off for ever.

The soulders from Heariford were at Lemster last thursday on theaire marche to theaire rendeuoues; the captaine not paying them all theare pay, they would haue returned into the towne againe, but all the towne rose, and thos that weare come out of chruch, and with thos arms they had, beate them back, but theare being a greate heape of stones out of toune, the soulders made vse of them as long as they lasted, in which time the townesmin did but littell good, till that powder was spent, and then the townesmen weare to hard; many weare hurt on both sides; the captaine would haue come into the towne, but was keep out.

Your letter this weake by the carrier was wellcome. I hope, if Mr Gower be at Oxford at the fast, that you may heare him preach that day; and I hope, we shall haue him shortly at Bromton. If Dagon begin to fall, it will downe. I thanke you for the paper you sent me; I haue not yet red it, and the booke I haue not yet seene; your father has it, and I haue not seene him much to day.

Deare Ned, take care of your self for my sake, and doo not goo to

be ouer heate in the crowed at the Act. The Lord in mercy blles you and presarfe you.
Your affectinat mother,   BRILLIANA HARLEY.

July 3, 1640. *Bromton Castell.*

I haue so scribeled that I thinke you will hardly reade it.
By this carrier I haue sent you a cape. I hope it will come well to your hand.

LXXXII.

For my deare sonne Mr. Edward Harley,
in Magdiline Hall, Oxford.

Deare Ned—I believe you doo as willing reseafe my letters as I rwit them, which makes me willingly to take all oportunitys to give you aschurance I am nowaye vnmindful of you. Your father has fully agreed with my cosen Vahan and her sister, whoo went from heance this morning, and about that biuesnes he now sends to Loundon; so that this bearer is to rest at Oxford, on the fast. We heare a confidente report that the kinge is agreed with the Scoths, and I hope it is true. Your father, I thanke God, is well. I have resued the booke you sent me, and thanke you for it. I beleeue I shall like it well, for the subiet is very needfull to be knowne, and the aughter of it, is of judgment, thearefore I beleeue he has doun it well. The wellknoweing how fure our pastions are good and how fure euill, and the right way to goworne them is dificule; and in my obseruation I see but feawe, that are stutidious to gouerne theaire pastions, and it is our pastions that trubells our selfs and others.

Deare Ned, I longe to see you, and I hope I shall with comfort. Mr. Salawewell is with your father. The Lord in mercy fitt you and us for the day of fast, and I hope Mr. Gower will preach at Oxford. Mr. Heath will be at Bromton on the fast. I looke that Mr. Pirkins should rwite to me when he will let you come home.

I pray God blles you and fill you with gras, which is the best riches.

Your most affectinat mother,   BRILLIANA HARLEY.

July 4, 1640. *Bromton Castell.*

Remember my loue to your worthy tutor. The messenger is not yet returned out of Linconscheer.

LXXXIII.

For my deare sonne Mr. Edward Harley,
in Magdeline Hall, Oxford.

Deare Ned—Mr. Gower came not home till saterday about 5 a colke. I, haueing no letters by the carrier, was something trubled, tell I reseued yours by Mr. Gower. I hope I shall now see you shortly, which I longe to do, and I pray God I may with much comfort.

I pray God blles you and bring you safe to

Your most affectinat mother,   BRILLIANA HARLEY.

July 27, 1640. *Bromton Castell.*

Remember me to your worthy tutor. I hope we shall see him at Bromton.

I reseued a letter the last weeke from my lord by M[r] Harbert. I thanke God he is very well. M[r] Harberd came but for 3 days, and is returned.

LXXXIV.

For my deare sonne Mr. Edward Harley.

My deare Ned—Your letters by the carrier I haue reseued, and I thanke you for them, and the kings speach and the versess. I hope the parlament will (by Gods mercy) haue as happy proseedings and endeing as it has a hopefull begining. I hope by the next you will send me the speakers speache. I much reioyce that your father and your self enioy your health, and I beceach the Lord you may longe doo so: but, my deare Ned, I would haue you rwite me word more at large, what my cosen Smith thinkes of that which trubells you, and wheather he thinkes a plaster will be sufficient for you. Deare Ned, beleeue it, my thoughts are much with you: be carefull to improuf your time. I know Loundoun is a bewitching place. I desire to knowe wheare your fathers lodging is, and wheather you lye at his lodging. I thanke God I am indeferent well, and your brothers and sisters are very well. Send me word wheather my cosen Hrry Pelham be of the parlament, and wheather my lord is to come or no to Loundoun.

I beceach the Lord to blles you, and presarfe you in all safety.

Your most affectinat mother,   BRILLIANA HARLEY.

The versess pleas me well, and to requite you, I haue sent you some.

Nou: 14, 1640. Bromton Castell.

Remember me to my cosen Smith and his wife. I haue sent to your man, to doo some biuseness for me. Good Ned, put him in minde to doo it.

Deare Ned, send me word what good men are of the parlament.

LXXXV.

For my deare sonne Mr. Edward Harley.

My deare Ned—I beceach the Lord to blles you, and to fill you with His gras, and that heauenly wisdom by which you may truely see, that the ways of the men of the world are but foolly.

I did much feare you would not haue endured your iourney so well, but my God was merciful to you and me in enabelling of you. Deare Ned, let me know whoo your father makes choys of to giue you some thinge, and I beceach the Lord to blles the means to you; and I dout not but that my cosen Smith will be carefull of you. Deare Ned, send me word wheare your father his lodging is.

I perswade meself, the enimes of Gods chruch will lay theair plots deep, but our God is aboue them, and to Him doo we looke, that neuer yet deserted His in the time of trubell. Nay, this is our comfort, that the time of trubell is a speciall time, in which the Lord has commanded His chillderen to seeke vnto Him; and the Lord dous not bide vs to seeke Him in vaine. I pray God presarfe the parlament and giude them in the good way, that they may counsell for the good of his chruch. I am glad you went to see my lady and my sister Wacke. I purpos, if pleas God, to keepe a day the next weake. I thinke it will be thursday; so I rest,

Your most affectinat mother, BRILLIANA HARLEY.

(No date.)

Deare Ned, rwit me word, how you found Ned Pelham. I thanke God I am indeferent well, but I haue not bine very well sence you went.

Your brothers and sisters are well.

I heare my lord of Northamton is to be lord presedent of Wailles; send me word wheather you heare so.

The chesnut gellding was grauelled and theare is a great hoole in his foote, but Martine thinke he will doo well.

LXXXVI.

For my deare sonne Mr. Edward Harley,
at Magdeline Hall, Oxford.

My deare Ned—Not being sartaine wheare you are, I haue sent one letter to Loundon, and this I send to Oxford, least you should not be at Loundoun. I pray God blles you, wheresoeuer you are. This night, I hard from my brother Pelham; he is well, but some of his chillderen haue not bine well. In hast, I rest,

Your most affectinat mother, BRILLIANA HARLEY.

Noue. 21, 1640. *Bromton Castell.*

LXXXVII.

For my deare sonne Mr. Edward Harley.

My deare Ned—I much reioce in the aschurence of your health with your father. I beceach the Lord continue your health and giue you thos choys grasess of His spirit, which He only bestowes vpon His chillderen. O deare Ned, it is most wellcome nwes that the parlament goos on thus happily. The Lord be with them still, and enabell your father for that greate worke. I was not sartaine wheather you would be goone to Oxford or no; becaus your father said nothing of it, which made me send this letter to Loundon. I thanke God your brothers and sisters are well. I beceach the Lord to blles you, as I desire my owne soule should be bllesed, and beleeue that I am,

Your most affectinat mother,   BRILLIANA HARLEY.

Noue: 21, 1640. *Bromton Castell.*

LXXXVIII.

To my deare sonne Mr. Edward Harley.

My deare Ned—I thanke you for your letter from Mr. Sallwells. I much reioyce that you so well endured so fare of the iourney, and I hope my God safe prouidence has brought you to London: my hart is much with you, and I desire to haue it much with my God, for you. It is my comfort that you desire to submite your self to the dispos of our gratious God; His way is best; and the Lord in mercy giue you allways the eye of faith to see it is so.

Deare Ned, be carefull of your self, and let me know how it is with you. Mr. Gower came home last night late and weet; and I feare your father and you had a weet day of it. I heare that parlament is ajourned for 10 days, but I defer my beleefe. I haue not bine yet out of my beed, but I thanke God I am indeferent well;

your brothers and sisters are well. I beceach the Lord to blles you and keepe you safe, under His holy protection; so I rest

    Your most affectinat mother,   BRILLIANA HARLEY.

Noue: 30, 1640. Bromton Castell.

Your truncke is sent to Oxford.

LXXXIX.

For my deare sonne Mr Edward Harley,
in Magdilen Hall, Oxford.—Endorsed, " For your deare selfe."

My deare Ned—This day I reseued your letter, which is much comfort to me. I longe much to see you, and I mise you as much; be carefull, of your self, and doo not neglect to vse the meanes, which is derected you. The last night I hard from your father by Morgan, who had bine at Loundon; I meane the apoticary; he left your father well, but full of buisness. He sawe Mr Prine and Mr Bourton come into Loundoun; they weare meet with 2000 hoors and 150 schochess, and the men wore rosemary that meet them. I haue heare sent you the 7 articells against my lord Straford; your father sent them me. The parlament goos on happily; I pray God continue it. Mrs Yats continues ill, but doctor Rwit hopes shee mendes; he is with her still. I haue sent your father a snipe pye and a teale pye, and a coller of brane, or elles I had sent you somethinge this weake. Remember me to my nephew Pelham and to your tutor. I pray God fitte vs all, for the day of fast. Your brothers and sisters are well, and I thanke God I am out of my beed againe. I pray God blles you and leade you in the path of life; and beleefe that I am,

    Your most affectinat mother,   BRILLIANA HARLEY.

Desem: 1640. Bromton Castell.

I haue not yet seene the glasses, they are not come from the carriers, but I thanke you for them, and I will and pleas God, send you mony for them.

Mr. James is not yet come downe; I hope he will come by you.

XC.

For my deare sonne M'r Edward Harley.

Deare Ned—I thanke you for your letter this weake by the carrier; it is my greet ioy to heare from you, and I pray God I may still heare well of you. I should be exceeding glad if your father could procure Wigmore to be a burges towne, and that you might be of the parlement. I reseued a letter from your father this night by M'r Morgan, but none by the carrier. I thanke God he is very well, but full of biusnes. He rwit me word that secrotary Winedibancke was fled. I heare it is likely to goo ill with the erle of Straford. My lady Veere rwit me a letter this weake; she was then gooing to my lady of Westmorland, whouo is bigg with child. My lord her husband has had the small-pox, but I heare not a word of my sister Wacke. Mrs. Wallcote was with me this weake; she tells me shee thinkes to send for her sonne thees holydays, but shee neuer asked me wheather I would haue any thing to Oxford. Shee toold me Dr. Toby Mathue was with Mr. Plooden, wheare theare was great resort of papis, which makes some feare they haue some plots; but I trust the Lord of Hosts will wacth ouer vs.

My cosen Cornewell is heare; but I thinke when the Ember fast is past, shee will be goone. If you goo to my brother Brayes theas holy days, I shall not be sorry, but I know not, wheather your father will be content. Deare Ned, let me know wheather you goo or no. My cosen Blany his wife is brought to beed of a sonne: your brother Robert was godfather. Your brother growes talle. Mrs. Yates is vpon recovery. Doctor Rwit dealt very kindely with them, and tooke much pains, and tooke but half his feese. I was sorry Mr. Griffits brought me no letter, but he aschured me you weare well. I thanke God I am reasnabell well, and your brothers and sisters are very well, and I pray God continue your health and fill your hart with gras, which will be much comfort to,

Your most affectinat mother, BRILLIANA HARLEY.

Desem: 11, 1640. *Bromton Custle.*

I thanke you for the glases you sent me. They came all very safe; and I hope to send you the 11th for them; they are fine glasess.

Deare Ned, remember me to my nephew Pellham, and my saruis to your worthy tutor; and I hope you are carefull of your owne health.

XCI.

For my deare sonne Mr. Edward Harley.

Deare Ned—On wednesday night last I receiued your letter from Mr James, and yesterday yours by the carrier, for both I thanke you; and do you beleue that your letters are uery welcome to me, and I hope that that will always make you willing to write.

Your father wrote me word that he did thinke to send for you, which I am very glad of, and that makes me send this letter to London, where I hope it will meet you. I wrote you nothing of what I haue heard of the parliament: bec: I hope you will heare it more fully at London. Deare Ned, tell your father that I desire him, if Mr Gower can be spared from comming to London, that I desire he may. Richard Sankie wrote to him to come up about the beginning of January. Mr Gower read Sankies letter to me, but I will not haue Sankie know this. I know not how this congregation will be well prouided for in his absence. I thanke God he is very well, but I see him but seldome: he kept wednesday last very worthely. Mr Tomms was at Brompton and helpt us in my family. I haue kept my bed since yesterday; I hope the Lord will bring mee well out of it. I thanke God your brothers and sisters are well. I pray God blesse you and preserue you in safety, both of soule and body.

Your most affectionate mother, BRILLIANA HARLEY.*

Brompton, December 19, 1640.

* This letter, excepting the signature of Lady Brilliana, is in the handwriting of another; probably that of her son Thomas.

I take it for a great blessing of God that you are so well. I pray God continue your health, and be carefull of yourselfe for my sake.

XCII.

For my deare sonne Mr. Edward Harley.

Deare Ned—On thursday night Miller came home, and brought me the wellcome aschurance of your being well, with your father: and I should be glad you weare of the parlament. I much reioyce that the parlament goos one so well. I trust the Lord will finisch this good worke begonne. I am sorry my lord keeper would goo away. I belefe others wisch themselfes with him.

I hard from my brother Pelham aboute a fortnight sence; the ocation of his sending was this; I hard that the minester of Brockellbe was deade, and the place was worth 50*l*. a yeare; I haueing a great desire to haue a good man theare, made offer to Mr. Volye. My brother liked the report I gaue of him, and sent to haue him come and speake with him; but sent me word it was worth but 30 pounds a yeare; neather would he haue him come with a hope that he would mend it; but if he sawe he weare painefull, it was likely he would consider him. Mr. Voly was loth to goo to so small a thinge, vpon so poore hopes, and he has so much wheare he is: it did much trubell me, that my brother semed to be so straight in so great a matter; he rwit me word he had many shuters for it; I thinke they are not worth the haueing.

My deare Ned, take care of your self: doo not goo by water this winter. I heare theare is a howes shut vp by my cosen Smith, which I am sorry for. If Rafe had not goone vp of his owne buisnes, I had sent vp Rise. I could wisch your father would make you another shute of cloths, for one shute is to littell.

I thanke God I am indeferent well, and all your brothers and sisters are well.

I pray God blles you and keepe you in His feare and leade you in the pathe of life, so I rest,

Your most affectinat mother, BRILLIANA HARLEY.

Janu: 2, 1640. *Bromton Castell.*

My cosen Cornewell is yet with me.

If you haue so much time, let Rafe tell you how the boys shut out Mr. Ballam out of scoule. I was very glad that your brothers weare not with them.

XCIII.

For my deare sonne Mr. Edward Harley.

My deare Ned—I hope this letter will finde you with your father: now I thinke it longe sence I hard from you; for this weake as yet I haue not hard. Send me word wheather my brother be in Loundoun, and how he does. Now your father and you are from me, my contentment is in the happy proseedings of the parlament, which makes a mend for your fathers longe absence. I longe to see him, and I hope in due time I shall inioy that comfort of seeing you both. I beleefe by this, you are somethinge aquanted with Londoun, and, deare Ned, send me word how you like it.

Yesterday wee keepe a priuet day; Mr. Gower, Mr. Yaits, Mr. Steuenson, Mr. Voile, and Mr. More, were at it. Mr. More's wife is very ill, as she was vsed to be, a shakeing all over her. I thanke God your brothers and sisters are well, and I am indeferent well; but it has bine extreme coold weather. I pray God blles you, and make you to see and finde that there is more sweetness in the seruis of God then in all the pleashurs of the world; and be aschured that I gladly will sheaw meself

Your most affectinat mother, BRILLIANA HARLEY.

Janu: 8, 1640. *Bromton Castell.*

Mr. Prise of Pilleth dyed on wensday last.

XCIV.

For my deare sonne Mr Edward Harley.

My deare Ned—I thanke you for your letter this weake; I reseued it not tell this morning, and then it was wellcome. I thought at the first I had no letter from you, becaus yours had no shuperscription; but I was well pleased to be so disceaued. It is a great comfort to me to hear the parlament goos on so happily, and that the kinge has consented that the insendereis should be judged. Mr Braughton is now at Bromton, and I beleefe, if Mr. Tomkins be not burges for Webly, he will on munday: Mr. Gower purposes to goo to Heereford, to consult aboute the scandolous ministers, and thos places which haue none. I am glad theare is likly to be so good a corespondency betwne us and the Duch. I am glad to heare my lord is well, but I haue not hard from him yet. Theare is a very fine discours rwiten in Italien, but translated in to Latine; it is dedicated to Oxsensterne, he that was tresure to the king of Sweden; if the book desarfe the comendation I could wisch you did reade it, but I can not send you the titell of the booke. I thanke God your brothers and sisters are very well. I pray God blles you, and keepe your hart aboue all the thinges in this life; so I rest,

Your most affectinat mother,   BRILLIANA HARLEY.

Janu: 9, 1640   *Bromton Castell.*

XCV.

For my deare sonne Mr. Edward Harley.

My deare Ned—This morning I reseeued your letter by Raphe, and I hope theas lines will finde you with your father, wheare I had rather haue you be then at Oxford. I am very glad that the parlament has defered priuet biusnes for a time, to settell the publike; in which I beseach the Lord direct them and giue them a vnanimous consent in thos things which may be for the glory of God and the peace of His Church; that all theas thinges, whithout which God may be sarfed without burdening the conscienc of any of Gods childeren, may be cast out, as thos things which haue to longe trubeled the peace of the chruch. I much reioyce that your father and you are well. I beseach the Lord continue your health. My cosen Smith rwite me word that you weare perfectly well, which is much comfort to me. I heare not a word of my sister Wacke. I am sorry my lord is gone into the North.

I thanke God, I am now out of my beed; your brothers and sisters are well.

I pray God blles you and keepe you in His feare, and giue you a comfortabell seeing of,

Your most affectinat mother,   BRILLIANA HARLEY.

Janu: 22, 1640.   *Bromton Castell.*

My cosen Dauis remembers saruis to you.

XCVI.

For my deare sonne Mr Edward Harley.

Deare Ned—I can not let such a sufficent mesenger goo without a letter to you. Mr. Gower had finisched but this day late. I beleefe your father will correct somethinge in it, or am deceafed. I sent Rice to carry this the more carefully, and I thinke your father may make some vse of him; for I feare on man is too littell for him. I pray God blles you.

Your most affectinat mother,   BRILLIANA HARLEY.

Janu: 23, 1640.   *Bromton Costell.*

Your sister Marget is not very well, but the rest are well. I feare her made vsed somethinge to her head.

XCVII.

For my deare sonne Mr Edward Harley.

Deare Ned—I am glad of all ocations to inquire affter your health, which I hope you inioye. Munday, as I hard from you and others, was to be the day of debate about bischops. We at Bromton keep the day to shue to our God for His derection of the parlament. I beleefe that herarchy must downe, and I hope now.

My cosen Keirle sent the petion he had at Hereford to Mr. Gower to geet hands; he rwit Mr. Gower word he sent it to my younge cosen Vahan; he singned it and goot threescore and 10 hands to it, but his father did not singe it. I longe to heare from you. I beceach the Lord to blles you, and that I may see you with much comfort; so I rest

Your most affectinat mother,   BRILLIANA HARLEY.

Junu: 28, 1640. *Bromton Castell.*

Your brothers and sisters are well; but your sister Brill has a very greate coold.

Deare Ned, let your man deliuer this letter to my cosen Pelham, as soune as you can; I haue rwit to him about a mariage for one of my neecess.

XCVIII.

For my deare sonne Mr Edward Harley.

My deare Ned—I thank you for your letter by the Wellchman and by the carrier. I thinke the Wellchman went vp on a sleepless arent, for he toold me he went vp about a petion against the minister wheare he liued, but the man that carried the petion was not come to Loundon, nor he knwe not wheare he was; as he went vp he said that he carried the petion, and that he would goo to your father about it.

I did much feare, when I hard first of the kings speach, that it would haue caused some allteration in the parlament, but I now theaire hands to. I am toold that it is the way in all cuntrys, and that Mr Macworths gaue such derections. To me it dous not sound reasnabell; for, in my opinion, such hands should be taken as vnderstand it, and will stand to what thay haue doun.

I heare my Lord Straford is aquesused of most abominabel maters, but I haue not hard any particulars. I had a letter from my cosen Harry Pelham, in which he dous much commend you. I beleefe you finde him to sauer more of religion than his brother Hurberd. I am glad my brother is not goon to the army, and that my cosen Farfex has the honner of knightwood added to him. My lady Veere rwit me word, that shee was glad that you weare with your father, for shee thought it would be an aduantage to you.

I hope the Lord will still gooalonge with the parlament, and tho wicked men wacth for theaire failleing, that they shallbe disaponted.

I blles God that you finde yourself well; I beceach the Lord to continue your health, and aboue all, that you may inioy a sound judgment, an vpright hart, large affectionons to your God, which is the true health of the minde. Deare Ned, be carefull of yourself, and the more for my sake.

Rwit me word what imployment your father puts Gorge Griffits brother to, which Mr Griffits toold me he sent vp the last weake to your father. I haue heare inclosed sent you 11th for the glases you sent me downe; they are very good and came very well to me.

I thanke God my coold is much better then it was, and I hope gooing away.

I am now out of my beed; this is the first day. I pray God blles you.

Your most affectinat mother,   BRILLIANA HARLEY.

Pheb: 15, 1640. *Bromton Castell.*

CI.

For my deare sonne Mr. Edward Harley.

Deare Ned—I should be glad I could as easely see you as rwit to you. I thanke you for your letter this weake. I reioyce that your father is well, and that is my comfort in his absence. I could wisch I could vndergoo some of the paines for him, but I would haue him act the vnderstanding part. I haue allways beleefed that the Lord would purge His chruch from all theas thinges and persons, that haue bine such a hinderance to the free pasage of His glorious ghospell; and I trust, now is the time. The death of the kinge of Spaine, I thinke, will make some alterations in thos parts. I much reioyce the parlament goos one so well. I pray God they may doo so still. Your brother Tomas red me the speach, which I can not vnderstand no further then to know I doo not vnderstand the nonesence of it. Your brother is very glad of his letter, but he is very soleme at the speach, as if he did not thinke that had bine spoken. Mr Gower is, I beleeue, with you. I did hope my cosen Daniel would haue come doune this weake, that so I might haue hard more fully from you. I haue sent your father some other cakes to put in his pocket. Rwit me word, how he likes them. I am sorry the biskets weare made wors in the carage; before they went of, all theaire falte was that they weare ouer backed. It pleases me well that you are with your father. Deare Ned, I beceach the Lord to blles you, and make you growe stronge in gras, which is ernestly desired by,

Your most affectinat mother,　　　BRILLIANA HARLEY.

Pheb: 19, 1640. *Bromton Castell.*

CII.

For my deare sonne Mr. Edward Harley.

My deare Ned—If you knwe how much I mise your company, you will conclude your letters are very wellcome to me. I thanke you for yours by the carrier and by the post.

I much reioyce that you and your father are so well. Deare Ned, still take care of your self, and put your father in minde to doo so.

I am sorry Irland is in so bade a case, and that the puting off of the land into a posture of defence, is so forslowed.

Mr Broughton, I beleeue, will tell you how they speake of the parlament, in the cuntry. I pray God open theare eyes, that they may see things a right. I should be sorry your father should put a stranger in trust with his estate, when he is not in the cuntry. I pray God direct him. I haue scase time to rwit any thing to you in this letter; Mr Moors man being in such hast. I pray God blles you.

Your most affectinat mother,   BRILLIANA HARLEY.

Pheb: 26, 1640.   *Brompton Castel.*

CIII.

To her son Edward.

Deare Ned—I haue rescued your letter by my cosen Dauis; it was wellcome tho it was short. My cosen Dauis telles me, your father is very well and that you are so, which is a great comfort to me; and I hope that the Lord will giue your father dubell strentgh, to vndergoo the waight of thos imployments which lye vpon him. And I hope you will not repent your being at Loundoun with your father, which I gees will be more aduantage to you, then if you had bine at Oxford.

My cosen Dauis is not cleere yet in his biusnes; for M`r` Edwards will not out; he slites what they say; and says M`r` Dauis goos about like a premouter. He says, he would be sent for vp to Loundoun, that he may informe the parlament with what vntruths my cosen Dauis has toold them. I never hard of a man that was not out of his sences, that was so careles to doo like a resnabell man, as M`r` Edwards is; he seames to let himself loose to be led by his pastions. I hope my cosen Dauis makes a ronge judgment; for he thinkes my lord Straford will not haue his sentence, and that some other thinges will fall out. My cosen Dauis charges dous not pleas him, becaus it is no more.

Your letter by Jhon Wall was very wellcome to me, and I thanke you for it. I hope the Lord will disapoint all the plots of thos that haue evill will at the prosperity of Gods chruch. Your letter has giuen me much content, for I feared that some would take ocation by the Scots declaration to vrge against them; but I hope the Lord will pasefy all distempers. I am glad to heare my brother is well, and I perswade meselfe he loues you. I hope my brother is not for lord Straford. I hard my lord Straford layed some of his actions to his charge; but I hope, if he did, my brother has cleered himself.

I am glad my cosen St. Jhons is to be maried. I beleeue it is for her aduantage; tho in my opinion, when one has chillderen, it is better to be a widowe.

M`r` Ballam is very sicke; I thinke it is an ague, but he eates, and so make his fits violent; he will take nothinge of Wodowes, nor Morgan, but is resouled to send to morrow for doctor Rwit, but he feares he will stay longer with him then 3*l*. will hoold out; that he is willing to giue, but he can spare no more, as he says: this 2 dayes he has bine debating of, as they tell me; but now in his fitte, he resoulfes to send for him, and dous not recken the charges. I hope he will doo well; he is so prouedent. Your brother Tome had a sharpe fitte on saboth day night, but I thanke God his last fite was but short; he is very cheerefull and hungry, but I suffer him to eate no meate, and I giue him glisters, which I thanke God has doun him much good.

I hope in good time your father will finde a chamber in the Tempell for you. Deare Ned, put your father in minde, to inquire of Mr Gwine.

I thanke you for your letter by the carrier; your letters gives me more satisfaction then any other. I did much feare, by what I was abell to gees, that the Scots declaration would giue the contrary party ocation to sheaw themselfes; but I blles the Lord, that He has ouer-ruled the harts of men, and I hope they goo now on well, to doo that greate worke they haue in hand. I thanke you for the paper the Scots put into the Lords. I haue taken a coppy, and heare-inclosed returned yours. I confes, I longe to heare the sugsess of the conferance. Many rumors are in the cuntry. If you haue bine to heare the Scots minesters, send me word how you like them. I am glad your father has not taken coold, this coold weather; for wheare your fathers loodging is, is the cooldest place I thinke about Loundoun. I reioyce that your father is well, tho I was sorry I had no letter from him; but when he is so biussy I would not haue him rwit.

I thanke God your brother Tomas scaped his ague yesterday, and he is indeferent well. Mr Ballam is ill, and so is Same Pinner. Deare Ned, send me word when you thinke that Mr Gower can come doune.

I haue rwit to Sanky about Hacklet; for I perseaufe shee may be brought to loue him. I haue keep my beed this weake, and as yet I haue not bine a whoole day vp. I pray God blles you, and giue you gras and comfort, the portion of His chillderen; so I rest,

    Your most affectinat mother,   BRILLIANA HARLEY.

Mar: 12, 1640. *Bromton Castell.*

CIV.

For my deare sonne Mʳ Edward Harley.

Deare Ned—Your letter was this morning a sweet cordiall to me, affter a great deale of sorrow I had for your brother Tom. It is Gods great mercy to me that your father and you are well; and I beceache the Lord to continue that mercy to you both, and then I shall be, so much the better.

I am sorry theare is that difference betwne bothe howes, and I feare theare will be more; but I trust the Lord will oner-rule mens harts. I am glad that the Bischops begine to falle, and I hope it will be with them as it was with Haman; when he began to falle, he feell indeede.

I am glad my lady Veere has caus to reioyce in my cosen St. Jhons second mariage.

Your brother Toms ague is much increesed, and he is very weake; his fitte on wensday heald him 22 oures; he is now in his fitte, and he has it very sharply; his noos has blled much at seuerall times, and they say is a singe, it is a feauor. I haue sent for doctor Rwit or doctor Bauer. Mʳ Ballam sent on munday for doctor Rwit, but then he was in Glostersheere. I had safed him that labor, but your brother was then reasnabell well. He lay in Mʳ Ballams chamber, and Blechely, whoo lookes to him and had wacthed with him, on monday night, shee left him a sleepe and prtly allmost out of his fitte, and would let them make no fier in his chamber, but when she was goon, the maid that shee left with him, made so much fier that it allmost burnt the clothes of the beed, and put him into a violent heate; now I haue him lye in the chamber by me, which pleases him very well. He weepe the other day in priuet, and toold on that he takes for his frrend, that his brother Robin was angry with him aboute the parlament nwes, and he feared he had made you angry with him; thearefore, deare Ned, rwite to him. Your brother Robin cares not to know how it goos in the parlament. I meane to know it, which I blamed him on day for, and then he rwit to you. Your brother Tom is the likest you, and loues you dearely.

I pray God blles you and giue you a comfortabell meeting with
    Your most affectinat mother,   BRILLIANA HARLEY.

Blechly giues him much content, and shee takes great pains with him.

Deare Ned, let this incolesed letter be deliuered to my brother. I rwit to him, becaus I hard he was expected in the North.

Mar: 19, 1640. *Bromton Castell.*

CV.

For my deare sonne Mr. Edward Harley.

Deare Ned—Sence I cannot haue the greater part of my comfort in seeing of you, I am glad to my parte in this, that is next it.

I much desire to heare the sugsess of this weakes debates in parlament; I pray God it may be a happy one.

Your brother Tom this morning is pritty well, but he had a very loonge fitt, from 2 a clooke wesday night tell 2 a clooke this thursday night; he is very weake, but doctor Rwit puts me in good hope of him: the doctor came yesterday to me. This morning he has giuen him a purge, and I hope the Lord will blles it to him: his noos bleeds every fitt. I see him twes or thrise a day. Blechly takes a greate deale of paines with him, wacthes every fite-night with him, rises euery night to him, giues him all his glisters. I did not thinke, shee had bine halfe so carefull. I beleeue you pray for him; some times in his fitts he speakes a littell idell; but he did not, I thanke God, in this fitt; but, poore hart! he is very weake. But the doctor puts me in good hope of him. Your brother Robin dous exceedingly neglect himself, which is a great greefe to me; he is still with the saruants, and grows tall and very leane, so that Doctor Rwit did not knowe him. I pray God blles you.

Your most affectinat mother, BRILLIANA HARLEY.

Mar: 20, 1640. *Bromton Castell.*

I haue sent your father by this carrier a turkey pye. Deare Ned, send me word wheather your father like it.

CVI.

For my deare sonne Mr. Edward Harley.

Deare Ned—That I haue no letter from you this weake puts me to a stand, and I should be very much trubeled, but that your father rwites me word you are well, which mercy, I hope, the Lord will still continue to you. I neuer more longed to heare how things goo then I did this weake. Many rumors we heare, but I biuld vpon nothing tell I heare it from you or your father.

I much desire to heare how the parlament tooke the ansure of the justices of this country, that sent word they knwe not by what aughtority the parlament did require the taking of the protestation. Sr William Croft is much against the parlament, and vtters his minde freely: he was much displeased that they would petition the Parlament: he toold Mr Gower he was a moufer of sedistion; and my cosen Tomkins was very hoot with him: they say the parlament dous theare owne biusness, and not the cuntryes. I shall long to heare from you. I thanke God, your cosen Smith has loost his ague, for I could not deserne he had any fite. On munday before Ester, Mr Kirll and some other gentellmen intend to seet forward with the petition, which I hope will be well taken.

I pray God blles you, and keepe you in His feare.

Your most affectinat mother, BRILLIANA HARLEY.

Mar: 25, 1641.

CVII.

For my deare sonne Mr Edward Harley.

My deare Ned—I know not wheather Mr Laneford will keepe his resolution, to be at Loundoun as soune as the carrier, and thearefore I desire to let you knowe how your brothers doo, which I perswad meself you longe affter. I thanke God your brother Tom is pritty well but weake; your brother Robine was ill all day yesterday. Doctor Rwit made haste backe, becaws he did not like your brother when he went away. This day he tooke a vomit, which rought very well with him, and I hope he will be much better for it; and I trust the Lord will be mercyfull to them and me, in restoreing them both to health; and I beceach the Lord to continue yours, and to blles you with all bllesinges, as I desire my oune soule should be bllesed. So I rest,

Your most affectinat mother,   BRILLIANA HARLEY.

Mar: 27, 1641.   *Bromton Castell.*

Your sisters, I thanke God, are well. This day Sr Williham Croft is at Wigmore aboute the subsedies.

CVIII.

For my deare sonne Mr. Edward Harley.

Deare Ned—I hope yon are well, and I am glad to heare you are so; but yet I know not what to thinke, that I had no letter from you, neather by the carrier nor by the post. I long to heare from you, and I beleiue you think I doo. I pray God blles you and keepe you from all euill, especially that of sinn. I thanke God your cosen Smith is well againe. So I rest,

Your most affectinat mother,   BRILLIANA HARLEY.

Mar: 28, 1641.   *Brompton Castell.*

I beleeue you hear that Mr Weafer, on of the burges of Hereford, is dead.

CIX.

For my deare sonne Mr. Edward Harley.

Deare Ned—The last night I receued your letter by the carrier which you rwite the last weake. I confes I was much joyed to see your hand, but I cannot but yet be sorry that I haue no letter from you this weake, nor from your father. I pray God I may heare well of you: it is my comfort, that in theas days of trubell you make the Lord your defence, and looke vp to Him, whoo goouers all the affairs of the world, and I am confident will bring this, His owne worke to a glorious end. I send this letter by the post of Loudlow, whoo is nwely seet vp; if you will rwite by him weakely, I will send, if pleas God, for the letters; for it will be eassyer then to send to Shreawesbury. I have bine ill, as I vse to be sence wensday. I pray God blles you and giue you wisdome both to walke before God and man.

Your most affectinat mother,   BRILLIANA HARLEY.

Apr: the first, 1641. *Brompton Castell.*

CX.

For my deare sonne Mr. Edward Harley.

My deare Ned—Your wellcome letter by Mr. Moore I receued the last night. I had longe longed for a letter from you; the last weake I had only a letter from you, but it was on that had bine rwite the weake before. We must all say, if the Lord dous not apeare in His allmighty power to ouer-rule the actions of men, we may feare woofull dayes. If such dayes should befalle vs, the woo would light on thoos that haue not walked with God, and Gods childeren should only tast of the sorrow of them. I am sorry for judg Mallet, I wisch he may be so wise as to see his error; but the soyle of pich will hardly be rubed of.

I haue sent Mr. Dauis of Wigmore, the derections you rwite me from your father, to Heariford; he went this morning. I pray God prosper him in it, and if it be His holy will, that you may haue that imployment. I beleeue my lord Scidmore stands for Mr. Witeny, and I beleeue Sr William Croft will looke after it; he is quite turned abowute. I purpos and pleas God, to send the keepers man to Loundoun on tusday, and then I hope to rwit you word what Mr. Dauis has doun at Heariford. You may beleeue I will rwite and doo all that I can, to further that which I do desire, and I am perswaded doctor Wright would doo all that weare in his power. I thanke God your brothers and sisters are well, and I pray God blles you with His choyest bllesings; and beleeue that you are most deare to,

Your most affectinat mother,   BRILLIANA HARLEY.
Brompton Castell. Apr: 9, 1641.

CXI.

For my deare sonne Mr. Edward Harley.

My deare Ned—Tho longe yet at last, I receued your letter sent by Mrs. Vahans man; it was very well-come, tho it bare an old date.

Mr. Scidmore the last night sent me your fathers letter, which he brought downe, and rwite me word you weare well, which was more wellcome to me then all his strange lines.

Now I know your father desires for your sisters comeing vp, I purpos, and pleas God, she shall begine her journy, without your father contradict it, on munday or tusday come senight, becaus I desire she should goo before the weather be so hoot. I am very glad your coold is gone. I beceach the Lord in His rich mercy to blles you, and keepe you from all euille and make you grow in wisdome, so that you may still giude all your actions with descretion: so I rest,

  Your most affectinat mother,   BRILLIANA HARLEY.

I send this by the post of Hariford, becaus I know not wheather the post of Loudlow euer deleuered my letter or no. Deare Ned, be carefull of yourselfe.

Apr: 14, 1641. *Brompton Castell.*

CXII.

For my deare sonne Mr Edward Harley.

My deare Ned—Tho your letter by the merser weare short, yet it had a longe wellcome. I much desire to heare how my lord Straford comes of; for I beleeue many thinges depend vpon it. Once againe I thanke you for his charge, and Mr Fines his speach, which I like very well. I need not tell you I had no letter from you by the carrier, but your father rwit me word you weare heareing my lord Strayfords charg, which was excuse susphicient; and that you weare well, was pleasing to me, tho I should haue bine glad of a letter. Your brother Tom, I thanke God, has loost his ague, but he dous not yet come abroode. Your brother Robine has is ague, but his fittes are short and much eassier then they weare. Mr Ballam is very ill; his is a feauor, if it be no thinge elles. The other day he resouled to make his will, and then to meddell no more with the world; but yesterday and to day he hopes better of himself. I am very sorry for him. Doctor Rwit, I thinke, will be with him on munday next, and then I purpos, if pleas God, to take something meself. Aske your father, wheather I shall send to Oxford for your beed and Gorgess and the sheets; I can hardly spare the beeds; for it may be, some will perswade that it is better sell them theare then bringe them home; but I am not of that minde. Your sisters are well, and I should be very glad to haue Brill goo to my lady Veeres. I hope Mr Gower will come downe shortly. I am much pleased that you are now with your father, and I hope it will be much aduantage to you; and I beceach the Lord to blles all the wayes of knowledg to you; for you now see the truth of Gods word, that tho men spread like a bay tree, yet they endure but for a time.

Deare Ned, be carefull of your self; and I beceach the Lord to blles you: so I rest,

Your most affectinat mother,   BRILLIANA HARLEY.

Apr: 19, 1641. *Bromton Castell.*

CXIII.

For my deare sonne Mr Edward Harley.

My deare Ned—It cannot but be much comfort to me to receaue the aschurance of your health, sence Loundoun is now so sikely a place, and thearefore I thanke you for your letter this weke by the carrier. It is an excelent thinge to carry a littell peece of meer in your mouth, to keepe you from any infection. Tell your father of it, it may be he will vse it; and I beceach the Lord to presarfe you, and giue me a comfortabell seeing of your father and you. In the cuntry they had broken the parlament and beheaded my lord Straford, which would not well hange togeather. I pray God remoufe all rubs that lye in the way, so that the worke can not goo forward. Our eyes must be to the Lord, whoo only can doo greete things.

Mr. Gower has not yet made an end of the relation of my lord Strafords charge; he is as much taken with the relation, as I thinke he was with heareing it.

Your brother Tom has loost his ague and is resnabell well. Your brother Robine keepes his old way in every . . . , in his dyet, and consealeing his being ill. Docter Wright left him well, but he is growne wors; but docter Wright calling of me as he came from a patient in Wostersheere, findeing him in that distemper, gaue him something, so that I hope the worst is past. This is the first day I haue take any time out of my beed. I will, if pleas God, haue some half shirts made for you. I longe to see you, and now I shall hope to doo so within thees 2 months. Your sisters are well. My cosen Dauis takes it exceeding kindely from you, and tells me he will rwit you word what he has doun. I pray God blles you as I would haue my owne soule blessed: so I rest,

Your most affectinat mother, BRILLIANA HARLEY.

I am glad your * * * has changed the Tempell to Linconsine, becaus theare is a better preacher.

Apr: 30, 1641. Bromton Castell.

CXIV.

For my deare sonne Mr. Edward Harley.

Deare Ned—I reseued your letter which you sent with your fathers by Heareford; it was doubly wellcome to me, in that it was yours, and that it brought me the wellcome hope of the two howesess agreeing about my lord Straford. I thanke God your brothers are pritty well. Your brother Tom has lost his ague, and your brother Robine I hope will doo his shortly. I thanke God I am reasnabell well, and I long to see you, and reioyce to express meselfe,

Your most affectinat mother, BRILLIANA HARLEY.

You did not rwit me word that you weare well, but I hope you are. Loue is watchfull. This man is in hast.

May 4, 1641. Bromton Castell.

CXV.

For my deare sonne Mr. Edward Harley.

Deare Ned—Sence my thoughtes are so much with you, I may easely writ offten to you. I take much content that I may hope to see your father and you within 2 months. I pray God giue me a comfortabell inioyeing of that my desire. Deare Ned, be carefull of your health, and aboue all, of keeping your hart cloos with your God. I did much reioyce that theare was hopes of a good agreement betwene the 2 howess, and I hope to heare more fully of it by Looker, who was looked for hard the last night; but he is not yet come. Your brother Tom, I thanke God, is so well that he comes into my chamber, and is mightyly a hungery, but your brother Robine has his ague still; his fittes are much lees. He was very ill, and I preuailed with him to take a vomit, which, he says now, if he had not taken he thinkes he had bine in his graue: but he was very vnwilling to take any more phiseke, so he did not: and I feare he is a littell corbuticall; for his teethe are loose; and I feare he had a littell touch of his old deases the other day, but he had no fitt: he is alltogeather against phiseke; he thinks an ague must be worne away by gooing abroode; but theas are not such agues. Mr. Ballam mends a paece, and so dous Sam Piner: your sisters are, I thanke God, very well, and your cosen Smith, whous only sorrow is, that I haue goot one to teach scoole for Mr. Ballam.

Mr. Gower toold me of the death of my good brother Bray. I am exceeding sorry for the loos of him; I hope my sister Wacke and my brother are well, and my lady Conway and my brothers chillderen.

I pray God blles you and keepe you in His feare: so I rest,

Your most affectinat mother,   BRILLIANA HARLEY.

May 7, 1641. Bromton Castell.

I thanke God, I finde meself much better for my phisek and being let blood. I haue bine to see your brother Robine, but I durst not goo to-day, becaus I haue taken a great coold.

CXVI.

For my deare sonne Mr. Edward Harley.

Deare Ned—I haue defered the mesenger so longe that I haue hardly time to write. I did hope Looker would haue bine in time, and now I hope he will bringe me the aschurance of your health, and your fathers, when he comes, which I longe for. Your brother Tom is well, but your brother Roberd had his ague to-day. We heare of great matters that has bine doun at Loundoun this weake, but I beleeue nothinge tell I heare it from a shure hand. I pray God blles you, and beleeue me to be,

Your most affectinat mother,   BRILLIANA HARLEY.

May 8, 1641.

Endorsed,—Conwey
    Carrage
    Cairage
    Caraige.

CXVII.

For my deare sonne Mr. Edward Harley.

Deare Ned—I haue resen to giue you thankes for your letters, for as I haue many ocations of sorrowes, so I thanke God your letters are greate refreschings to me. I am very sorry to heare that the sikenes is so much increesed. I beceech the Lord stay that judgment that it may not goo through the land; and the Lord in mercy presarue you from all infections. And deare Ned, be not so boold in gooing into plases where the sikenes is. I haue some hope that the parlament will ajourne, that your father and you may come doune within this fortnight or 3 weakes at the farthrest, which I should be glad to be assured of. I am glad my lord Saye is master of the wards. In the cuntry they haue in report hanged the archbischope. I am glad that Mr. Gwine has giuen a better imprestion of himself. I could wisch with all my hart, that my cosen Harry Pelham weare aquinted with him. My brother Pelham is a good father, but yet my dear sisters chillderen want theare mother.

I feare my brother is not ouer willing to part from his money. My nephewe Edward is now returned to Oxford from Brockellsbe. Deare Ned, I could wisch your chamber weare in Linconsine and not in the laine ouer against it; those lains weare the vnsweatests places in Loundoun, and allways the siknes is in thos places. I could wisch you had rather bine in the Tempell or Graseine. Grasein mythinkes is a fine place. I would haue you tell your father what I thinke of your chamber and the howes. I would haue write to him about it meself, but that I thought it might trubell him to reade so longe a letter. I longe to heare how you are prouided for a man, and whoo shall mainetaine Gorge at Oxford; for I heare he has not write to his father aboute it this mornig. Merredifes hows that Mr. Simons lined in fell on firer, but thankes be to God, theare was not much hurt doun, only the walls of the kichen burnt and pulled doune; the loos is thought to be about 3l. Mr. Ballam is fallen sike againe; he is no ouer wise man. I thanke God your brothers and sisters are well. The protestation was taken on sabath day last at Bromton, Wigmore and Lainterdine, with much willingnes. I desire to know wheather you tooke it. I pray God blles you, and giue you a comfortabell meeting with

Your most affectinat mother, BRILLIANA HARLEY.

May 21, 1641. *Bromton Castell.*

I haue sent you a peace of angelica rooat: you may carry it in your pocket and bite some times of it.

CXVIII.

For my deare sonne Mr. Edward Harley.

Deare Ned—The shurenes of the carrier, tho he is slow, makes me writ by him, tho I purpos and pleas God to write by the mersser, whoo goos towards Loundoun on munday. I am glad that justice is excicuted on my lord Straford, whoo I thinke dyed like a Senneca, but not like one that had tasted the mistery of godlyness. My deare Ned, let theas exampels make you experimentally wise in Gods word, which has set forth the prosperity of the wicked to be but for a time; he flowreschess but for a time in his life, nor in his death has peace; but the godly has that continuall feast, the peace of a good contience, and his end is peace, and his memory shall not rot. I thanke God that I hard you weare well, for I haue bine in feare of it all this weake. I thanke God your brothers and sisters are well. I haue keepe my beed sence munday. Deare Ned, be carefull of your self, and I pray God blles you. So I rest,

Your most affectinat mother, BRILLIANA HARLEY.

May 21, 1641.   *Bromton Castell.*

CXIX.

For my deare sonne Mr. Edward Harley,
in Wesmester, neare the Parlament Howes.

Deare Ned—I thanke you for your letter by the Wellcheman; beleeue it, your letters cannot come to offten to me. I blles God that you are well, and I hope the Lord will keepe you so, and in good time giue me, whoo longes for it, a happy seeing of you. I knwe not of Mr Yaits his gooing to Loundoun tell this day. I hope buisnes in the parlament will goo one smouthly, and I hope your father will come downe and you in June. I was allways of the minde, that Gorge would not stay with you but to sarfe his owne turne. I pray God send you a religious and a good natured saruant. Deare Ned, take my counsell, I beleeue you will not finde it beest to take Gorges his brother; it is a most teadious thinge to be sarued by a chillde, without you had other saruants that might healp out his defects; they want witt and discretion, and haue theair pastions unbrideled, wich all togeeather makes them teadious saruants;

and I consider when you are at the ends of court, and nobody about you but a child, if you should not be well, you would finde it a trubell; and so you would being well; when you imploye him in any saruis you would tast his childeischness in all he did. I speake from experience. I haue had chillderen sarue me; and I finde very yonge men and women no good saruants; and then at the end of a yeare or 2, you will haue him doo as Gorge dous; but if you weare sure he would not, yet I would not haue you take such a youth; you would finde no content in it. If Samuell weare of a good nature, I could wisch you would like him; but he has a sower nature. Pleas yourself in your choyce, and I shall be pleased; but take my word; boys are trubellsome saruants.

I thanke God your brothers are well, and so is your sisters. I am very glad to heare my lord is well, and that my lady Veere is willing to haue Brill; it is my greefe that my condition in health is such, that I can not be of more aduantage to you all than I am. I thanke you for the sparigous you sent me. I pray God blles you, and keepe you in His feare; and, deare Ned, beleeue me to be,

Your most affectinat mother, BRILLIANA HARLEY.

Mr. Ballam has made shift to geet his ague againe. Roger Beeb like a wise man is goon to be maried. I haue not bine out of my beed sence munday. I pray God bringe me well out of it.

May 22, 1641. *Bromton Castell.*

CXX.

For my deare sonne Mr Edward Harley.

Deare Ned,—I thanke you for your letter by Jelly and by the carrier; it is my greate comfort that you are well, and I hope the Lord will continue that mercy to you. I much reioyce that the Lord has sheawed Himself so mightyly for His peopell, in heareing theare prayers; that it is come so fare as that the bischops and all theiare traine is voted against. I trust in God they will be inacted against, which I longe to heare; and I pray God take all thos thinges away which haue so longe offended. I longe much to see your father and you. I did hope to haue seene you the later end of this month; but now I heare, it will be not tell the begineing of July.

I thanke God your brothers are well, and so are your sisters. Mr. Ballam is abroad, and has begoun to keepe scoule; but as you thought when you weare in the cuntry that he was not wis, so I finde him. Sr William Croft has promised me to come to Bromton at the faire, when I beleeue I shall want your father and you.

On tusday night I had a greate fitt of the stone, but now, I thanke God, I am better. Deare Ned, be carefull of your self, and I beceach the Lord in mercy to blles you, and giue you a happy meeting, with

Your most affectinat mother,   BRILLIANA HARLEY.

I am sorry that your father was displeased for not haueing his mony souner: but I did what I could, and so will doo still.

June 5, 1641. Bromton Castell.

CXXI.

To her son Edward.

Deare Ned—Had I not this weake reseued a letter from *** by which I heare you and your father were well, I should haue bine very much trubelled; for this weake I haue reseued no letter from your father, nor from you. I know you are careful to rwite to me, becaus you know what a comfort it is to me; thearefore I beleeue your letter has miscarried.

I very much desire to heare how the affaires goo; for I thinke theaire was neuer a more doutfull crisise; but it is the Lord who hoolds the bridell vpon all men, so that they cannot doo what they desire, but in aduancing at theare owne endes, they still bringe to pas the Lords work.

Deare Ned send me word wheather your father * * * * * * * *

the man for a steward or no. I am grieued with all my hart that the tenants doo not pay theaire rents, that I might send it to your father, whous ocations I hard rather a hundred times weare supplyed then my owne. I should be very glad, if your father would be pleased to bye a coach and haue horrses. I thinke it would not cost him much: and insteed of other horsess, if he keepe coach horsess, which would be of as much vse as other horsess, I thinke I shall be abell to take the ayre in it; and I beleeue it would be much aduantage to my health. And good Ned, tell your father so, and let me pray you to put him in minde of it. The maire and one or two horsess are sike, and so will not be fite to be sould as yet. Your cousin Smith has some remembrance of his ague againe, but I hope it will not last longe.

I pray God blles you and presarue you in health, and giue you a happy and comfortabell meeting with

Your most affectinate mother,   BRILLIANA HARLEY.

1641. *Brompton Castell.*

The letter you rwit to me last weake I had this weake.

CXXII.

For my deare sonne Mr. Edward Harley.

Deare Ned—I cannot let doctor Deodat goo, without leting you know my thoughts are much with you, and I hope I shall see you shortly. I receued your letter by Mr. Griffits: it brought me wellcome nwes, in that it asshured me of your health, which I pray God continue to you. I thanke God your brothers and sisters are well. I am still in beed, but I hope I shall be abell to rise with in thease feawe days. I am sorry doctor Deodat has left the cuntry.

Deare Ned, be carefull of your self for my sake. I pray God blls you and giue you a comfortabell meeting with

Your most affectinat mother,   BRILLIANA HARLEY.

June 14, 1641. *Bromton Castell.*

CXXIII.

For my deare sonne Mr Edward Harley.

Deare Ned—I thanke you for puting me in minde of takeing the ayre; I beleeue it would doo me good, but as yet I haue not made triall of it; but I hope to doo, and if your father weare with me I should doo it with more cheerefullness. I thanke God I am now abell to site out of my beed, and finde meself indeferent well. Every weake begeets nwe desires in mee, for now I very much desire to heare what is become of the biusness of the bischops, which I hope shall downe; but I feare it will finde mighty opotion; but the Lord can make hard things eassy. We must all acknowledg Gods greate mercy in the discouering of so great a plot against His poore peopell. I pray God we may still make God our refuge; that so He may wacthe ouer vs, and then we shall be safe. Deare Ned, rwit me word how the pasage was of Mr Harberds Pris his carage in the parlament, becaus theare is such various reports of it. I beleeue you father takes greate pains. I beceach the Lord strentghen him and direct him in all his ways, and give me a happy and comfortable meeting with your father and you.

Mr Ballam I thinke is a very silly man; he has discouered himself what he is, in his sikness.

I feare your brothers loose theare time very much. Your brother Robrert is very much growne, and I feare spends littell time in gaineing of knowledg, which trubells me much. I hope your father will thinke of some cours for them.

I much wonder at Gorge Griffits, whoo has had so many tyes to you, that he so neglects what you would haue done. I hope your father will not let you goo to Linconsine as longe as he is in Loundoun. Mr. Edwards, you will heare by my cosin Dauis, has by fors keept Bucknell, and cars not for the order of the parlament, which I thinke will be of very ill exampell, if it be not reproufed in him. I will and pleas God, send you some handchorchers as soune as I can.

I pray God blles you, and giue you thos choys bllesings which He only bestowes vpon His beloued ons in Christ: so I rest,

Your most affectinat mother, BRILLIANA HARLEY.

Jne: 19, 1641. *Bromton Castell.*

I pray you tell your father that the cooke I tooke, I was enforsed to put away, he was so naught.

CXXIV.

For my deare sonne Mr. Edward Harley.

Deare Ned—Mr Doughty his stay something affter my cosin Dauis, giues me leaue to begine this weake with a letter to you. I pray God blles you and presarue you from all things that may hurt you eather within or without.

I hard this morning that your father had taken my cosin Wigmors estate into his hand, and vndertaken to pay all his deets. I hope it is not true: send me word wheather you heare any such thing. I would haue write to your father, but I thinke many letters would trubell him: be carefull of yourselfe for my sake.

Your most affectinat mother, BRILLIANA HARLEY.

June: 21, 1641. *Bromton Castell.*

Just nowe Mr Ballam tell me he is not abell to teach scoule. I pray you tell your father so.

CXXV.

For my deare sonne Mr. Edward Harley.

Deare Ned—Your letters must needs be dubly wellcome, sence they come from you, and make a supply for your fathers not writing. I acknowledg Gods greate mercy, that your father and you are well, which mercy I hope the Lord will continue to you. I am glad corenell Goreing did so well cleere himself. We heare of many more plots; one that Loundon should haue bine seet on firer, and many plots against the parlament; that theare weare porters apointed to take notice of euery parlament mans lodging. I pray you write me word wheather it weare so or no. I desire to trust in the Lord, and that dous stay my hart, or eles I should be much trubeled. I hope the Lord will direct the parlament in such a way as that they may seetell theare affairs, so as that they haue a time to goo into the cuntry, wheare I longe to see your father and you.

I haue written to your father to desire him that your brothers and cosin Smith may goo to Mr Voils tell the scoule be better prouided, or that Mr Ballam returne from Oxford: they loos theair time extremely. I make them translat some thinge out of Latin into Inglisch, but it is but a litell which they doo. Mr Griffits was with me this day; he tells me he will alow Gorge at Oxford 20l. a year; his elledest sonne is to be maried shortly to Mr Knights daughter. I haue writen to your father aboute your brother. Put him in minde to sende me an ansure, for I shall longe for one. I hard a post came downe to Loudlow on tusday, but I had neuer a letter. I thinke it now longe sence I had on from your father. I thanke you for the patterne of worke you sent me. I like it very well, and so well, that if pleas God, I purpose to woorke a shute of chars of it, and I hope you shall inioy them.

I thanke God your brothers and sisters are well, and I am indiferent well.

I pray God blles you and keepe you in His feare, and presarue you in all safety.

   Your most affectinat mother,   BRILLIANA HARLEY.

June: 25, 1641. *Bromton Castell.*

I haue sent you halfe a dusen of handcherchers, tell I send you more.

I thanke you for sending me word that your fathers bisket was goon. I hope to send him more the next weake. I am sorry the meath is not good.

CXXVI.

For my deare sonne Mr. Edward Harley.

Deare Ned—This weake I receued a letter from your father by a man of Kinton. I hope you weare well, tho you did not wirite; and this weake I haue receued no letter by the carrier. Just as I write this, the carrier sent me your letter from Loudlow, which giues me great content; for, deare Ned, you are a great comfort to me, and I hope the Lord will blles you for it. I much reioyce that your father is so well; and I trust the Lord will still inabell him to vndergoo thos waighty affairs which lye vpon him. I feare, as you doo, that it will be Augst before your father will haue time to come downe. I hope you ride some time into Hide parke to take the ayre; and for my sake be carefull of yourself. I thanke you for giuing me some hope of the bischops bill paseing this weake. I pray God effect that mighty worke. My cosen Wigmore was with me yesterday. He tells me your father was very well, but full of buisnes, and that he was 3 times to see him at his loudging, but found him not at home. He tells me you are very much growne, which I am very glad to heare. When he toold me he neuer spake with your father at his loudging, I thought what I had hard was not true. I thanke God I haue found meself much better of late then I haue bine this yeare and halfe, but not so well as I was before that time; and I thinke if your father and you weare with me, I should, I thinke, be better. Mr Ballam is goon to Oxford, and I know not what to doo by your brothers. I thanke God, they and your sisters are very well.

I haue sent your father by this carrier a box, in which is 6 pise, Mrs Osbersons pise. I hope he will like them, but I feare theare is too much spice in them. In that box, and another littell box, I haue sent your father some biskets; theare are 23—6 of them are for your self; the meath was mistaken; it was that which was of the combs; thearefore if your father doo not like it, he may have other sent vp, which is better.

I haue not hard a great while from my sister Wacke and my brother Conway. I desire to heare what your father has doun with Mr. Gwine. I pray God blles you and keepe your hart cloos to Him, so that you may experimentally know the ways of God to be the beest and pleasants way. So I rest,

Your most affectionat mother, BRILLIANA HARLEY.

I desire to knowe how your littell man pleasess you.

July 2, 1641. Bromton Castell.

CXXVII.

For my deare sonne Mr Edward Harley, at Sr Robert Harley, loudging at Mr Gay his howes, Woolstaple, in Wesmester.

Deare Ned—Let theas lines tell you I am glad of all opertunitys by which you may be ashured my thoughts are with you. I hope it will not be longe before I haue the comfort of seeing your father and you, tho when I consider the biusness the parlament is in hand with, I then feare it will be longe. I pray God blless you, and giue you such a true knowledg of the thinges heare below, that you may know them to be but transetory. Your brothers and sisters are well, and I pray God keepe you so.

Your most affectinat mother, BRILLIANA HARLEY.

July 3, 1641. Brompton Castell.

Piner forgot to seet doune Edward Dallys rent in the rent rolle, thearfore he has now sent it: for the rest of the tenants of Kingsland, he says he can make no rent role. Giue this note to your father.

CXXVIII.

For my deare sonne Mr. Edward Harley.

Deare Ned—I thanke for your letter: it was loaded with good newes; so that I may well say it did much cheere me. Your letters are great comforts to me; and tho I want my owne health, yet that your father and you are well makes vp much of mine.

I desire to giue our gratious God the glory of thos great things that has bine doun in the parlament; that the king has past the 3 bills, in which the high commistion goos downe; and that they haue proseeded so fare against the bischops. The Lord our God, who can doo great things, I hope will perfect that greate worke. I thanke you for the acts of parlament, and for doctor Dowing booke. I did hope you would haue sent me word this weake when your father had meent to haue come downe, which I longe to heare, and more to see. Your brothers and cosen Smith went on munday last to Wallcot, and so on wensday to Clanuer, wheare they haue a very good chamber, and I hope they will do uery well theare. I thanke God I am reasnabell well, and I roos souner this time out of beed then I vse to doo. Doctor Wright came to see me, and it feell out to be when I keepe my beed. He perswad me to rise, and gaue me some cordiall; but that night I was something ill, but the next day I was well; and I thanke God this day I have bine out of the gate, but no further; and sence it pleased God I was so well affter riseing, and that it feell out accedentally that doctor Wright came to me, I haue entreated him to be with me the next time I am ill; hopeing by Gods mercy to gaine some more liberty out of my beed, which I thinke the keeping of it dous me much hurt. I promis meself your prayers. I am glad you haue toold Mr. Gwine, and I thinke it strange that his father has such an estat and will asshure so littell of it in his elldest sonne. I pray God blles you, as I desire my owne soule should be bllesed.

Your most affectinat mother,   BRILLIANA HARLEY.

July 16, 1641. *Bromton Castell.*

CXXIX.

For my deare sonne Mr Edward Harley.

Deare Ned—I thanke you for your letter, which I receued the last weake by one of your fathers soulders, and for this weakes letter by the carrier; it is my great comfort that your father and you are well. I hope the same comfortabell hand of Prouidence will still keepe you in all safety; and deare Ned, be carefull of yourself that you doo not ouer heate your selfe, nor to goo into any infected places, and the Lord in mercy presarue you. I did hope to haue seene you and your father shortly, but now I heare theare is littell hope of the agurning of the parlament. I could wisch and desire, if it be so, that your father would aske leaue to come into the cuntry for a littell time. I thinke it would doo you and your father much good. I much reioyce that theare is hope of pasing the bill against bischops; the Lord say Amen to it; we doo not desarue to see such a mercy; but our God, I hope, will worke for His owne name sake. I hope the quene will stay her journy. I forgot to rwit you word that Mr Husbands is maried, and a most abundant loueing cuppell they say they are; and old Mrs Hubbins is goone to liue with her daughter. Mr Gower is goen into Schescheere to his sister Mrs Bursell, whoo has beuried her husband. I thinke Mr Gwine no wis man, that would not haue bine glad, with all his heart, to haue giuen any condistions to haue maried his sonne into such a famely and to such a wife.

Mr Ballam is returned from Oxford, but says he feares he shall not haue his health to teach scoule, thearefore he would only stay tell your father be prouided of a good one. Your brothers are very well at Clanuer, and I think they will learne better theare than at home; but as your father pleases, so I shall be content. Your sisters are very well: I thanke God I haue this weake goon a littell a broode, and I purpos, if pleas God I am any thinge well, and the weather dry, to goo to chruch on saboth day next. I pray God in mercy, if it be His holy will, make me partaker of thos sweet preueleges of His publick ordinancess. I pray God blles you and keepe your hart aboue all the thinges of this life, and I pray God giue you comfortabell meeting with

    Your most affectinat mother,   BRILLIANA HARLEY.
July 23, 1641. *Bromton Castell.*

I beleeue you heare that Mr Griffitt is a maryed man. I thanke you for the kings manifest.

CXXX.

For my deare sonne Mr. Edward Harley, at Sr Robert Harley his Loudging in Wesmester.

Deare Ned—I heare Mr Moore is come downe. I long to heare from him, how your father and you doo. I pray God I may heare well of you, and that I may see your father and you with comfort. If the howes will site still, yet I hope your father will come down for a littell time. I thanke God I was yesterday at chruch, in the morning, but the aftternoune was so weet I durst not goo, and I thanke God I finde myselfe reasnabell well to day. Your brothers are well at Clanuer, and your sisters are well. I pray God blles you, as I desire my owne soule should be bllesed. So I rest,

    Your most affectinat mother,   BRILLIANA HARLEY.
July 26, 1641. *Bromton Castell.*

When you see my brother, tell him I present my saruis to him.

CXXXI.

For my deare sonne Mr. Edward Harley.

Deare Ned—I thanke you for your double letter, which was very wellcome to mee. It is Gods great mercy, for which I desire to be thankfull, that your father and you enioye your health. I am sorry that there is no hope of an aorgment of the parlament, for then I feare your father will not come into the cuntrey, where I longe to see you and him. Mr More cam to see mee vpon tusday last. Hee tells me that your father and you are very well: it gaue mee much content to spake with so good a frind, that could tell me how your father and you are. Hee telle mee the queene has stayd hir iorney. I pray God prosper the affaires in the parlament, and the Lord giu a good isue to the bill of the bishops. I was very glad to reciue a letter from my brother. I thinke to send for your brothers home vpon tusday next, and Mr Ballam shall teach them tell your father can get a good on. I haue keept my bed sence thursday last. I pray God bring mee well out of it. I thanke God your brothers and sisters are well. I pray God blese you and giue mee a hapy seeing of you. So I rest,

Your most affectionnat mother,   BRILLIANA HARLEY.*

July 31, 1641. Bromton Castell.

CXXXII.

For my deare sonne Mr. Edward Harley, in Westmester.

Deare Ned—This weake I haue receued three letters from you, which made the weacke more cheerfull. Sanchky came to Bromton on tusday morning, and this day the boy Rise brought me your letter. I take it as a great mercy that you haue your health, which I hope the Lord will continue to you, that though I wante mine, yet I may haue the comfort that you inioy yours. I am sorry theare is any differance betwne the tow howesess. I beceach the God of peace to presarfe peace betwne them. I am very sorry that the sikness and small pox dous so increes, and I hope you will be willing to come into the cuntry, sence your stay in Loundoun may be of such danger to you. I can not blame you to be vnwilling to leaue so deare a father; yet remember, you come to a mother that loues you. I beceach the Lord to presarfe you from all infextions, and to

---

* The date and signature of this letter are alone in Lady Brilliana's handwriting.

bring you with much safety into the cuntry; and the Lord I trust will be your keeper in all placess. Deare Ned, if you come downe, be very carefull that you doo not ride to hard; for it is very dangerous to doo so this hote weather, for feare you should ouer heate your blood. The diet was so bade, as Mrs. Wallcote told me, at Clanuer, for your brothers, that I sent for them home on thursday last. I feare it has doun your brother Tome some hurt. He dous not looke well, and his stomake is goon. They did eate nothing but salt meate. Mrs. Wallcot has taken home her sonnes. I am in greate trubell to geet on to teach them; but as yet I can heare of none. Mr. Ballam has not his health, and is resoulued to goo to Oxford.

This time that I keepe my beed I was so ill, that I was constrained to send for doctor Wright; it was an inclination to the stone. I thanke God, I am now indifferent well, and abell to goo out of my chamber. My deare Ned, the Lord in mercy blles you and giue you a happy and comfortabell meeting with,

Your most affectinat mother, BRILLIANA HARLEY.

Augt: 7, 1641. Bromton Castell.

CXXXIII.

For my deare sonne Mr. Edward Harley.

Deare Ned—I knwe not of this bearers gooing to Loundoun tell it was very late, thearefore, in short, let thease tell you, I longe to see you and your father. I beceach the Lord to keepe you in all safety, and giue you a happy meeting with

Your most affectinat mother, BRILLIANA HARLEY.

Augs: 9, 1641. Bromton Castell.

CXXXIV.

To her son Edward.

My deare Ned—You cannot tell with what joye I rwite theas lines, in that hope to see you, though it should be but for a littell time. I hope, vnder Gods holy protection, you will have a safe journey downe, and that you will be at Brompton on wensday or thursday. Deare Ned, to see you will much reuiue me in the midst of many sad thoughts. It has very much trubelled me to see the affections of this cuntry so against your father that is worth thousands of them; and he has desarued so well of them: but you are in the right. It is for Gods caus, and then it is an honnor to suffer; * * * * * * to trubell me. * * * * * since I conseaue true patience has loue joyned with it, to the persons that doo one rong, yet I thinke as the case stands thus, I shall not be very glad to see any of them. Doctor Wright came to see me on saturday last. They hate him as much as any; and if Petter doo but goo into Heareford, they call him fresch roundhead. They haue hated doctor Wright ever sence he stood for you; and I haue bine toold by some that has bine by, that if any spooke against your father, he would tell them he could not indure it; that now they durst not speake before him. He toold me that Mr. Dewe did defend your father very much, and that he loued him for that, though he did not before. I had not seen him in a great while before. He is resolued to giue nothing, but he dous not knowe how it will goo with him.

I hope the horsess will come well to you. Your nag I haue giuen order should be leed, and the younge geldinge.; but, deare Ned, I pray you doo not ride vpon gray-shephard, for he has throwne Samuele twis very desperately. I hope you will be carefull of yourself, and not ride too hard in the heate of the day. I haue not toold any body that you are comeing downe. I pray God blles you, and giue you a most comfortabell meeting with,

Your most affectionate mother,   BRILLIANA HARLEY.

I pray you aske Anthony * * * * * what Mr. Hauor proclaimed in Shobden chruch. I haue scribbled this letter. I was at the dutys of this day at the fast, so that it is late. When Dr. Wright went away he prayed me to remember his saruis to you. I haue given

Colborne 5*l.* I pray you let somebody bye a littell barrel of anchouies, becaus you loue them, and a bottell of salad oyle.
(No date.)

CXXXV.

For my deare sonne Mr. Edward Harley.

My deare Ned—I rwite to you yesterday, and doo it as willingly this day. The last night Bagly came home; you will beleeue I had longed for your fathers letters before they came. I now desire to heare of your safe comeing to Loundoun. I hope my lord was not goone before you came, and I hope you will make acquaintance with Sr Jhon Conyars, whoo loue, first for my sake, and then for his owne.

My deare Ned, the Lord of heauen blles you and presarue you from all euill.

Your cozen Cornewell dous not remember her loue to you. Put your father in mind to be carefull of himself: so I rest,

Your most affectinat mother, Brilliana Harley.

Your 2 boxes are not sent vp this weake; becaus I sent your father a desell of Meath, and they could not carry them; but the next weake, and pleas God, I will send them.
Pheb: 5, 1641.

CXXXVI.

For my deare sonne Mr. Edward Harley.

My deare Ned—I did the last night, with much contentment, receaue your letter by Jhon Coolborn. I take it for a greate bllesing that you came so well to Loundoun, and that you meet with so good newes theare, as that the bischops are voted in both howes to lous theaire vots theare. I hope the Lord will perfect His owne glorious worke. You know how your fathers biusnes is neglected; and, alas! it is not speaking will sarue turne, wheare theare is not abilltise to doo other ways; thearefore I could wisch, that your father had one of more vnderstanding to intrust, to looke to, if his rents are not payed, and I thinke it will be so. I could desire, if your father thought well of it, that Mr Tomas Moore weare instrusted with it; he knowes your fathers estate, and is an honnest man, and not giuen to greate expences, and thearefore I thinke he would goo the most fruegually way. I knowe it would be some charges to haue him and his wife in the howes; but I thinke it would quite the chargess. I should be loth to haue a stranger, nowe your father is away. Deare Ned, tell your father what I haue rwiten to you, and I pray God derect him in his resolutions; and what he resoulues of, I shall be contened with; so doo not forget to tell your father. I did not rwite him word of it, becaus I would not make my letter so longe to him, and I am not very well at this time; being ill, as I vse to be. I haue, by this carrier, sent vp your rwiteing boox, and your boox of bookes. I pray God blles you, and beleeue you are most deare to,

Your most affectinat mother, BRILLIANA HARLEY.

I thanke God my coold is goone.

Pheb: 11, 1641. *Bromton Castele.*

CXXXVII.

For my deare sonne Mr. Edward Harley.

Deare Ned—The last night, as I went to super I receued your letter, sent by the Shwsbury post, and you may beleeue mee, it made mee eat my super with a better stomake then any sause could haue done. I doe much recoige in the kings answer to the petcion of both houses, and that my brother was one of the sixe and threetie lords that voted against the bishopes. I haue sent vp too your father, in youre boxe of books, 2 paire of riding stockings, and I haue sent by this carry, a boxe of pies for my brother and 2 chees fore him. I pray you, if hee bee not gone, doe you take car to haue them sent to my lords from me; and I haue sent your father 2 boxes of biskates. I pray God bles you: be carfull of yourselfe, and let mee heare from you as often as you can, for it is a greate comfrot to,

Your most affectionat mother,   BRILLIANA HARLEY.*

Brompton Castel, Pheb: 11, 1641.

I am not well, as I writ to you last night, therefore I haue made vse of anothers pen.

CXXXVIII.

For my deare sonne Mr. Edward Harley.

My deare Ned—I send theas by the post of Hariford, becaus I desire your fathers ansure aboute the seeting of his grounds at Kingsland, becaus the yeare is so fare past, thearefore, I pray you, put your father in minde to rwite aboute it, for if his land be not seet, it will be greate loos to him.

I mise you very much; and deare Ned, sometimes thinke of me, tho you cannot mise me. Your brother Robine seemes to be extremely discontented. I wisch your father would rwite to him, to take his minde of it. Your frind, my cosen Cornewell, is no changeling. I thanke God, my coold is goone, and I am now abell to goo out of my chamber againe; but this was the first day. I much desire to heare what is become of our Harifordsheare petetion for bischops; but I more longe to heare the kings ansure to the petetion to take away the bis: vots in parlament.

In Hariford, they haue turned the tabell in the cathedroll, and taken away the cops and bassons and all such things. I hope they begine to see that the Lord is about to purg His church of all such

---

* The signature of this letter is alone in the handwriting of the Lady Brilliana.

inuencions of men. Deare Ned, be carefull of your self, and I beceach the Lord of heauen to blles you, and keepe you, as I desire my owne hart should be keepe.

Your most affectinat mother, BRILLIANA HARLEY.

Pheb: 17, 1641. *Brompton Castell.*

CXXXIX.

For my deare sonne Mr. Edward Harley.

My deare Ned—You desarue many thankes for your letters to me this weeke, which was exceeding wellcome to me, both for the good newes they contained, and becaus they came from you, whoo I mise; for I may booldly say, I haue not bine very merry sence you went. To me, theas mercys of God are such, as may make our harts stand amased at the goodnes of our God, and they are strong bands to tye vs in obedience to our God; for howe can we sinn against so gracious, so mercifull a God, whoo is thus pleased to put forth His wisdome and power, for the healp of His poore chillderen.

I am exceeding glad that Sr Jhon Conyars is leftenant of the tower. I hope you are acquainted with him, and I hope you haue deleuered my letter to my brother. They are now aboute a petecion to the parlament, which I hope will be ready to send vp the next weake. My deare Ned, the Lord of heauen blles you and presarue you from all euill. Put your father in minde to be carefull of himself; and I desire to know wheather he likes the meath, and wheather my brother had the pyes I sent him. We heare of letters that weare intersepted from my lord Digbe. I desire to know wheather theare was any such thing or no. My deare Ned, still beleeue I am beest pleased, when I can expres meself to be,

Your most affectinat mother, BRILLIANA HARLEY.

Pheb: 19, 1641. *Brompton Castell.*

CXL.

For my deare sonne Mr. Edward Harley.

My deare Ned—I can not lette the carrier goo without rwiteing to you, tho I rwite yesterday by the post of Heariford; for could I heare from you and send to you every day, I should be glad.

By the carrier I haue sent a box in which is a cake and 2 schees with the box; they are directed to you. I pray you scrape out the derection to you, and rwite vpon them for my lady Conyars, and let me put you in trust, to send the cake and schees to her from me, without your father contradict; for I pray you tell your father of it. I purpos to rwit to my Lady Conyars by my cosen Dauis, whoo says he will goo on munday. Mun cries out to be goon, because of his carage. I pray God blles you; so I rest,

Your most affectinat mother,   BRILLIANA HARLEY.

Mar: 6, 1641.

CXLI.

For my deare sonne Mr. Edward Harley.

My deare Ned—I allways longe to heare from you, but this weakes inteligence in the cuntry made me more ernest to heare, and thearefore, I with much joy receued your letter last night by the carryer: that your father and selfe inioye your health is much comfort to me; and, deare Ned, be carefull of yourself for my sake.

Many feares did aris in the cuntry, because the kinge gaue such a refusall to the requeste of both howes, but I hope the Lord will be gratious to this poore land; it was a most remarqabell thinge that shpe was cast away, in which thos fopperis weare. I wisch they may have eyes to see Gods hand.

I haue no desire at all, that a stranger should come to looke to your fathers biusness. Now your father is away, you know that I have no body I can speake to; and if Piner goo away, whoo I dare trust with any thinge, and whoo I know loues your father and me, I should much want him; thearefore I desire not to haue any other, that must so wholy put Piner away. I should haue bine glad to haue had Mr Moore, the time your father was away. I am very glad you like your cosen Conway so well. Your cosen Smith is ill, which has something trubeled me; it is not an ordinary ague he has; he is now in his fitt. I thinke doctor Wright will be with him this day.

I rwite by the post, becaus there is a man that would lay out a 1000*l*. on something for liues, and he desire a speady ansure.

I was ill affter I rwite last to you, as I vse to be, so that I can not yet make the pyes for your father. I pray God blles you, as I desire the soule should be blles of

  Your most affectinat mother,   BRILLIANA HARLEY.
Mar: 12, 1641.

CXLII.

For my deare sonne Mr. Edward Harley.

My deare Ned—I did thinke to haue made Hall stay tell munday, that so I might haue had so much time more to haue rwite to you in; but Piner sends vp 20*l*. to venture in the Irisch wars, and thearefor they desire he might goo with the carryer. I hope things goo one well in the parlament, and that the discontent with the Loundoners is not so much as it is said to be in the cuntry. I am exceeding glad that the affaires goo so well in Ireland. They are about a petecion, but they can not so well agree aboute it, and thearefore I know not when it will be ready.

I will, if pleas God, make the pys your father sends for. I wisch your father would bye a cooch and haue cooch horsess; I should hope to be abell to take the ayre sometimes. To-morrow theare is a sacrement, and I hope to be at it, thearefore I can say no mor at this time, becaus it is late.

Deare Ned, be carefull of yourself, and I beceach the Lord to blles you and to fill you with gras, and give me a comfortabell seeing of you.

Your most affectinat mother,   BRILLIANA HARLEY.
(No date.)

Deare Ned, send me word wheather your father venturs any thinge in Irland, and wheather you thinke that it will be sure and profitabell aduenture into Irland, and wheather it may be doun without much truebell.

CXLIII.

For my deare sonne Mr. Edward Harley.

Deare Ned—I thanke you for your letter by Hall. I did much long to receaue the declaration to the kinge. I thanke you for it; I am sorry the kinge is pleased yet, not to conseaue anny better thoughts of this parlament. The Lord be mercifull to this poore land, and to this cuntry wheare I ame; for I thinke theare is not such another. I heare the justices haue sent vp theare ansure, why they would not take the protestation. Sr William Crof gouerns all of them. Mr Braughton tells me you had taken coold and weare not very well with it. I shall longe to heare how you doo. Deare Ned, be carefull of yourselfe, and I pray God blles you and presarue you in health. I am very well content your father should take another, that his estate might be well looked to, but I desire Piner may stay to receaue the mony, and to lay it out. I thanke God, your cosen Smith is much better. I will, if pleas God, prouid your linnes as soune as I can. I haue by this carrier sent your father 12 pyes and a schees. Mr Braghton brought me no letter from you, which made me sorry; but more sorry that you weare not well. I hope shortly you will have the peticion for this county, but Sr William Croft disswaded it, as a thing vulawfull to petecion. So I rest,

Your most affectinat mother,   BRILLIANA HARLEY.
Mar: 19, 1641.

CXLIV.

To her sonne Edward.*

* * * * * * * * * *

by your * * * * * by the keeper. I see thinges stand in a doutful maner, and our healp must be from our God, and I trust the Lord will presarue His poor childeren. I haue not bine well theas 2 days, or elles I could rwite much more to you. Mr Smith toold what I rwit to you by Mr Braughton. I do not * * * * * * your sister Brill * * * * * * * * * journey * * * *. I hope Mr Moore will goo munday come sen-night, and Mr Yaets is resolued and pleas God to goo then; and becaus of the fast of the next weake, I am desirous she shoude stay till that be past. I pray God blles you, as I desire the soul should be bllesed of

Your most affectinat mother,   BRILLIANA HARLEY.

April 22, 1642.

I haue made 2 shirts for you till I make more. I purpos to send them this weake.

CXLV.

For my deare sonne Mr. Edward Harley, at Mr. Cooles howes, in Chanell Row.

My deare Ned—I cannot let Mr Moore goo without a letter to you, tho I rwite to you yesterday by the post of Ludlow. I am perswaded thinges are now come to theaire ripenes, and if God be not very mercyfull to vs, we shall be in a distressed condistion; but the Lord has promised to heare His chillderen in the day of trubell, and to deliuer them, which I am perswaded He will doo nowe.

I longe euery day to heare from you; I beceach the Lord to presarue you; and deare Ned, be carefull of yourselfe. I haue receued a box with macth and 2 bandeleres; but the box was open, befor it

---

* This letter is much injured by damp.

came to me. I purpos, and pleas God, that your sister Brill shall begine her journey to Loundoun on munday comsenight, and Piner and Hackelet shall goo with her. Mr Yeats, I beleeue, will goo with her; your cosen Smith has not bine well, tho his ague was goone, so that I was faine to send for doctor Wright for him. He came when the keeper brought your letter, which was on friday, so he meet your letter, for which he returnes many thankes, and would not now rwite to you, becaus he desires when he dous, to rwit aboute Potters biusness, which he will, when he has spoken with a lawer. He desires you would doo him the fauor to bye him 2 muskets and rests and bandeliers, and 15 or 16 pound of poweder in a barell, and he desires you would send them by Lemster carrier, and so derected them to Brompton, and he will giue order to haue them sent to Heariford, and will send you what they cost.

I am not yet very well, and yesterday I was something ill. I pray God blles you and presarue you in all safety; so I rest,

Your most affectinat mother, BRILLIANA HARLEY.

Apri: 23, 1642: Brompton Castell.

Doctor Wright telles me that Mr Weafer is still sike, and for his part he would haue doun his vtmost, that you might haue had that place.

CXLVI.

For my deare sonne Mr. Edward Harley.

My deare Ned—You cannot conceaue how wellcome your letters are to me; yet beleeue I give you thankes for them. I receued one by the post and another by the carrier this weake. I see the distance is still keepe betwne the kinge and parlament. The Lord in mercy make them one, and in His good time incline the kinge to be fully assured in the faithfull counsell of the parlament. Our God has doun greate thinges, and I hope He will still glorify Himselfe in exerciseing of His mercy to vs His poore saruants. And, my deare Ned, it is my greate comfort that you haue made your God your confidence; and this is most sure, He will neuer faile you. I purpos, and pleeas God, your sister Brill shall begine her journey to Loundoun on munday next, and I hope shee will be abell to reache Wickam by wensday night; wheare I hope shee shall meete you at the Catterne wheele; shee much longes for this journey. Piner and Hackelet and Prichard goo vp with her, and Mr Yeats and his wife. This night Mr Old tells me that Mr Nweport is maried; for my Lady Nweport sent to Shrewsbury to haue the bells rounge for it. I wishee, and please God, I had the like ocation of reioyceing. Your cosen Smith is now well. Doctor Wright stayed with him 3 or 4 dayes, and gaue him somethinge, which has doun him much good.

I was ill when docter Wright was with your cosen Smith, and so I haue bine sence he went; but I haue taken nothing of him sence you went.

Deare Ned, be careful of yourselfe, and I beceach the Lord in much mercy to blles you whith all His bllessings, and I wisch you much ioye in your nwe lodging in Lincons Ine. I beleeue your father misess you, and I am sure I doo. I pray you send me word how you like your commons; so I rest,

Your most affectinat mother,   BRILLIANA HARLEY.

Apr: 29, 1642, Brompton Castell.

Mr Gower is very well pleased that he is chosen on of the ministers.

CXLVII.

For my deare sonne Mr. Edward Harley.

My deare Ned—But that I loue to say something to you my selfe, I might thinke this letter might be spared, sence your sister is the bearer of it, whoo can tell you how how all dous at Brompton; but, becaus shee cannot giue me the content by her discours with you, as if I did so, I am glad to take this way of discours; for I exceedingly long to see you, and I hope God will, in His good time, giue me that comfort. I haue sent you 2 shirts by your sister and haue sent for cloth to make you 4 more, which shall be sent you, as soune as I can, if pleas God.

I hope theas will meete you at Wickam, wheare I know and at Loundon, you will be very carefull of your sister; shee is yonge, thearefore, deare Ned, obsarue her carage, and let not your counsell be wanting to her, and I hope shee will have so much wisdome to take it. I am toold that Sr William Croft shall be burges if Mr Weafer dye, whoo they say is very sike. I cannot but let you know what hapned the other day, which may shame all the rest that haue spoken ill of your dear father. I was toold, that on Mr Fox spake ill of your father, which he hard of, and came to me to excuse himself, with many protestations, that he neuer did so, and how ready he would be to doo your father saruis: he is Mr Foxes sone, that is at Creete; your sister Brill can tell you all the story of it. Let your father know of it. I pray God blles you with all the grases of His spirit. So I rest,

    Your most affectinat mother,   BRILLIANA HARLEY.
Apr: 30, 1642. Brompton Castell.

On the back of the letter are the following arithmetical processes.

```
    b   Ll   b
    216 — 9 — 767                216
              9                   31
          ─────                 ─────
       216)6903                  216
           — 42                  648
       31¹ ────                 ─────
            207                 6696
           ─────                 207
            216                 ─────
                                6903
```

CXLVIII.

To her sonne Edward.

My deare Ned—I beleeue some buisines hindered your rwiting this weake or ells I should haue promised myself a letter from you; for you know how much I loue to have a letter from you. I should wisch you would begine a letter on monday and take the whoole weake to rwite it in, that so I might know from you how thinges goo, and how your sister Brill pleases my lady Veare. I feare theare will be blowes struck. I pray God prepare vs for thos times.

Deare Ned, tell your father that the plumer of Woster is now casting the leads; the timber was very rotten; he seems to be an honest man. I wisched you with me to day, to see him cast it. I thanke God your brothers and sisters are well. I pray God blles you, and giue you a comfortabell meeting with

Your most affectinat mother,   BRILLIANA HARLEY.

I hope you doo not forget to spend some time to learne French. I pray you send me word wheather you doo. I hope you haue reseaued the letter I sent by Mr Moore.

(No date.)

CXLIX.

For my deare sonne Mr. Edward Harley.

My deare Ned—Your letter by the post and by the carrier are both very wellcome to me; for besides the knowledge you giue me of the publicke affaires, the assurance of your health is very deare to me. We all are ingaged deepely to pray ernestly to our God, that He will giue both wisdome and corage to the parlament, and I hope the Lord will so giude them that the mouths of thos that would speake euill of them shall be stoped. I thanke you for desireing me not to beleeue rumors. I doo not; becaus I assure meself I shall heare the truth of thinges from your penn. It is the Lords greate worke, that is now a frameing, and I am confident, it will be finisched with much beauty, so that the very enimyes shall be enforsed to acknowledg it has bine the Lord that has rought for His caus and chillderen; against home they will finde that theare is no deuination nor inchantment.

We hard that the Kenttiche peticion was brought by 3000 men, and that 3000 Loundoners meete them vpon Blacke Heath and theare fought, and many weare killed. And now we heare that Sr Francis Wortly drwe his sword and asked whoo was for the king, and so 18 foolowed him. I thinke this later may be true; but for the fight vpon Black Heath, I know it is not true.

I am glad our Heariford peticion is come to Loundoun, and I hope deliuered before this: your sister, I hope, meet you at Wickcam on wensday last. Deare Ned, send me word how my ladey Veere vsess her, and how shee carriers herself.

I pray God blles you with a large measure of gras and with all the comforts of this life.

 Your most affectinat mother,   BRILLIANA HARLEY.

May 6, 1642.

CL.

For my deare sonne Mr. Edward Harley.

My deare Ned—Tho my letter can bring you no other inteligence then of the deere affection of a mother that loues you dearely, yet I will beleeue it shall haue a wellcome. By this time, I thinke your sister has lefte wondering at Loundoun. I long to heare how she dous: deare Ned, put her in minde to be carefull of herselfe.

Mr Gower is very well pleased that he is chosen. I pray God derect them all, that theare may be a full reformation. I purpos, and pleas God, to send you 4 more shirts as soune as I can. I haue taken on to waite vpon your cosen Smith and your brothers. It is on that came out of Schescheere; he borded at Mrs Pirsens; his name is Raphe; he dous it for his diet without wages, and yet he dous it very well; he is a very honnest man; I beleeue you remember him. I pray you tell your father of it; they did much wante one to looke to them. Your sister Doll has not bine very well, and shee lookes very lamentabell. Deare Ned, I longe to see you, and I pray God giue me a comfortabell inioying of that comfort.

I pray God blles you, as I desire the soule should bee bllesed of
    Your most affectinat mother,   BRILLIANA HARLEY.

They haue so mocked at our Hearifordsheere petion, that I long to heare what they say to it at Loundoun.

May 7, 1642. *Brompton Castell.*

CLI.

For my deare sonne Mr. Edward Harley.

My deare Ned—Mr Voile is in hast, so that I haue only time to let you know you are much in my thoughts; and as I think of you, so I much longe to see you. I pray God derect the parlament, and the Lord of heauen blles you: so I rest,
    Your most affectinat mother,   BRILLIANA HARLEY.
May 7, 1642.

CLII.

For my deare sonne Mr. Edward Harley.

My deare Ned—I doo so much desire to see you, that I take offten rwiteing to you, in the place of it, tell I can see you. Piner says littell, which makes me thinke that your father said some thing to him. I pray you send me word wheather your father will take another or no: and, deare Ned, aske Mr. Smith whoo toold him what he toold Mr. Braughton. I desire much to knowe whoo it was. I hope something will be doun to docter Rogers.

I haue sent you, by the carrier, 8 botteles of cider in a box derected to you, and a runlet of sider to your father. I pray you send me on of your scokes, to make you nwe onse by. Your shirts you shall haue shortly, if pleas God. I desire to heare how Sr Jhon Conyars comes off for Onells escape.

I pray God blles you and keepe you in His feare, and giue you comfortabell seeing of

    Your most affectinat mother,   BRILLIANA HARLEY.

(No date.)

CLIII.

For my deare sonne Mr. Edward Harley.

My deare Ned—I am glad your sister Brill has the joy of seeing you, tho I can not: but I hope God will againe giue me that comfort. Your sister Brill did looke much paler; I thinke, by resen of her ernest desire to goo vp to Loundoun. I much desire to knowe how my lady Veere likes her. I thanke you for your letter by Piner; it was wellcome; but I had no letter from you by the carrier or post: but your father rwiteing to me by the post, and letting me knowe you weare to see the soulders on tuesday last, I tooke it, that that hindered you.

Deare Ned, I sent you a letter to your father from Mr Gower; I hope you receued it; and I hope it will be thought fitt that the publischers of such ventings of such matter as the enclosed sermon was, will be thought fite to be sencured; and I thinke if Mr Schirbere be reproufed, it would be very well. I pray God blles you, and giue you a comfortabell meeting with

    Your most affectinat mother,   BRILLIANA HARLEY.

Deare Ned, send me word how Sr Jhon Conyars ansured Oneles gooing out of the Tower.

May 13, 1642. Brompton Castell.

CLIV.

For my deare sonne Mr. Edward Harley.

My deare Ned,—A short letter will sarue to let you know how Harifordsheare stands, when Mr. Braughton is the bearer of it: thearefore I will say nothing of what is doun abroode, only tell you of your frindes at Brompton, wheare I longe to see you.

This day I hard out of Linconscheere: I thank God they are all well: but I see my brother Pelham is not of my minde. I thinke now, my deare sister was taken away that shee might not see that which would haue grefed her harte.

Sr William Pelham rwites me word he has giuen vp his liftenatcy and his gooing to Yorke, to the king; being his saruant, as he rwites me word, and so bound by his oth.

Deare Ned, send me word wheather your sister lookes as pale as shee did. I haue not bine well theas 3 dayes, but it is as I vse to be. Your sister Dorrity has bine exceeding ill: shee fell ill about 10 days sence. I was very unwilling to send for any docter, tell shee grwe very ill, and so ill, that I much feared her; and I sent for docter Wright, whoo went away this morning. I hope now shee will recoruer, tho I still feare her: shee lookes most lamentabell, and is growne weake; but I hope God will be mercifull to her.

I hope to send you your shirts shortly. I pray God blles you and presarue you in all safety: and deare Ned, let me heare the truth of thinges, tho it be bade. We heare that the kinge will sommon all that will be for him, to come to him.

I pray God compos thinges to His glory and His chruches advantage.

Your most affectinat mother,   BRILLIANA HARLEY.

I haue receued docter Wrights armes you sent downe.

May 17, 1642. Brompton Castell.

CLV.

For my deare sonne Mr. Edward Harley, theas Loundoun.

My deare Ned—The ocation of this letter is to let you knowe that Mr. Weafer is dead. Doctor Wright has exprest a very greate deale of frindeshipe to you in this biusnes, more then this short time will let me tell you. This mornig doctor Wright came to me presently affter 7 a cloke; he thinkes that if your father can make Mr. Seaborne ferme to him, and gaine Mr. Ellton to preueale with yonge Mr. Weafer, that you will haue it. I will, in the meane time, rwite to Mr. Ellton, and doctor Wright will carry the letter to him. But this is the question, that you must be a burges of theare towne, which I bide Mr. Davis tell them you would: but it seemes he did not so cleerely; for that was one reson that made doctor Wright come to me, to let me knowe, that if you weare not burges, you could not be one. Doctor Wright is so ernest that you should haue this, that he perswaded me to send to your father, that nothing might be left vndone. If your father be displeased that I send so to him, you must healp to make my excuse. If please God, I should be very glad you might be in this imployment. The Lord prosper our indeuors and blles you. In great hast,

Your most affectinat mother,   BRILLIANA HARLEY.

Samuell promises me to be with you on saterday . . I pray you rwit doctor Wright thankes, and pray your father to doo so. I did not tell now thinke he had borne so much good will to Brompton, as I see he dous.

May 19, 1642.

Deare Ned, put your father in minde, if he thinkes best to doo so, to rwite to Sr William Croft for his healpe.

CLVI.

For my deare sonne Mr. Edward Harley.

My deare Ned—I thanke you for your letter this weake by the carrier, and for your promis of one by the post; but I receued none by him. I beleeue you weare hindred from rwiteing. Samuell, I hope, came to you on saterday. I was vnwilling to leaue any thinge vndone that might further your being chosen for the parlament; in which, if it be the Lords will, I should be very glad you might acte your first saruis for the commonwellth. To tell you now what has bine doun; I must first let you know that doctor Wright is very ernest in it; as soun as Mr Weafer was dead, he sent his man to let me know so; and when I rwite him word that I desired he should try his frindes for you, he did so. When Mr Dauis came to towne, as Mr Davis toold me, he found no incoragement; but I had directed him to goo to doctor Wright, and he put him in such a way, that he had good hopes of it. Doctor Wrights frinde, as Mr Dauis toold me, was very desirous to haue you, and saide you must be made free of theare towne, to which he would giue all his assistance.

As I rwit yesterday to you, doctor Wright staid diner and tooke a letter from me to my cosen Ellton, which he saide he would delever himself. It was his counsell to me to rwite to him; for his daughter has married Mr Weafers sonne, and yonge Weaffer has power ouer many voces. Doctor Wright perswaded me to rwite to my cosen Vahan, whoo has interest in some of the alldermen. I haue doun so; and if the mesenger returne to night, I will rwite you word, what hope theare is. Mr Dauis spake of himself to Sr William Croft; he toold Sr William Croft that he, heareing in Heariford of the death of Mr Weaffer, he desired his masters sonne might haue that place, and desired him that he would be pleased to giue his assistance to it. It was doctor Wright counesele to Mr. Dauis. Sr William Croft ansured, hee would not medel in it; he would leaue all men to themselfes; and such an ansure your sweet hart made Mr Dauis. Antony Child, whoo I sent to my cosen Vahan, brought me this inclosed leter; by which you will see Mr Vahan is not come home. Childe tells me, they say at Heariford that Sr William Croft or Mr Allderne shall be. Deare Ned, let you and me commite this to the wise directions of our God, and be well contented with the issue He shall pleas to giue. I pray God blles you.

Your most affectinat mother, BRILLIANA HARLEY.

May 20, 1642 : Brompton, at night.

CLVII.

For my deare sonne Mr. Edward Harley, thease Loundoun.

My deare Ned—I hope you are well, though I had no letter from you by the post, and I shall longe tell I receaue the assurance of yours and your fathers being well. This day doctor Wright rwite me word, he made no question but that you would haue voices enowe in Heariford; yesterday he spent in gaineing as many as he could; this day he went to Leadbury with my letter to my cosen Ellton. Doctor Wright rwite me word, that some of the alldermen toold him that it would be very well, if you did come downe, to be 2 or 3 dayes in Heariford; but that is as your father shall thinke fite; but if pleas God, that you be made free of theare towne, and to be so you must haue Mr Seaborns assistance; if he be constant to your father, it will I hope, doo well. I was very sorry that I had not an ansure from Mr Ellton before I rwite this letter. Doctor Wright rwit me word, he hears none spoken of to haue it besides you, but Mr Prise of Wistanstone (Mr Prises father, that is of the parlament), and Mr Hoskins; but they stir not yet. I pray God blles you, and the Lord in mercy giue you suich a large porcion of wisdome, that you may be very abell to doo your cuntry saruis. I thanke God I am reasnabell well, and your brothers and sisters are well; only Doll is not well, and has bine very ill this night. Deare Ned, put your sister in minde to be carefull of her self.

Your most affectinat mother, BRILLIANA HARLEY.

May 21, 1642: Brompton Castell.

CLVIII.

To her son Edward.

My deare Ned—I must tell you once againe, that I haue had no letter from you this weake, but Sankey rwites me word that you are well, and that makes me glad. I should haue bine very glad to haue receaued derections from your father, wheather I should doo any more in getting voices for you about Heariford. I haue spoken to many who haue promised me, and young Mr Weafer, if hee doo not stand for it himself.

If Mr. Ellton is nowe in London, I pray you tell your father, that if it pleas him, he may speake to him. If you did rwite any letter by the post, he has played the naughty fellow, and then I pray you rwite no more by him. I pray God blles you, and giue you a most comfortabell meeting with

Your most affectinat mother, BRILLIANA HARLEY.

May 27, 1642: Brompton Castell.

CLIX.

For my deare sonne Mr. Edward Harley.

My deare Ned—I did very much longe to heare from you, and I thanke God this night I receaued your letter by Samuell. I will doo no more in the biusness for Heariford, tell I see what my lord Scidmore sonn will doo.

You are much behoolding to doctor Wright, for he has stood very hard for you, tho some threaten him much for it, that they shall loose theare frindshp. If you have not this, I hope you shall haue another.

I pray God blles you: so in great hast, for it is very late, I rest,
Your most affectinat mother, BRILLIANA HARLEY.

May 28, 1642: Brompton Castell.

CLX.

For my deare sonne Mr. Edward Harley.

My deare Ned—I am very sorry I haue had no letter from you this weake. Deare Ned, rwite to me, tho it be but 2 or 3 words. I sent to Heariford to let them know that I hard that my lord Scidmors sonne would stande for the burgesshp, and then I did not further desire it for you; but gaue them many thankes for theare good will to you, and desired if my lords sonne did not stand, that then they would giue you theare vosies, which they then promised they would, and tooke my thankes very well. I pray God blles you and giue me a joyfull seeing of you: so I rest,
Your most affectinat mother, BRILLIANA HARLEY.

June 3, 1642.

CLXI.

For my deare sonne Mr. Edward Harley.

My deare Ned—Now I thanke you for your letter by Mr Braughton, whoo brought it this day somethinge late, so that I am shortned in time to rwite to you.

I thinke we must all acknowledeg Gods greate mercy that the plot for the takeing of Hull was discouered. I pray God derect the parlement what they ought to doo, for they haue enimyes enough to looke with on euill eye at what theare actions.

At Loudlow they seet vp a May pole, ana a thinge like a head vpon it, and so they did at Croft, and gathered a greate many about it, and shot at it in deristion of roundheads. At Loudlow they abused Mʳ Bauges sonne very much, and are so insolent that they durst not leaue theare howes to come to the fast. I acknowledg I doo not thinke meself safe wheare I am. I loos the comfort of your fathers company, and am in but littell safety, but that my trust is in God; and what is doun in your fathers estate pleasess him not, so that I wisch meselfe, with all my hart, at Loundoun, and then your father might be a wittnes of what is spent; but if your father thinke it beest for me to be in the cuntry, I am every well pleased with what he shall thinke beest. I haue sent you by this carryer, in a box, 3 shirts; theare is another, but it was not quite made; on of them is not wasched; I will, and pleas God, send you another the next weake, and some handchersher. I rwite yesterday to you by the post of Loudlow, how my thankes was taken at Heariford.

I pray God blles you and keepe you from sinn, and from all other euills, and giue you a joyfull meeting with

Your most affectinat mother,   BRILLIANA HARLEY.

Your sister Doll is not well, shee has a great weakenes vpon her; yet I thanke God this day shee is somethinge better than shee was.

June 4, 1642: *Brompton Castell.*

CLXII.

To her son Edward Harley.

My deare Ned—You haue now made amens for not rwiteing the last weake, becaus you haue rwite by the post and promis me another letter by Hacklett, whoo I hope will be with me this night. I longe to see her that shee may let me know how you doo, which I should be glad to be an eye witness of meselfe; for beleue me I longe to see you, and I wisch you were with me to morrow on the faire day. I hope they will be quiet, tho I somethinge feare it. I am sorry you finde that paine in your head. I beseach the Lord to free you from it, and to blles the phisecke to you, which you haue taken. I shall extremely longe to heare how you are affter it; and pray, deare Ned, send me word particularly how you doo, or elles I shall not haue much contentment. I pray God that it be true, that the lords will return to parlament, which I thinke will much work upon others. Your brothers and sisters are well, only your sister Dorroty. I hope you take care of your sister Brill, and pray let me pray you to send me word, how my lady Veare likes her.

Mr Braughton is now come that he may keepe the faire quiet, and Mr Floyd has mustered vp his fors; and then you must remember he is a buissy man. My cosen Cornewall is goone. I pray God blles you, as I desire my owne soule should be bllessed: and rest

    Your most affectinat mother,   BRILLIANA HARLEY.

June 10, 1642.

CLXIII.

For my deare sonne Mr. Edward Harley.

My deare Ned—I thanke you for your letter by Hackelet; I much reioyce to heare you are well, and longe to see you. Your fathers horses could not be sould at the faire, thearefore I thinke and pleas God, to send them vp on munday or tusday, when I hope to rwite to you more at large, for now I haue defered rwiteing tell it be late, that I might let you know howe the faire went. I thanke God heatherto it has past quietly, but I was somethinge afraide, becaus they are growne so insolent.

I hope this night will be as quiet as the day has bine. I pray God blles your phiseke to you; and, deare Ned, let me know how you doo in euery particular. I hope to send you your other shirt by Martaine, when he bringes vp the horses.

I pray God blles you and keepe you in all safety; so I rest

Your most affectinat mother, BRILLIANA HARLEY.

I haue sent your father a box of Shrewsbury cakes.

Just as I am rwiteing theare is a quarell begoun.

June 11, 1642.

CLXIV.

For my deare sonne Mr. Edward Harley.

My deare Ned—I thanke you for your letter by the carryer. I hope your phisek has doun you good, and I pray God it may. We must all ioyne our sorrows togeather that the kinge yet hoolds of. I dout not but that the Lord will perfect His great worke, He has begoun.

I purpos, and pleas God, to send Martane with the horsess your father sent for, on munday next. I doute not but that your father will giue to his vtmost for the raiseing theas hoors, and in my opinion it weare better to borrow mony, if your father will giue any, then to giue his plate; for we doo not know what straits we may be put to, and thearefore I thinke it is better to borrow whillst on may, and keepe the plate for a time of neede, without your father had so much plate, that he could paret with some, and keepe some to sarue himselfe another time. This I doo not say, that I am vnwilling to part with the plate or any thing ells in this case; if your father cannot borrow mony, I thinke I might finde out some in the cuntry to lend him some. Deare Ned, tell your father this, for I haue not rwite to him aboute it. I haue not bine very well this day, but it is as I vse to be, and I thanke God so much better, as I keepe not my chamber. Your sister Dorroty is much better then shee was, and I hope shee will doo well, though I was much afraide of her.

I pray God blles you and giue you a comfortabell meeting with

Your most affectinat mother, BRILLIANA HARLEY.

June 17, 1642. *Brompton Castell.*

CLXV.

To her son Edward.

My deare Ned—If you beleaue how glad I am to haue this paper discours with you, you will read it as willingly as I rwite it. Since your father thinkes Hearefordsheare as safe as any other country, I will thinke so too; but when I considered how long I had bine from him, and how this country was affected, my desire to see your father, and my care to be in a place of safety, made me ernestly desire to come vp to Loundoun; but since it is not your father's will, I will lay aside that desire. But, deare Ned, as you haue promised me, so let me desire you to let me know how thinges goo. This night I hard that my lord Savile was dead. I desire to know wheather it be so or no; and wheather my lord Paget be goon to York. I heare that on Mr Mason carride a letter from the justices of this country to the king at York, to let him know that they would sarue him with theare lives and estats. I thought it had bine with the petition they made for the bischops, but they say, it was with a letter. When d{r} Wright was with Mr James, he toold me you had rwite to him aboute Petters bill, and that it was well if some lords weare spoken to: he desires me to make some means to speake to my lord Brooke, which I promised him I would; thearefore, good Ned, eather speake yourselfe to my lord Brooke, or get somebody to speak to him, that when the bill comes into the lords he may further it. This day Mr. Dauis came from Heareford, wheare he went to preach, by the intreaty of some in the town, and this befell him: when he had ended his prayer before the sermon, which he was short in, becaus he was loth to tire them, 2 men went out of the chruch and cryed "pray God blles the kinge; this man dous not pray for the kinge;" vpon which, before he read his text, he toold them that m[isters] had that liberty, to pray before or after the sermon for the chruch and state; for all that, they went to the bells and range, and a great many went into the chruch-yard and cryed "roundheads," and some said, "let us cast stones at him!"

and he could not looke out of doors nor Mr Lane but they cryed "roundhead." In the afternoon they would not let him preach; so he went to the cathedral. Thos that had any goodness weare much trubelled and weepe much.

Mr Yats dous much lament doctor Wrights being theare, and says, if he can preuaile with him, he will persuade him to goo to Shreawsbery; which I should be very glad of, becaus he has gained him enemys in standing to geet voices for you. You may see by this how wicked they are growne. I think it beest to let doctor Rogers alone till it pleas God to giue a fairer correspondency between the kinge and parlament, and then I wisch he may be soundly punished.

I thanke God I have bine very well, and so well, that I am abell to goo abroode, when I am not well as I used to be.

I haue sent you a shirt and hafe a dusen handcherchers and some powder for your hair.

I haue rwitten so misrabell that I feare you will hardly reade it, but I hope, this will be leagabell to you, that I desire the Lord to blles you, as I desire my own soul should be bllesed: so I rest,

Your most affectinat mother, BRILLIANA HARLEY.

I hope I shall see you this summer; I long for it. I thanke God your brothers and sisters are well. Deare Ned, send me word wheather my cosen Dauis has lost Bucknell or no; he says he has not, and Mr Edwards says he has.

June 20, 1642. *Brompton.*

CLXVI.

For my deare sonne Mr. Edward Harley.

My deare Ned—Your two letters this weake weare exceeding wellcome to me. I thanke God, that you finde yourselfe better affter your pihiseke. Deare Ned, for my sake take care of your ———.

I am very glad to heare that your sister has so much fauor from my lady Veere. I had no letter from your sister this weake. I hope the horsess are come well to your father: and by this carrier I purpos, and pleas God, to send the 2 pistolls you rwite me word your father would haue, and the gillt plate which he has sent for. I am exceeding glad to heare that my lord of Sallsbery and my lord of Clare is come to the parlement. It is a greate comfort to me to see you fixe your thoughts in theas times vpon your God. Your brother Tom has bine extreme ill, and it pleased God, that docter Wright was with Mrs Litellton, and so came to see me as he went home, which I thought fell out happily for your brother. Yesterday I was exceeding fraid of him, but this day, I thanke God, he is better, so that I hope docter Wright may leaue him to-morrow. He fell sike on tusday last; so that, deare Ned, I finde that on trubele foolows another.

Mr William Littellton being at Loudlow last weake, as he came out of the chruch, a man came to him and looked him in the fase and cryed "roundhead;" he gaue the fellow a good box of the eare and steep to on that had a chugell and tooke it from him and beat him soundly. They say, they are now more quiet in Loudlow. I pray you put your father in mind to consider of that I rwite to him about Mr Yates, and send me word what he says, for I desire they may be punisched.

I pray God blles you and giue you a comfortabell meeting with
    Your most affectinat mother,   BRILLIANA HARLEY.

Jne: 24, 1642. *Brompton Castell.*

Deare Ned, send me word wheather my lady Veere giues any thinge in this prouicione for raizing of hors for the good of this poore kingdome.

CLXVII.

For my deare sonne Mr. Edward Harley.

Deare Ned—I loue to rwite to you, and thearefore, my deare Ned, be somethinge glad to receaue my letter.

Sr William Croft came to see me: he neuer asked how your father did; spoke slighty, and stayed but a littele.

I heare that he has commanded the beackon nwe furnisched, and nwe piche put into it. I haue sent to inquire affter it; if it be so, I will send your father word. When Sr William Croft came to me, he came from my lord Harbert. . . . I pray God blles you, and the Lord in mercy send you a comfortabell meeting with

Your most affectinat mother, BRILLIANA HARLEY.

Jun: 25, 1642.

CLXVIII.

To her son Edward.

My deare Ned—This morning I rwite to you by Mr Greene, but I cannot so offten haue an opertunity as I haue a desire to let you know my thoughts are much with you, and my prayers are for you.

I sent to Mr. Dauis, to enquire about the beackon, but he could not heare that any piche was put into it; only piche was in the howes, wheare the beackon was. I neuer hard of a man so changed as they say Sr William Croft is. He gaue me a slight visit.

I haue sent vp the pistolls your father sent for, by the carrier, which bringes up the littell truncke in which is your shirt and handcherchers, and a bundell derected to your sister. I thanke God your brother Tom is much better, and your sister Dorrity is exceedingly mended. I pray God blles you, and giue you a happy meeting with

Your most affectinat mother, BRILLIANA HARLEY.

June 25, 1642. *Brompton Castele.*

I pray you tell your father that the dublet he sent for is in the truncke.

CLXIX.

For my deare sonne Mr. Edward Harley.

My deare Ned—I am not willinge to make an excuse for not rwiteing to you becaus I did so offten the last weake; but I am glad to doo it now. I hope we shall haue better nwes of the affaires than yet we haue, and I am confident the Lord will finisch this His greate worke. And the Lord in mercy hasten it, that the mouths of wicked men may be put to silence. Heariford is growne now wors than Loudlowe. You may gees wheaire they haue theaire incoragement. I haue sent your father another sermon of d^r Rogers. In my opinion, it weare a most just work to punische him: but your father knows beest what is to be doun: but sure it is pitifull that a man should goo on so.

I wisch with all my hart that the howes of lords would send for him, and that would make them startell in this cuntry; and I thinke the lords will be very sencibele of what he says, for he lays lyes enowe to theaire charge. Good Ned, put your father in minde of it. I doo longe almost to haue him punisched. I feare your father dous much neglect himself. Deare Ned, put him in minde of eateing in the morning. I pray God blles you, and giue you a comfortabell meeting with

    Your most affectinat mother,   BRILLIANA HARLEY.

June 27, 1642. *Brompton Castell.*

CLXX.

For my deare sonne Mr. Edward Harley.

My deare Ned—I hard very late this night that Mr Moore would goo to Loundoun, and I cannot let him pas without a letter; for, my deare Ned, beleeue me, I long to see, and how glad should I be, if you weare heare at the fast. Docter Wright was send for to Mr James, whoo was very ill, and he, seeing Mr Moore with him, toold me he was to goo to Loundoun: but it was late, and if I doo not send very early, he will be goon; so that I can say no more but that I am,

Your most affectinat mother, BRILLIANA HARLEY.

Jun: 27, 1642.

CLXXI.

For my deare sonne Mr. Edward Harley.

My deare Ned—Had not I hard that you weare well, I should haue allmost haue feared it, becaus I had no letter from you this weake. I did hope eather Martaine or the vnder keeper would haue bine in the cuntry this weake; but, this being saterday, I haue no hope they will come.

I feare your father in theas great biusness will neglect himself; thearefore, deare Ned, put him in minde to eate something in a morning.

I long to see you, and yet, when I thinke you are a comfort to your father, I cannot wisch you from him; yet I desire you weare with me for a littell while; now euery day begeets a nwe longeing in me to heare from you, and to heare how thinges goo.

I pray God blles you and fill you with the grasess of His spirit, and the Lord in mercy presarue you in health, and giue you a comfortabell meeting with

Your most affectinat mother, BRILLIANA HARLEY.

July 2, 1642. *Brompton Castell.*

I beleeue the mending of the howes will cost a greate deale, for the plumers haue 5 sh. a day, and 5 sh. a hundered for casting the leade, besides the carpenters and masons, but I thinke your father will not repent of it when it is doun.

CLXXII.

For my deare sonne Mr. Edward Harley.

My deare Ned—The resen why I send this bearer to your father is, to let him knowe that the kinge has sent a commission to 12 of the justices to settell the milica. I haue rwite your father theare names. I did not heare it tell late this night. I herd it presently affter diner, but it was but a flyeing report; but now I heare it from one that was at Rudall, when my cozen Rudall was sent for; tell your father that the other as I thinke is Mr Wigmore of Shobdon. I pray God derect your father and the parlament what to doo, and I thinke, if any cuntry had need of some to haue bine sent doun into it, it is this. Your father they are growne to hate. I pray God forgiue them. My deare Ned, I am not afraide, but sure I am, we are a dispised company.

I pray God blles you; in hast I rest,

 Your most affectinat mother,   BRILLIANA HARLEY.

July 5, 1642. Brompton Castell.

I thanke God your brothers and sisters are well.

CLXXIII.

For my deare sonne Mr. Edward Harley.

My deare Ned—I receued your letter by Mr. Hill yesterday, and I thanke God that I heare you are well; the Lord in mercy continue that comfort to me.

They goo on with the milica in this cuntry; the sherafe has sent out warents that they apeare on the 15 of this month at Herifrd. Your fathers company, I heare, they meane to make offer to you, and if you will not haue it, they will giue it to another. They trihumfe brafely, as they say, and threaten poore Brompton; but we are in the hand of our God, whoo I hope will keepe vs safe. I pray God blles you, as I desire the soule should be bllesed, of

    Your most affectinat mother,   BRILLIANA HARLEY.
July 8, 1642.

CLXXIV.

For my deare sonne Mr. Edward Harley.

My deare Ned—I haue bine so longe in puteing vp the plate to send your father, that I haue no time to rwite any more than that I longe to see you. I am confident you are not troubled to see the plate goo this way; for I trust in our gratious God, you will haue the frute of it.

I pray God blles you.

    Your most affectinat mother,   BRILLIANA HARLEY.

I pray you send me word wheather my lord Clare be come to Loundoun.

I doo long allmost to be from Brompton.

In the hamper with the plate, I haue sent your father a cake; it whas sent me this morning.

July 9, 1642.   *Brompton Castell.*

CLXXV.

For my deare sonne Mr. Edward Harley.

My deare Ned—Beleeue it, your letter by Raphe and Mr. Longly and the post this weake weare very wellcome to me. It is true, as you aprehend it, that I haue great caus to blles God for His great mercy in giuing me, now at this time, a fare more full measure of health then I haue had, ever sence I was ill; for now, I thank God,

I can goo abrood at thos times that I was inforsed to keepe my beed, and this last weake was abell, at that time, to keepe a priuet fast, and the Lord that has doun this for me, the vnworthyest of all His scruants, I trust and am fully assured, will doo much more for His chruch. I haue offten toold you, I thought you would see trubellsome times; but, my deare Ned, keepe your hart aboue the world, and then you will not be trubelled at the changes in it; and haveing your God for your porcion, which I am confident you haue, and it is my comfort that I can beleeue so, you are happy; for I can experimentally say, that the Lord will sheawe most mercy, when we stand in most need of it; and I am confident, the Lord will not faile His poore saruents at this time. I wisch you with me, but, deare Ned, I am glad you are at Loundoun, becaus that is a safer place.

I sent Samuell to Heariford on tusday, to obsarue what was doun. Yesterday the soulders weare called. He is not yet come home, which makes me thinke it very much, for he was seene this day at Lemster, at 4 a cloke. I did hope to haue sent the relation of all to you in this letter by the post.

Mr. Dauis of Coxall did not goo to Heariford, and Mr. Dauis of Wigmore went, but did nothinge: he says but a feawe of your fathers company did apeare. They speake bigg words, but I hope the Lord will keepe theare harts lowe.

I haue receued the box with 20 bandeleres, but the boxes with the muskets and rests the carrier has left to come in a waggon to Woster; he promises I shall haue them shortly. I pray you tell your father the reson, why I did not send the truncke of plate by Lemster carryer was, becaus the last I sent to Lemster, they said it was plate; but Bagly, that went with it, not knowing what it was, only I toold him theare was a cake in it, and so he toold the carryers wife. I hope your father receued it. I haue derected this truncke to Mr. Smith, in the Old Bayly, and I haue desired Will Griffets to deleuer it to the carrier and to take vpon him that he sends it. I pray you bide Sankey be carefull to speake to Mr. Smiths man to goo to the carryer of Loudlow to looke for the truncke; it is sowed vp in canues. I haue sent your father a note of what plate is in the truncke.

I pray God blles you and giue you a comfortabell meeting with
    Your most affectinat mother,   BRILLIANA HARLEY.

I pray you tell your father the bay gellding he sent to haue taken vp, is so, and he is in very good case.

Remember me to your sister. I haue sent her bibell in the truncke with the plate. I wisch some parlament men might be sent into this cuntry to settell the milica, and that my lord of Essekes would make Mr. Shirborne hoold his peace.

Gloues and pattern for me.   M. Instrum^{ts}.
July 15, 1642.

CLXXVI.

To her son Edward.

My deare Ned—By the enclosed paper to your father, you will knowe how poore Hearifordsheare is affected; but, deare Ned, I hope you and myself will remember for whous caus your father and we are hated. It is for the caus of our God, and I hope we shall be so fare from being ashamed of it or trubelled, that we beare the reproche of it, that we shall binde it as a crowne upon us; and I am confident the Lord will rescue His chilldcren from reproche.

I sent Samuell to Heariford to obsarue theaire ways. He had come home last night, but that he had a fall from his hors and put out his shoulder.

He tells me that they all at Heariford cried out against your father, and not one said any thinge for him, but one man, Mr. Phillips of Ledbury said, when he hard them speak so against your father, "well," said he, "tho Sir Robert Harley be lowe heare, yet he is aboue, wheare he is." My deare Ned, I can not thinke I am safe at Brompton, and by no means I would haue you come downe. I should be very glad if your father could geet some religious and discreet gentleman to come for a time to Brompton, that he might see sometimes what they doo in the cuntry. I trust the Lord will direct your father what way is beest, and I doute not that we shall pray, on for another.

I could wisch that my cosen Adams weare out of the howes, for I am perswaded he will give the other side what assistance he can. If you thinke good, tell your father so: your father dous not know what counsells they haue in Hearifordsheare, and what way they goo.

The captaine of the voluntiers is one Barell, he was a tradesman, and once maire of Heariford.

It is so late I will but wisch you a good night, and I pray God blles you, and in His good time giue you a comfortabell meeting with

  Your most affectinat mother, BRILLIANA HARLEY.
July 17, 1642. *Brompton Castell.*

CLXXVII.

For my deare sonne Mr. Edward Harley.

My deare Ned—I longe to see you, but would not haue you come downe, for I cannot thinke this cuntry very safe; by the papers I haue sent to your father, you will knowe the temper of it. I hope your father will giue me full derections how I may beest haue my howes gareded, if need be; if he will giue the derections, I hope, I shall foolow it.

My deare Ned, I thanke God I am not afraide. It is the Lords caus that we haue stood for, and I trust, though our iniquitys testify aganst vs, yet the Lord will worke for His owne name sake, and that He will now sheawe the men of the world that it is hard fighting against heauen. And for our comforts, I thinke neuer any laide plots to route out all Gods chillderen at once, but that the

Lord did sheawe Himselfe mighty in saveing His saruants and confounding His enimyes, as He did Pharowe, when he thought to haue destroyed all Israell, and so Haman. Nowe, the intention is, to route out all that feare God, and surely the Lord will arise to healpe vs: and in your God let your confidence be, and I am assured it is so. One meet Samuell and not knoweing wheare he dwelt, Samuell toold him he was a Darbesheare man, and that he came lately from thence, and so he did in discours; the papis toold him, that theare was but a feawe puretaines in this cuntry, and 40 men would cut them all off.

Had I not had this ocation to send to your father, yet I had sent this boy vp to Loundoun; he is such a rogeisch boy that I dare not keepe him in my howes, and as littell do I dare to let him goo in this cuntry, least he ioyne with the company of vollentirs, or some other such crwe. I haue giuen him no more money then will sarue to beare his charges vpe; and becaus I would haue him make hast and be sure to goo to Loundoun, I haue toold him, that you will giue him something for his paines, if he come to you in good time and doo not loyter; and heare inclosed I haue sent you halfe a crowne. Giue him what you thinke fitte, and I desire he may not come downe any more, but that he may be perswaded to goo to seae, or some other imployment. He thinkes he shall come downe againe. Good Ned, do not tell Martaine that I send him vp with such an intention. I haue derected theas letters to you, and I send him to you, becaus I would not haue the cuntry take notis, that I send to your father so offten; but when such ocations come, I must needs send to him, for I can rely vpon nobodys counsell but his. I pray God blles you and presarue you in safety, and the Lord in mercy giue you a comfortabell meeting with

 Your most affectinat mother, BRILLIANA HARLEY.

July 19, 1642. *Brompton Castell.*

My cosen Dauis tells me that none can make shot but thos whous trade it is, so I haue made the plumer rwite to Woster for 50 waight of shot. I sent to Woster, becaus I would not haue it knowne. If your father thinke that is not enoufg, I will send for more. I pray you tell your father that my cosen Robert Croft is in the cuntry. My cosen Tomkins is as violent as euer, and many thinke that her very words, is in the Heariford resolutions. I beleeue it was Mr Masons pening. He is gone to Yorke, for when he carried the letter from the gentellmen in this cuntry, he was made the kings chapline.

CLXXVIII.

For my deare sonne Mr. Edward Harley.

My deare Ned—I did hope that Richard Sanky would haue come downe this night, which made me defer my rwiteng tell now that it is time to goo to beed. Mr Ellton came aboute 4 a cloke: he tells me that the commiscioners desires to haue mony for three months pay for a hors. Sr Richard Hopton comes not at them, nor Sr Ihon Kirle; Mr Wigmore stands much vpon his points, he will scase looke vpon any one; and your cosen Tomkins made the most slightest ansure that on could make, when shee was toold, that I would goo out of the cuntry. I pray God blles you, and giue you comfortabell meeting with

Your most affectinat mother,   BRILLIANA HARLEY.
July 23, 1642.

Remember me to your sister; it is so late I could not rwite to her.

CLXXIX.

To her son Edward.

My deare Ned—I must needs thanke you for your two letters this weake; for, beleeue me, in this trubellsome time and your fathers absence and yours, your letters are of much comfort to me. My deare Ned, at first when I sawe how outrageously this cuntry carried themselfes aganst your father, my anger was so vp, and my sorrow, that I had hardly patience to stay; but now, I haue well considered, if I goo away I shall leaue all that your father has to the pray of our enimys, which they would be glad of; so that, and pleas God, I purpos to stay as long as it is poscibell, if I liue; and this is my resolution, without your father contradict it.

I cannot make a better use of my life, next to saruing my God, than doo what good I can for you. Wigmore faire is to be on munday next. You may gees at the resons why I would not speake to Mr Wigmore or his asociats to be at the faire; and thairefore I sent for Mr Ellton, whoo promised to come this night. I stayed supper till past ten a clocke, but he came not. I did hope to haue sent you word by him what they did at Heariford * * * * * horsess at Roos * * * * bought 30. Sr William Croft and Mr Wigmore, as they say, will goo with him to the kinge.

I pray you tell your father that they sent to the kinge on thursday, and till they haue an ansure they are not resolued what to doo. It is very late, theairefore I can say no more; but I pray God blles you with all His bllesinges, and I hope you will alwaies be the joye of your

   Most affectinat mother,   BRILLIANA HARLEY.

July 2, 1642. *Brompton Castell.*

I thanke God all your brothers and sisters are well. I haue reseued this night the hamper with the powder and macth, but I haue not yet the muskets, but will and pleas God, enquire after them.

CLXXX.

For my much honnored frinde Mrs. Wallcote, at Wallcote.

Most worthy frinde—I had rather intreate a kindenes from you then from any I knowe; assureing meselfe you will doo the same to me, in home you have as much interest in, as in any.

I haue had of late in the mending of the leeds of my howes bine inforsed to lay out an extriordary some of money; and Edward Dally with others, oweing me rent, I can not as yet geet it; if you can lend me 40*l.* for halfe or a quarter of a yeare, I shall take it as a greate kindenes, and I will pay the interest of it with all my hart, and giue you any securety my sonne and I can giue you, which I hope will be enough for a greater some. So recommending you unto the protection of God, I rest,

Your most affectinat frinde,   BRILLIANA HARLEY.

Augs. 18, 1642.

I desire to haue my saruis presented to Mr Wallcote and your sonne.

CLXXXI.*

For my much honnored frinde Mrs. Wallcote, at Wallcote.

My much honnored and deare frinde,—I acknowledg this as a greate fauor, and I shall be ready to expres my thankes with all the

---

* This Letter is accompanied by Mr. Walcot's acquittance, endorsed thus in Sir Edward Harley's handwriting:—

M^m. That I heard not of ye 20 ll within specified but of late: and though I was not by cours of law obliged to ye payment, yet, reckoning myself by ye law of conscience (wch is true honor) bound to pay it, if due, I bless ye Lord who hath enabled mee to pay it.

E. H.

Also in Mary Walcot's handwriting, on a separate paper:—

Whereas I am informed that there is some question between the hon^{ble} Sr Edward Harley and John Walcot Esq. concerning twenty pounds lent by Humphrey Walcot Esq. in the time of the late warres to the Honble the Lady Brilliana Harley, I can testifie that seuerall times since the decease of the said Humphrey, I have heard my mother in law Ann Walcot, his relict, mention the said twenty pounds, as certainly lent and never repaid.

Witness my hand this 31st of Decem. 1667.   MARY WALCOT.

Acq't'ce fro Mr Walcot:—

Received this twenty-first day of March 1682 of Sr Edward Harley of Bramton Castle in the county of Hereford k^t of the hon^{ble} order of the Bath by mee John Walcott of Walcott in the county of Salop Esq. the sum of twenty pounds of lawfull English money in full of all moneys debts reckonings and accompts whatsoever due vnto my late ffather Humphrey Walcott, Esq. dec^d or vnto my late mother Ann Walcott (the relict of the sa^d

testimony of true respets, and I acknowledge, that for the vertues you haue, I much loue and honnor you. I haue receued the 20*l.* you are pleased to lend me, and I haue made a bill of the resaite of it, and my sonne and meselfe haue put our hands to the resaite of it, and I will and pleas God pay you very shortly.

I desire to haue my saruis presented to Mr Wallcote and your sonne; and desire you to beleeue that I am most vnfainedly

Your most affectinat frinde,   BRILLIANA HARLEY.

Augt: 22, 1642. *Brompton Castell.*

CLXXXII.*

To her son Edward.

My deare Ned—My hart has bine in no rest sence you went. I confes I was neuer so full of sorrow. I feare the prouicion of corne and malt will not hoold out, if this continue; and they say they will burne my barnns; and my feare is that they will place soulders so

---

Humphrey Walcott) decd or unto mee the said John Walcott from sd Robert Harley late of Bramton Castle aforesaid in the said county of Hereford kn{t} of the Bath decd or from dame Brilliana Harley decd or from the said Sr Edward Harley by bond bill promise agreement or otherwise from the beginning of the world untill the day of the date of these p'sents and the said John Walcott doe for me my heirs executors adm{ors} and assigns and every of them acquitt release and for euer discharge the said Sr Edward Harley his heirs ex{tors} and adm{rs} and every of them by these p'sents of and from the said sume of twenty pounds and every part and parcell thereof and of and from all bonds bills reckonings and accompts for or touching the said sume of twenty pounds or any part thereof or for or touching any cause matter or thing whatsoever due or payable as aforesaid In witness whereof the said John Walcott haue hereunto put my hand and seale the said twenty-first day of March in the five-and-thirtieth year of the reign of o{r} sovereign Lord King Charles the Second over England &c. a°q' D'ni 1682.

J. WALCOT. (S).

Signed and sealed and delivered
   in the presence of
NEH. KETTILBY.
J. FUMDWEN.
THOMAS PROSSER.

* The original is written on cloth.

neare me that theare will be no gooing out. My comfort is that you are not with me, least they should take you; but I doo most dearly mis you. I wisch, if it pleased God, that I weare with your father. I would haue rwite to him, but I durst not rwite vpon papaper. Deare Ned, rwite to me, though you rwite vpon a peace of clothe, as this is. I pray God blles you, as I dsier my owne soule should be bllesed. Thears a 1000 dragonears came into Harford 5 owers affther my lord Harferd.

Your mother, BRILL: HAR.

Desem: 13, 1642.

CLXXXIII.

To her son Edward.

My deare Ned—I thanke you for your letter by Proser; he is a trusty mesenger. I must now tell you how gratious our God has bine to vs: on the soboth day affter I receued the letter from the markis, we sett that day apart to sceeke to our God, and then on munday we prepared for a seege; but our good God called them another way; and the markis sent me word he remembered him to me, and that I need not feare him, for he was gooing away, but bide me feare him that came affter him.

Mr Connisbe is the gouernor of Heariford, and he sent to me a letter by Mr Wigmore. I did not let him come into my howes, but I went into the garden to him. Your father will sheawe you the letter; they are in a mighty violence against me; they reueng all that was doune vpon me, so that I shall feare any more parlament forsess comeing into this cuntry: and deare Ned, when it is in your power sheaw kindenes to them, for they must be overcome so. Bardlam has played the very traitor to me, and Richard Bytheway neuer comes at me: Mr Phillips takes much care and pains. Deare Ned, rwite him thankes tho it be but in a littell scripe of paper. My deare Ned, I pray you aduis with your father wheather he thinkes it best that I should put away most of the men that are in my howes, and wheather it be best for me to goo from Brompton, or by Gods healp to stand it out. I will be willing to doo what he would have me doo. I neuer was in such sorrows, as I haue bine sence you left me; but I hope the Lord will deleuer me; but they are most cruely beent against me. I thanke you for your counsell, not to take theair words; the Lord in mercy presarue you, and if it be His holy will, giue me the comfort of seeing you, in home is much of the comfort of

  Your affectinat mother,   BRILLIANA HARLEY.

Desem: 25, 1642.

CLXXXIV.

To her son Edward.

My deare Ned—Your wellcome letter I receued on munday last, but Hopkis was taken at Rickards Castell, but sent me your fathers letter and yours. But I heare he had 6 other letters, and they weare carryed to Mr Coningsby. He is still at Heariford. How he will be used I knowe not; for poor Griffits was cruelly used, but he is now seet at liberty. But the poore drumer is still in the dungon, and Griffits says he fears he will dye. I cannot send to releas him.

My deare Ned, I know it will greeue you to know how I am used. It is with all the malice that can be. Mr Wigmore will not let the fowler bringe me any foule, nor will not suffer any of my saruants pas. They haue forbid my rents to be payed. They draue away the yong horsess at Wigmore, and none of my saruants dare goo scarce as fare as the towne. And deare Ned, if God weare not mercyfull to me, I should be in a very miserabell condistion. I am threatened euery day to be beseet with soulders. My hope is, the Lord will not deliuer me nor mine into theair hands; for surely they would use all cruellty towards me, for I am toold that they desire not to leaue your father neather roote nor branch. You and I must forgiue them. Deare Ned, desire the prayers of the godly for us at

Brompton. I desire to * * * * * * * as it is poscibell that I may keepe the possestion of your fathers howes for him.

I know not wheather this will come to your hand or no, but this I know, that I longe to heare from you, and I pray God blles you, as I desire the soule should be bllesed, of your

Most affectinat mother,   BRILLIANA HARLEY.
Jany. 28, 1642.

CLXXXV.

For my deare sonne Mr. Edward Harley.

My deare Ned—I am confident you longe to heare from me, and I hope this will come to your hand, though it may be it will be long first. We are still threatned and iiniured as much as my enimyes can poscibell. Theare is non that beares part with me but Mr Jams, whoo has shouwed himselfe very honnest; none will looke towards Brompton, but such as truely fears God; but our God still takes care of vs, and has exceedingly sheawed His power in presaruing vs. Nine days past my lord Harberd was at Heariford, whear he stayed a weake; theare was heald a counsell of ware, what was the beest way to take Brompton; it was concluded to blow it vp, and which counsell pleased them all. The sherife of Radnorsheare, with the trained bands of that county and some of Hearifordsheare soulders, weare to come against me. My lord Harberd had apointed a day to come to Prestine, that so his presence might perswade them to goo out of theare county. He had commanded them to bring pay for vitals for 10 days. The soulders came to Prestine, but it pleased God to call my lord Harbrd another way, for thos in the forest of Deane, grwe so strong, that they weare afraid of them.

Now they say, they will starue me out of my howes; they haue taken away all your fathers rents, and they say they will driue away the cattell, and then I shall haue nothing to liue vpon; for all theare ame is to enfors me to let thos men I haue goo, that then they might seas vpon my howes and cute our throughts by a feawe rooges, and then say, they knewe not whoo did it; for so they say, they knewe not whoo draeue away the 6 coolts, but Mr Connigsby keepes them, though I haue rwite to him for them. They haue vsed all means to leaue me haue no man in my howes, and tell me, that then I shall be safe; but I haue no caus to trust them. I thanke God we are all well. I long to see my cosen Hackellt. I pray God blles you.

Your most affectinat mother,   BRILLIANA HARLEY.

Feb. 14, 1642.

CLXXXVI.

For my deare sonne Mr. Edward Harley.

My deare Ned—Your littell vollome of paper sent by Bonde had a long wellcome. I am very glad that your sister is recouered. If Mr Moores man Makelin has told you nothing, I pray you aske him, what Mr Moore bide him tell you. Docter Wright and his wife presents theare saruis to you, and Mr Phillpis has bine, and is very carefull. Mr Hill has vndertaken to bring the water into the mote. I ventured but 20th but he has had many oposits, but Mr Gower was for him. I hope it will be doun. I pray God blles you with all blessings.

Your most affectinat mother,   BRILLIANA HARLEY.

I thanke God your brother and sisters are well.

Feb. 23, 1642.

CLXXXVII.

For my deare sonne Mr. Edward Harley.

My deare Ned—I rwite to you the other day by Mr Taylor, and I am as glad to doo it now, and I hope this will come safe to your hand.

I am in the same condistion as I was; still amongst my enimys, who now threeten me not with forsess, becaus the soulders are goon before Gloster; theaire randevous is S^r Ro. Cookes howes. My deare

Ned, desire your father to send me word what he thinkes I had beest doo; for if I should put away the men in my howes, I should be eury day plundered, and as basely vsed as it is poscibell, and I can receaue no rents.

Sam Piner toold who went with you, and so Leeg and Poell are indited.

Mr Yaets and Mr Lowe and Edward Pin. goo towards Loundoun the next weake. Edward Pin. biusnes is to speake with your father aboute the legacy he should pay Mr Poells daughter; he has sould land to her husband, and he would haue him take the mony of your father. I would not haue had him goo vp to Loundoun, becaus I thinke it is not a time for your father to take vp mony to pay that legacy, that the land is still in question; but your brother tells me Piners intentiene is to geet more lives on Buckton for that mony. If your father pleas to consider it, I thinke it is not so much for his profit to let on man haue so many liueings in his hand; for then they put poore tenants into them, and let the howses goo downe, and your father has but on tenant, for his tenant haueing 2 or 3. I pray you speake to your father about it. Good Mr Bayley is come to me. They rage more then euer. I pray God keepe vs from them; and, deare Ned, pray for vs and desire all good Christians to doo so. The Lord in mercy blles you, and giue me, a comfortabell seeing of you, who hoold you as deare as my owne soule.

Your most affectinat mother, BRILLIANA HARLEY.

I longe to see your sister Brills sonn.

I think it seuen yeare tell he come.

I sent you all your linnens the last saterday.

Mr William Griffits tooke them with him, and promised to send them to his brother Gorge.

I purpos to send your man vp to you, when Piner goos, for I beleeue you will hardly haue on that is better and loues you more.

Feb. 25, 1642.

[1642-3.]

CLXXXVIII.*

For Mr. Edward Harley.

Deare Ned,

[*I desire you*] imagin to [*would pray*] all strength and [*your father*] go all to geather; why did I rong my judgment so as to [*to send me*] let vs the [*word what*] world. As for to loue wheare I did know [*he would haue*] all be it [*doo: if I put*] it is strang [*away the*] theare was no hoold to be taken for what my wisches [*men I shall*] thirst if [*be plundered*] once of it my hart can bost straight by her [*and if I*] is [*haue no*] forsaken [*rents, I know*] off haue I wisched that when theare had bine some [*not what*] all mineche [*cours to*] for to haue seene when loue with her had bine [*take*] in season [*If I leaue*] but I [*Brompton*] perseaue theare is no art, can finde the [*all will be*] of that [*ruened*] hart that loues by chance and not by reson. [*Mr Coningsby*] if and [*swore he*] violent [*would be*] Cato Johannes, the Grecian emperour, vp with came [*in Brompton*] with a [*within five*] wast Army of hors and foote, and demand [*days*] cold and [*I heare*] with diemns [*he has*] to resign vnto him all places of strentg, togeather [*a commition*] with all the [*to displace*] forse he had, and then he seet forward to [*all ministers*] he too [*and put*] them [*in others*] all places without resistance as you haue hard [*so it be*] to the greef [*doun with*] of many I cannot heare what is to be doun, and

---

* This Letter is read by a key of cut paper, the openings of which correspond with the words within the brackets.

[*the bischops*] that is [*consent*] all I can [*I would*] heare at this time, as I lived on an [*not haue y^o*] penny [*beleeue*] yeare as frinds togeather, but now thee [*all that will*] is gon [*be toold*] I know [*you about*] not wheather could I but gees; I doo protest [*the bringing*] I speak [*of the water*] it not to flatter of all the women in the [*Mr Hill has*] world [*undertaken*] I newer [*it, and I*] would come at her tho grecionce came in [*hope will*] all has [*effect it*].

You must pin that end of the paper, that has the cors made in incke, vpon the littell cros on the end of this letter; when you would write to me, make vse of it, and giue the other to your sister Brill. I beceach the Lord to blles you, and deare Ned, be carefull of yourselfe. I did not send your man, whoo has a greate desire to be with you, becaus I did not know wheather you would haue him; if you would, send me worde, for I thinke you will hardly geet a better in theas days. I shall long to heare from you.

Your most affectinat mother, BRILLIANA HARLEY.

I haue sent you your linen. Doctor Wright and M^rtris Wright presents theare saruis to you.

Mar: the first, 1642.

CLXXXIX.

To her son Edward.

My deare,

[*This day I*] went a [*heare that*] great way [*Sr Wm Cro*] so that they all pudd and watters weare when first [*has sent forth*] I sawe and [*a warent to*] hard from the yong men giue, and Rich they are of the

[*that somens,*] same year [24 *to come*] they are [*into Her:*] and sisters chillderen are not, and are of opinion as thos [*on munday*] that are [*next, to wittnes*] of a more constants mind and testament the next in degres [*to dismanors*] can come [*and crimes*] are brother [*laide to the*] the more kindred the greater affinity the more a man is [*charge of*] honoured is [*your father*] they must as well become kindsmen or frindes [*yourselfe*] to theair [Mr *James*] frindes as [Mr *Dauis*] it self is satisfied and redeemed with a sartane number of [Mr *Gower*] beasts [Mr *Lowe*] which contenteth the whoole famely, and is profitabel [Mr *Yaets*] to the for [Mr *Beale*] common [*by Dickien*] good for wheare liberty is theare is priuet of [*the vnder*] are not I [*shereffe,*] and entertainements in no weare more beautifull [*so that it*] then theare [*seemes the*] to beare [*under-sherefe*] any man his howes, and not giue him meate or [*is the*] and drinke [*accusor of*] when all is spent the last host will be to the next [*you all. The*] howes and [*butler saw*] for united [*the warent*] and are recewed with like curtesy and respect hospetallity [*in the baylefes*] of theare [*hand, and*] make you no diferance wheather it be of or from or a [*he rent it.*] greate and [*Meredife the*] or not [*ranger, and*] if any thing the manor is to grante it demand or if so [*Tom Child*] you and he [*and Daile*] as thinges aske the as thinges that pleas but thos that well [*of Lainterdin*] doo not [*and Hopkis*] thinkee [*of Dounen*] they you and not bond or beholden for them they enter [*are some*] theare gees [*of the* 24.] which they wasch in warme haueing long winter [*The rest of*] and when [*the names*] they full [*I know not*]. to eate euery man stoul and to himself.

Then full [*Hellische plots*] to theare [*they haue,*] biusness and make good cheere to seet and stvnd [*but I hope*] the a day is [*the Lord will*] not disgras [*disapoint*] to many and commonly it hapneth but selldome with offten [*them. I am*] with mirth [*still threatned.*] of all and make and chuse meate when neuer more [*I heare you*] vpon to [*are to haue*] plaine [*a company*] dealeing or more stirred vp or the neathe carefty or sutell end [*of hors. I pray*] dous not [*you send me*] discours or say nothing and the euery mens minde bring [*word wheather*] or is to [*it be so*] or the next [*or no.*] shall with or regard

I hope Edward Piner is come to Loundoun, and that you haue receaued my letter by him, and then you will not maruell at this nonesence, which I haue writen to you to make you merry. I beceach the Lord in much mercy to blles you, and that I may haue againe the comfort of seeing you, whoo are very deare to me. Your brother is much better than he was, and does much reioyce that you wisched him with you. Tell your father what I haue writen; he may eassyly gees at the reson why I did not wright to him. I thanke God, we are all well, and I long to see your sisters sonne come downe. Deare Ned, tell your sister I pray God to blles her; and present my saruis to my brother; so I rest

Your most affectinat mother, BRILLIANA HARLEY.

Mar: 3, 1642.

CXC.

For my deare sonne Mr. Edward Harley.

My deare Ned—By what I haue writ to your father you will see what they meane to doo with me and mine. You will see my ansure, and I hope the Lord will derect me what to doo when the time comes, and I trust He that has deleuerd me will deleuer me.

The Lord in mercy presarue you and keep you, and in His good time giue vs a comfortabell meeting; and, deare Ned, pray for Brompton, and

Your most affectinat mother, BRILLIANA HARLEY.

Mar: 4, 1642.

Mr. Phillips carries himself very well, and all in my howes are of good corage.

CXCI.

For my deare sonne Mr. Edward Harley.

My deare Ned—I should haue bine very glad to haue receued a letter from you by Mr. Taylor; and deare Ned, finde some way or other to rwite to me that I may know how the world goos, and how it is with your father and yourselfe; for it is a death to be amoungst my enimys, and not to heare from thos I loue so dearely.

Heare I haue sent you a coppy of the sommons was sent me; I wisch with all my hart that euery on would take notice what way they take: that if I doo not giue them my howes, and what they would haue, I shall be proseeded against as a trator. It may be euery onse case to be made traytors; for I beleeue eury on will be as vnwilling to part with theare howes as I am. I desire your father would seariously thinke what I had beest doo; wheather stay at Brompton, or remoue to some other place. I heare theare are 600 soulders apointed to come against me. I know not wheather this sessation of armes will stay them. I cannot tell what to think, that I heare nothing of your sister Brills sonne, nor that you did not write me word, that he was come to you. I heare captaine Jeferes is drowned. I am very much behoolding to docter Wright, for he will not goo from Brompton tell he sees me out of my trubell.

Mr. Phillips carrys himselfe very well, and Mr. H   as he was vsed to doo. Good Mr Baughly is faine to come to Brompton.

Mr Legg is still at Brompton, and Mathes and the Wellchmen and Staney and 2 of Knights brothers, who were faine to fly out of theare owne cuntry. My deare Ned, I will promise meselfe a letter from you by this bearer, whoo has carried himselfe very well to me; thearefore I pray you giue him thankes for it. I pray God blles you, and in His good time giue vs a joyfull meeting, which I beleeue you thinke is longed for, by

  Your most affectinat mother, BRILLIANA HARLEY.

I heare they have put vp proclamations in this cuntry, that theare shall be no sessation of armes.

Docter Wright and Mrs Wright remember saruis to you.

Mar: 8, 1642.

CXCII.

For Mr. Edward Harley.

My deare Ned,

[*When*   *the*] in trihumph [*judges came*] to Woster [*not to Hearifrd*] then in haste in the more courtly to what purpose lately trained otherwise [*so that theare*] the viccount [*was nothing*] enriching themselfes vnited vnder erle Simons and Richards to the hassard of [*doun against me*] or any [*at the bench,*] when I sent [*they sent for*] come protesting which now in feareing fell fomented by the supposed [*the*   *trained*] vp in pride [*bands, and haue*] not cared to speake as they from him and her, so they goo one [*taken*   *away*] meate colthes [*thearie armes;*] sowords [*some say to*] gaine as much as can be thought and haue ended the a greete to [*giue the armes*] vp and [*to my lord*] Crauen so when all is doun it comes all togeather [*Harbreds soulders*] and the [*that wante.*] mony? [*They*   *say*] so when all was sould the mony came short and that was so [*that they gaue*] gloues of [*half a crowne*] a peace to comfort them for all loses so they went away [*to every soulder*] howes [*to looke for*] the more [*enimyes*] wheare to the joy of ons hart to the greefe of frends [*every day. They*] went out [*haue taken*] fisch good store which may last a greate while [*Mores lad,*] not bine [*and he is in*] a good howes [*prison at*] wheare is a greate many that loues tobacco came to [*Heariford,*] to liue a time [*becaus he*] neuer thought it had bine so hard a matter hogg and dich [*was with*] Poell to [*me. If I had*] hard of the [*mony to*] come to morrow I had then sent it so now they must [*buy corne*] at another place [*and meale*] somewheare elles, or it will not doo well; but it is strange [*and malt*] I should not [*I should hope*] to render it [*to hoold*] as long as any but brauely and beaten and reduced to obedience [*out, but then*] write [*I haue* 3] yeares heance will be acknowledged to the ioy of all and greefe of [*sheeres against*] which for [*me . . .*]

When you have laught at the nonsense, pleas your self with this, that is reson; I thanke God we are well, though all would not haue it so. I longe to heare from you. Desire your father from me to be carefull of himselfe, and I pray God blles you, and giue you a comfortabell meeting with

Your affectinat mother, BRILLIANA HARLEY.

Mar: 11, 1642.

CXCIII.

For my deare sonne Mr. Edward Harley.

My deare Ned—I was very glad to receaue a letter from you by Proser and by Samleman, but I did hope you would haue bine more at large, for I doo exceedingly long to heare what you doo, and what is beest for me to doo. I heare some say, you haue an imployment, but I will beleeue nothing tell I heare it from your selfe or father. The report in this cuntry is, that my lord Capell comes very shortly to be gowernor of Shrewsbury, and the qu: is to come to Loudlow. I thanke God we are all at Brompton, and desire to knowe when you meane, and pleas God, to moue this way.

I pray God blles you and giue you a comfortabell meeting with

Your most affectinat mother,   BRILLIANA HARLEY.

Doctor Wright and Mrs Wright, whoo yet make me so much behoolding to them as that they are with me, remember theaire saruis to you.

Mar: 25, 1643.

CXCIV.

For my deare sonne Mr. Edward Harley.

My deare Ned—Your wellcome letter by the carrier I haue receued; and deare Ned, let this tell you, God has mightyly bine seene in Hearifordsheere. Mr Conningsby and Sr William Croft and Sr Wallter Pye are at Gloster. I will with all speede send Mr Hill to you. The Lord in mercy blles you.

Remember my deare loue to your father, and my bllesing to your sister. I pray God giue you a happy meeting with her that longes to see you.

Your most affectinat mother,   BRILLIANA HARLEY.

May 6, 1643.

I thanke God we are all well. To my greefe I must tell you that honnest Petter is taken. 6 seet vpon him; 3 shot at him as he was opening a gate not fare from Mortimers Cros. He fought with them valliantly and aquited himself with corage: he hurt 2 of them, and if theare had not bine 6 to on, he had escaped: he is wounded in the head and sholder, but not mortally; he is in prison at Loudlowe. I doun all that is poscibell to get him out, but it cannot be; but I hope the Lord will deleuer him. I haue found him very faithful to me, and he desired to haue come to you.

CXCV.

For my deare sonne Mr. Edward Harley.

My deare Ned—Sence God has put into your harte that you haue taken this imployment vpon you, the Lord in much mercy blles you, and make you to doo wisely and valiently: and now, my deare Ned, you may be confident my very soule goos alonge with you; and becaus I cannot be with you myselfe, I haue sent you on, to be of your troope, and haue furnisched him with a hors. You know he came at the first to Brompton, when our trubells begane, and has faithfully stayed with me, and carried himselfe honestly and with very good corage. He had a desire to come to you, and I as good a desire he should come, and I hope you will find him such a one as I say he is, if not more: the hors coost me 8*l*. I hope it will come safe to your hande, with his rider. I read your letter very well, which came by Looker; but if you would let the paper you write vpon be of the same breath of the cute paper, it would be much better. From this place make vse of the cute paper.

+ [*I pray you*] take into [*consider that*] it has [*Mr. Hill is*] all ways ready and will be still, which I know will reioyce [*much given*] and in [*to keepe*] the beest and richest and wisest so that some weare much [*company and*] to eate [*so to drinke,*] and sleepe [*and I feare*] this day Captaine Croft and his wife weare to see me and so [*will put his*] but all [*minde much to*] no purpos I long to see you more than you can thinke. [*plundering.*] but doo [*Consider well*] and that [*of it.*] Pray God blles you, and giue you comfortabell meeting with

    Your most affectinat mother,   BRILLIANA HARLEY.

May 9, 1643.

Mr Moore is come to stay at Brompton, which I am very glad of. Your brother Robine goos aboute as if he weare discontented, but I know not for what. Mr Phillips carrys himselfe very honestly and carefully, and is impatient to have you come to Brompton, wheare I should be glad to see you. Petter is still in prison at Loudlow. 5 men seet vpon him; he fought very valiently with them all; they had carrabins and pole axes. I am very sorry for him, and I haue doun all I can to geet him out. I will trye once againe what my lord Capell will doo; he was hurt in three places. Deare Ned, take it well that Mr Legg is so willing to come, and I hope you will vse him kindely.

CXCVI.

To her son Edward.

My deare Ned—I receaued your letter by the carrier of Lemster, and beleeue me, it was extremely wellcome to me, and therefore, let me prenaile with you to rwite to me as offten as you can. I am sorry you say nothing of Mr Leggs coming to you: if you doo not like him, he will willingly returne to Brompton. For Mr Mountaine (I beleeue you understand that name in France; I mean he that you thought of, for a place in your trope) I find, he was altogether given to shifting, and I dout his faithfulness. Any thing shall be digested for mony with him. I beleue it is true; thearefore deare Ned, take heede of your choys.

I hope you will let me know as soune as you can when you begine your journey; and the Lord in much mercy blles and prosper you, and giue me in His good time a joyfull seeing of you, which I long to doo; . . . as much longes for you. The water is brought quite into the greene court, and I thinke you will like the worke well. I like it so well, that I would not haue it undoun for a great . . . Petter is still in prison theare;

. . . . fident that I cannot well . . . which the ocation that all the Wellchmen are goone from me. Good Mr Moore is with me and is much comfort to me, and so is Doctor Wright and his wife, whoo promises not to leaue mee till my trubells are past.

I am confident you pray for us at Brompton, and I pray you doo so, and the Lord in mercy blles you, as I desire the soule should be bllesed, of

Your most affectinat mother, BRILLIANA HARLEY.

Deare Ned, remember me to your sister Brill. I was very glad to receue a letter from my brother. . . .

Poore Petter wisched himselfe many times with you before he was taken. He is used better nowe then he was at Loudlow.

May 28, 1643.

CXCVII.

To her son Edward.

My deare Ned—I did hope I should haue had a letter from you this weake, by the carrier, but I mised of that comfort; but I was so much beholding to Mr Moore that he rwite me word you weare well.

I pray God send you well into the cuntry. Take heede of your choys of that man, I haue rwrite you of hearetofore.

We are pretty quiet, but still in the . . . condistion. We are still threatened. Some soulders are billeted in Pursla. I pray God send the faire well past ouer. The worke aboute the court is almost ended, and I thinke you will like it well. I rwite to my nephewe Pelham, whoo is cornet to my lord Capell, but he has not goot Petters releas. He write me an ansure with some hope of his releas. I am very sorry for him; he has bine used pittifully.

I could say much more, but I know not wheather this will come to your hand. I pray God blles you, and giue you a comfortabell meeting with

Your most affectinat mother,   BRILLIANA HARLEY.

June 3, 1643.

I pray you remember me to your sister Brill. Doctor Wright and his wife remember theaire saruis to you.

CXCVIII.

To her son Edward.

O! my deare Ned—that I could but see you! I liue in hope that the Lord will giue me that comfort, which I confes, I am not worthy of. I heare from a good hand that you are ready to come out of Loundoun. The Lord in much mercy goo with you and make you to doo worthyly; and deare Ned, beleeue my hart and soule is with you.

I hard from Gloster on thursday last, by on I sent a purpos. Sr William Waller went on tuesday towards the west. Lef.curenell Massy is commanded to be gouerner of Gloster by my lord jenerall. I haue and am exceedingly behoolding to corenell Massy, as much as I was ever to on, I did not know; and I pray you tell your father so, and pray him to giue him thankes. I sent to him to desire him to send me an abell soulder, that might reguelate the men I haue, and he has sent me on that was a sargent, an honnest man, and I thinke an abell soulder; he was in the Jerman wars. He came to me on thursday last, but your brother has the name of the command. I writ to you the last weake, that the Wellchmen weare goone from me; this bearer will tell you the reson. Honnest Petter is come out of prison. He was greeuiously vsed in Loudlow. Turkes could have vsed him no wors; a lefftenant corenell Marrow would come every day and kicke him vp and downe, and they laied him in a dungon vpon foule straw. Mr Goodwine sheawed him kindnes. In Shreawesbury he was vsed well for a prisoner; but he is very glad he is come home againe, and so am I. The Lord in mercy blles you, and giue you a comfortabell meeting with

    Your most affectinat mother,   BRILLIANA HARLEY.

Mr Phillips is very carefull, and longes to see you.

June 11, 1643.

I shall be full of douts tell the fare be past. Some soulders are come to Knighton; my old frinds that weare theare before.

CXCIX.

For my deare sonne Mr. Edward Harley.

My deare Ned—I hard from Loundoun that you with Sr Arter Hasellrike left Loundoun on Friday was senight, and that your intentions weare to hast to Sr William Waller. I haue some hope that theas lines may meet with you, which if they doo, my deare Ned, let them assure you my hart is with you; and I hope my God will blles you. This bearer can tell you the state of Heariford-schere. You know you are the comfort of my life, thearefore thinke it not strange, if my thoughts are so much with you.

The Lord in much mercy blles and presarue you, and giue you a comfortabell meeting with

    Your most affectinat mother,   BRILLIANA HARLEY.

June 19, 1643.

I thanke God we are all well at Brompton.

CC.

For my deare sonne Captaine Harley.

My deare Ned—I receued your letter dated the 17 of this month, which was dearely wellcome to me, becaus it brought me word that you weare safely come to Sr William Waller, wheare the Lord of heauen and earth blles you and presarue you. My hart is with you, and I know you beleeue it; for my life is bonnd vp with yours. My deare Ned, sence you desire your brother to come to you, I cannot be vnwilling he should goo to you, to home I pray God make him a comfort.

If Mr Hill be with you, and you would be free of him, you may if pleas you, tell him I desire he should come to me, and so you may send him to me: if your brother will speake freely, he can tell you of his carage. My deare Ned, if you wante any thinge that I can healp you to, I pray you send to me; and be sure I will wante myselfe, before you shall. Your brother will tell you how this cuntry is, and I pray you take care of your brother, and I beccach the Lord to blles you and him, and in His good time to giue me a joyfull meeting with you.

Your most affectinat mother,   BRILLIANA HARLEY.

Your father was, I thanke God, very well on tusday last. I had not a letter from him, but Mr Moore wrote me word so. I am very sorry that my brother has doun what he has. I haue bide your brother tell you what I haue hard.

CCI.
To her son Edward.

My deare Ned—On saterday I receued your letter by Raphe. Your being well is mine, and thearefore you may beleeue I reioyce in it. That you left me with sorrow, when you went last from Brompton, I beleeue; for I thinke, with comfort I thinke of it, that you are not only a child, but on with child-like affections to me, and I knowe you haue so much vnderstanding that you did well way the condition I was in; but I beleeue it, your leaueing of me was more sorrow then my condition could be; but I hope the Lord will in mercy giue you to me again, for you are both a Joseph and a Beniamin to me, and deare Ned, longe to see me; and I hope when you haue spent some littell time in the army you will come to Brompton. Sence you desired your brother to come to you, I could not deny it, though I was loth to leaue him. I hope he is come, before this, safe to you; and I pray God blles you both togeather, and that I may agene haue you returne in safety with your deare father. In this cuntry they begine to rais nwe tropes, and they haue seast the country at 1200*l.* a-month. My lo. Harbert and colonel Vaueser whoo is to be gouerner of Heariford, is gone vp into Moungomeryscheere to rais soulders. All of them are returned into Hearifordsheere; Sr Wallter Pye, Mr Brabson, Mr Smaleman, Mr Wigmore, Mr Ligen, and Mr Stiles and Gardnas, whoo has quartered soulders in Kingsland, and they say, that besides the 1200*l.* a month, theare must be free quarter for soulders. They counsell, but the Lord in mercy defeate theaire counsells. I must looke for nwe one-seets, but I hope I shall looke to my rocke of defence, the Lord my God, from home is deleuerance. Out of Chescheere, I heare from a sure hand, that on the 19 of this month Sr William Brerton sent out a party of hors into Sharpschere, but when they weare plundering at Hanmere, the lo. Capells tropes supprised them; they hasted to theaire horsess and fleed, but theare was taken prisnors of them the leftenan colonell and captain leftenant Sanky, and 13 more taken prisners, and about 12 slaine, and many more wounded. They vsed the prisnors very barborously. All Lancascheere is cleered, only Latham howes. My lord of Darby has left that county, which they take ill. My deare Ned, I know you loue to heare how I doo. I thanke God, beyond my expectation or that of some in my howes, my prouistions has heald out; and I haue borrowed yet not much mony, though my tenants will not pay me, and Coolborn deales very ill with me, and will pay me no mony; and Mr Connisbys steward sent to him to know wheather he would receaue the 6 coolts, and he neuer toold me of it, but sent them word he durst not. This Mr Eaton rwite me word of yesterday.

Your brother can tell you I sent for a sargent to colonnell Massey, and he sent me one, and I hope he will doo very well. As you desired to haue some honnest man sent you, I did as much desire to send you some. Those that I thought would haue gone gladly, findes out excusses, but theas 3 desired to goo, to venture theair liues with you, or elles they would not goo from me. Doctor Write asked his man the question, but the poore gardner and Stangy desired it of themselfes, and they seet forward with good corage. I will endeuor to see wheather any will contribute to buy a hors; but thos that haue harts haue not means, and they that haue means haue not harts. I doo not send you Jack Griffets, becaus I thought you might like Phillip Loouke, whoo is a pretty inienious fellow, but if you would haue Griffets, I pray you let me know by Raphe, and I will, if pleas God, send him to you. By Raphe and the rest I haue sent yon your bookes. Deare Ned, I could say much more to you, but I haue run out my paper. The Lord of Heauen blles you and presarue you, and make you to doo worthely and to outliue all theas trubells.

Your most affectinat mother,   BRILLIANA HARLEY.
June 30, 1643.

I am confident you will hate all plundering and vnmercifullness. I pray you aske your brother what I bide him tell you concerning Mr Hill.

CCII.
To her son Edward.

My deare Ned—My cosen Dauis has desired much to see you, and thearefore I am so much behoolding to him that he dous me the kindnes to be the bearer of these lines, by which I am glad to let you know I haue reseaued your letter by Raphe. You may beleeue, it was welcome, for I had long desired it. I acknowledge the greate mercy of my God that He presarued you in so sharp a fight, when your hors was killed. The Lord my God presarue you still, and I trust that He will still continue His mercy to . . . . that I may againe see you with comfort.

I am sorry you haue lost so many hors out of your trope; but I hope they will be made up againe. I knowe not what they will doo heareafter, but, as yet, I can get but very little towards the byeing of a hors; what it is, I haue sent you inclosed. If you want any thing I can possibilly healp you to, let me knowe it, and I will . . .

I hard this day that your father and sister weare well this day senight. What is to be knowne of theas parts this bearer will tell you. Out of Schesheare I heare that Haughton Castell is still besieged by Sir William Breerton, and it is thought cannot hoold out. Two tropes of hors went out of Chester to rais the siege of Haughton Castell, but they weare beaten backe.

My deare Ned, the Lord in mercy presarue you in all fights, and giue me . . . .
and which is . . desired by

Your most affectinat mother, BRILLIANA HARLEY.

July 11, 1643.

CCIII.

To her son Edward.

My deare Ned—I cannot but venture theas lines, but wheather you are at Loundoun or no, I know not. Now, my deare Ned, the gentillmen of this cuntry haue affected theair desires in bringing an army against me. What spoyls has bine doun, this barer will tell you. Sir William Vavasor has left Mr Lingen with the soulders. The Lord in mercy presarue me, that I fall not unto theair hands. My deare Ned, I beleeue you wisch yourself with me; and I longe to heare of you, whoo are my great comfort in this life. The Lord in mercy blles you and giue me the comfort of seeing you and your brother.

Your most affectinat mother, BRILLIANA HARLEY.

August 25, 1643.

Mr Phillips has taken a greate deale of paines and is full of corage, and so is all in my howes, with honnest Mr Petter and good Docter Wright and Mr Moore, whoo is much comfort to me. The Lord direct me what to doo; and, deare Ned, pray for me that the Lord in mercy may presarue me from my cruell and blood thirsty enemys.

CCIV.

For my deare sonne Mr. Edward Harley.

My deare Ned—I receaued your most wellcome letter by Mr Greens man, but I had none by Fischer, which did trubell me. I hope before this, you are assured of the Lords mercy to vs in deleuering vs from our enimys.

My deare Ned, a thousand times I wisch you with me, and then I should hope, by Gods assistance, to keepe what is left your father with comefort. It is true, my affection makes me long to see you, and my reson tells me it would be good for you for to employ yourselfe for the good of your cuntry, and that which I hope shall be yours. My deare Ned, if the Lord should be so mercifull, it would be such a comfort, that it would reuive my sad hart and refresch my dryed vp spirits.

The Lord in mercy derect you and presarue you, and giue you a comfortabell meeteing with

Your most affectinat mother,   BRILLIANA HARLEY.

My deare Ned, let me know your minde wheather I had beest stay or remoue.

Remember me to your brother.

Sep. 24, 1643. *Brompton Castell.*

CCV.

For my deare sonne Colonell Harley.

My deare Ned—Your short but wellcome letter I receaued by Prosser, and as it has pleased God to intrust you with a greater charge, as to change your trope into a regiment, so the Lord in mercy blles you with a dubell measure of abillitys, and the Lord of Hosts be your protector and make you victorious. My deare Ned, how much I longe to see you I cannot expres, and if it be possibell, in parte meete my desires in desireing, in some measure as I doo, to see me; and if pleased the Lord, I wisch you weare at Brompton. I am now againe threatned; there are some souldiers come to Lemster and 3 troopes of hors to Heariford with Sr William Vauasor, and they say they meane to viset Brompton againe; but I hope the Lord will deleuer me. My trust is only in my God, whoo neuer yet failled me.

I pray you aske Mr Kinge what I prayed him to tell you conserning Wigmore.

I haue taken a very greate coold, which has made me very ill thees 2 or 3 days, but I hope the Lord will be mercifull to me, in giuing me my health, for it is an ill time to be sike in.

My deare Ned, I pray God blles you and giue me the comfort of seeing you, for you are the comfort of

    Your most affectinat mother,   BRILLIANA HARLEY.

Octo: 9, 1643.

APPENDIX.

No. I.

LETTERS FROM SIR ROBERT HARLEY, LORD CONWAY, LADY VERE, THE EARL AND COUNTESS OF WESTMORLAND, EDWARD HARLEY, AND MARY HARLEY.

To Mr. EDWARD HARLEY, at Magdalen Hall in Oxford.

Ned Harley—Comend my service to M^r provost and Mr Rouse, and lett them know that I do receeve it as an honor to mee y^{er} intentions to set up my armes in the colledge. I will go (God willinge) send it to them.

There is another seruice which I have impartid to your worthy tutor, which if you like not, new counsailes shal be taken, for I would willingly shew myself, as time shall trie, and truth shall prove, and occasion shall rest contented, your obedient father. But, if otherwise or so, the horses shal be with you on Wednesday, the 11th of the next month, that you may be heere the 14th; and, if you have taken the schoolinge so farr as that you have learned any rhetoricke, file your tong, and bestowe it all on your tutor to p'suade hym to come along with you. In which attempt if you faile, I may say you have spent your time and I my money to small purpose, if your tutor hath not taught you to overcome hym at his owne weapon. Howsoever, *fac periculum*, use your skill, and if you prevayle, send me word by the next, and I will send a horse for the good tutor allso. The Lord in mercy sett and settle His holy feare in your heart, then which nothinge can more inlarge the joye of,

Your most lov'ge father, RO. HARLEY.

Bro'pto: Castle, 18mo 9^{bris}, 1639.

For Mr. EDWARD HARLEY,
at Magd: Hall, in Oxon.

Ned Harley—By my last I acquainted you of my purpose to send horses for you and your worthy tutor, if your logicke or rethoricke can prevayle with hym to honoure you heere with his presence, and my resolution hereby (God will'ge) to send them that they may arrive with you on the 11th of the next month. But if the tutors affaires stand calculated for an other meridian in the verticole point of this yeare, then let this berer, in his returne from London, bring mee a cleere understonding of it, and beseeche your good tutor to be the good genius for a schoolmaster heere. Remember, you haue set saile for heaven: let Ch: be your north starr, His holy word your card, and keepe your canvase pregnant with His feare, and upon my life, you will make a happy voyage. In which hope I joye and rest,

Your most affectionate father,   RO. HARLEY.

Bro'pto' Cast: 25^t 9*bris*, 1639.

For my sonne Mr. EDWARD HARLEY,
at Brōptō Castle.

Ned Harley—I canot advertise you any thinge of your chamber, but I intend to provide one for you as soone as I can. Whilst you are at Brōpton lett no day pass *sine linea*. Walke as an example in love before your brothers and sisters, that they may honoure you next mee and your good mother. See the worship of God kept up in the familye, greeve not your heavenly Father by s——ge agst Hym. So you wilbe the joye of your earthly,   RO. HARLEY.

Comend my love to your brothers and sisters, and to your cossin Smyth.

Little Brittan, 18mo 8*bris*, 1641.

For NED HARLEY.

Ned Harley—I thanke you for your lettre, which you will understande I hope to be an incouragēt to write to mee. I am sorry for the sad accident at Leyntwardine. It is fitt that Pyner should th^{ke} how to provide an other tenant for the mille, and let hym cõferr with Thos. Davyes of Wigmire abote the death of the man.

Divide my blessing betweene yourself and your brothers and sisters, and, if you challenge a double parte, strive to walke worthy of your title to it, which you can never do, unless you feare all s——e, which the Lord in mercye settle in your heart, that you may be the joye of your father,

Ro. Harley.

Com^d me to your cossin Smyth.

London, 30° 8bris, 1641.

LADY VERE to EDWARD HARLEY.

Good Nephew—I am very sory to hear by yor sistars leter of the weakn^s in your arme. I am glad you ar in London, whear you may have the meanes wich I pray God to bles to you, and m'k vs to se the mercy in preserveing yor life with this mark of honor. I did writ latly to you about my sad busnis, it is lick to be very burdensom to me, for I shall not know what to do, if that plas faill me. My hope is in God, who will never fail them that ar His. I know you will not be wanting in any thing wherein you may be helpfull in the busines, wich I beleue you vnderstand so well as to know what is to be done in it, and I know your fathers love and care of me. I hear not it that my nephew Tracy be come, and tell then I hear nothing can be don. God geve me a good end of it, and menes to expres the senserity of my affections, wich shall never faill in loveing and esteming you, and in aproving myself,

Yor most faithfull true loving avnt, Mary Vere.

LORD CONWAY to COLONELL HARLOW.

Nephew—I heare that you are returned to London, hauing heard that your hurte in your arme did grow worse, when it was conceived it was in an estate of melioration. I doubt that you comme to London that you may haue a good chirurgion. I send therefore this to enquire of your health, of which I am very desirous, not onely bycause of your neereness to me, which inciteth euery one to wish wele without other reason, but bycause that I thinke your health will not be ill bestowd on you: and it is very mutch wished to you by,

Your most affectionat vnkle to serue you,

CONWAY AND KILULLA.

Sion, Sep. 28. (1643?)

The EARL of WESTMORLAND to COL. HARLEY.

Cosen—Ther needs noe apollogising wher the inconsiderablenes of your mushrom frends and seruants heer ought and must giuue way to those sublimer occations wherein you with many more heroes or worthyes are wrap. I wish I were but a hewer of wood or a water tanker in this great work begun of reformation, wherein y̆e divel and wicked men cause yet soe many rubbs. But the vpper orbes are wise, and know what sphear is sutable to every p'portion of light. I am fixed in resolution, I assure you; noe roaming, wandring plannet; and therefore it may be, to weak sight may appear a twinkler, though I was born high and a gentleman, though not altogether Welch; therefore must needs say, I contemn y̆t monster parety, soe much now seeks to domineer. I am sorry the treaty ends without beginning. The summer will be the hotter if God (who alone can) p'uent not.

My wife is yet soe weak she sitts not vp, and therefore I thanke you for and from her, and wish you all happiness whither you goe. Resting euer,

Your poor yet truely affectionat kinsman to serve you,

WESTMORLAND.

My love and seruice to y̆r good father. Doe not tel him that I am going afoot this morning to Malling Lecture, least he conclude me a Puritan.

Februar: 22.

The COUNTESS OF WESTMORLAND to COL. HARLEY.

Deare Cousin—I here this afternone that Hulle is beseged, and my Lord Fairfax and my brother in danger. Pray if you doe here any thing send me word, for I am very much troubled, and whether Beverley be taken by my Lord Nacastell: what news you hav, pray comunicat, and lay a farther obliggation one,

Your affectionat cousin, M. WESTMORLAND.

Directed—" To my very much esteemed cousine, Coneranell Harlow."

The EARL of WESTMORLAND to COL. EDWARD HARLEY.

Cosen—Pray acquaint your father with what I was entertained with, all this day—heer coming one of the officers of Douer Castle with Sir Nicholas Miller to church, they dined with me and assure, that ther is a great plott discouered at Douer, which was to have seised on the castle upon Wensday last for the K—— without P——. The gentleman tells me he saw the kinges com'ission for it, which, vpon search, they found in a fether bed: it was directed to Captain Collins and others: some of them taken, and the maior there in hould. This Collins com'aunded the blockhouse iust vnder the castle in the dukes time, and had been easd of that charge sithence. I fear this will not sound well in times of treaty. But stil our God workes marvailously for vs: to whŏ be praise.

If your intents hould westward, let me know for Robins sake.

Soe rests at your com'and, WESTMORLAND.

Mer: 10—23. (1644.)

Directed—" For my cosin, Collonell Harley,
at Westminster."

The EARL of WESTMORLAND to COL. EDWARD HARLEY.

Cos. Col. Ned—I take this opportunety again to thank you for that favour you did vs heer, which must not be forgotten. It seems the world is pregnant with mischiefs, soe that treaty and treachery are coupled, and

216   APPENDIX.

plotts generative begetting plotts. I was tould of the Douer busines that morning I came out of toun, but knew nothing to w^t now; for I haue spoken with one who sawe the com'ission itself, which was directed to one Increse Collins, quondam captain of the blockhous ther vnder the D. of R. and L. his gra. The partees apprehended, as ye Maior of Dover, &c., were brought to Maidston and ther examined yesterday, from whence I heer they will send them vp. I strain to lode intelligence, that we may be refreshed with some by return from the Mint. My wife came from church very ill on Christmas day, but, God be praised! is better now (a good condition for all the sex). Freedom bids me salute you with what I conceived vpon the coniunction of the two great planetts (which you may impart to Spencer, that great astronomer,) Christmas and Fast:—

> Quondam festa dies nunc jeiunantibus apta es,
> Ut queis non prosunt gaudia, moesta invent.
>
> A holy day I was: and am soe still.
> For holy fasting sanes wher riotts kill.

Soe rests,
" Tuus dum sum,"
WESTMORLAND.

St. Thos day (1644?).

Directed—" To my loving cosen, Collonell Edward Harley,
at Westminster."

Col. HARLEY to his brother Thomas.

Deare Brother—I have now exchanged the sweet country aire and sports for the dirt, fogs, and trouble of the city. The employment there, is to chase the poore hare, or crafty fox; heere, to pursue one another. The forest whence I came, hath not beasts more savage as we meete every day. The lustfull goat, fawning dog, greedy wolf range freely, and what is worst, every one abounds with these wild inhabitants, and want sagacity to pursue and courage to destroy them. If every private person would be an honest hunter, we should not complaine of so many Nimrods. If you have re-

covered, and can spare your *watry hunter*, I shall be very glad to receave him from you. The assurance of your health will be very wellcome to,
Your most affectionate brother,
EDW. HARLEY.

Westminster, 6 *Martii*, 1650-1.
For his deare Brother,
    Mr. Thomas Harley.

ED. HARLEY to his father.

Sir—I trust the same mercy which conducted me safely hither hath comfortably preserved you. If that confidence did not refresh me, this journey would be very sad; but I dare not doubt the tender compassions of our heavenly Father to you, because I have alwaies experienced your tenderness to me. Thus, I beseech you, give me leave according to our Lord and Saviors precious logick to make some return for your fatherly love to me, with an assurance of an infinite Fatherly love to you. Sir, if our Lord God see it good to permitt Satan to discover his malice, be pleased to consider that your age and weakness, which encourage Satan to assault you: they doe much more assure you of victory, because all the retrenchments from your own ability to resist, doe place you more closely and imediately under the secure protection of the Lord of Hosts, who I doubt not will graciously avenge you of your spirituall adversary; will make His candle shine upon your head, and having sanctified all His dispensatins towards you, will fully assure you, that having given you His son, how shall He not with Him also freely give you all things. Thus humbly prayes he, who begs your blessing for, Sir,
    Your most obedient son,   EDW. HARLEY.

Birmichem, Feb. 2, 1653-4.
    To his most honored father,
Sir Robert Harley, Knt. of the Bath,
        at Ludlow, present these.

EDW. HARLEY to his father.

Sir—I bless God for your letter and for the testimony of His goodness to you, which I trust will be graceously continued and enlarged. I am not yet at a certainty whether I shall procure the money by the security of an assignation of your statute to the Earle of Lincolne, or by a new statute, but I doubt not a speedy dispatch, through Gods goodness. Wednesday last, the lord Protector rode in great state from Temple-bar to Grocers Hall. The lord Mayor rode bare, with the sword before him, and was knighted by him after the banquet, and the sword the Protector did then weare, he bestowed upon the Mayor. The Recorder his speech I present to you, enclosed. I beseeche the Lord in mercy confirme your health, according to His abundant mercy, which is the prayer of him, that humbly begs your blessinge, and is,

Sir,
Your most obedient Son,
EDW. HARLEY.

London, Old Bayley, 11 *Feb.* 1653-4.
For the Right Worshipfull
Sir Robert Harley, Kt. of the Bathe,
at Ludlow, Shropshyre.

EDWARD HARLEY, on the day of his marriage, to his Father.

Sir—Although I have not heard since I parted from Ludlow concerning your health, I trust our gracious God continues your health towards a further degree of confirmation and strength. This day according to your leave, and by Gods mercy to me, I have consumated this great affaire heere, and my dear heart and I joyn in humbly begging your blessing. The most part of the 3000*l.* will be in a fewe daies at London. 1500*l.* of it is for Mr. Sherwyn. I desire to know whether Mr. Lacy shall have his money out of the remainder. My Lady Button is very desirous to have the joynture immediately settled, which I doubt cannot be wel-done before you speak with Mr. Powys, who is now on the circuit; therefore if please you, I think you may give my lady satisfaction for the present, if you acknowledg a statut of 8000*l.* to my Lady Button, with a defesance that you will settle a joynture within three or six months of 500*l.* per an. This may be done at Ludlow; and if you aprov it, I beseech you that it may be speedily dispatched hither. I think Mr. Davies of Wigmore can draw the defesance wel. My Lady Button is very desirus of a letter from you. She presents her service to you. When you think fit to writ of any privat business, I think, Sir, it may be better, if you pleas, to mak use of my sister Stanleys penn. Sir, I beseech the Lord in mercy continue your health and enlarge all spiritual comforts to you. So prayes, Sir,

Your most obedient son,

EDWARD HARLEY.

Tavistock, June 26, 1654.

Sir—I beseech you y^t our maryag may be kept privat.

To his most honored father,
Sir Robert Harley, Kt. of the Bathe,
 At Ludlow, present these.

MARY HARLEY to her husband, Col. ED. HARLEY.

Deare Heart—I was very ill on Saturday last, and not abrode till to day. The duty as you desierid of the fast was this day performed, and the other of prayer every second Thursday shall be, if God pleas—it being your fathers command as well as yours. Mr. Shilton tells me Hurse cannot have either of the livings. I was forced to borrow money to paye Rutley 15*l.* 12*s.*; and I must borrow sume and the rest in my gold must pay Mr. Shiltons bill to Mr. Cloggie. The steward tells me none will be had. I know not what to doe for the house. I believe I must be forced to leve it, tho I should gladly do any service I am able. I have given your directions concerning the church to Mr. Davis, and to the steward for to bring hay, which he thinks, as he tells me, very difficult alredy, and it will be impossible, by that time he hath done plowing: so he would have too of the coach horses sent to be kept at Brompton. My brother came well home last Satturday, but the coach brook at Eacham, and came not till yesterday. Sir Robert and all are well, but your sad (and in your absence, deare heart,)

 Unhappie, MARY HARLEY.

Sep. 16.

Pray write to my mother—my service to my brother, with my prayers for his health. We prayed for his recovery, which we hop will be sudaine. My brother presents his love to you. If you write to my mother, and send the inclosed you'll doe a great favour. My mother is grieved she heard not from me.

Sir EDWARD HARLEY to his Brother, announcing the birth of his son Robert, afterwards created Earl of Oxford.

Deare Brother—I thanke God I can give you the notice of the great mercy God hath pleased to vouchsafe us. Thursday, 5 Dec. between 7 and 8 in the evening my wife was very well delivered of a lusty boy, who was next day baptized and bears my fathers name, and through mercy my brother was recovered to so much strength as to be present. I desire you to joyn with us in thankfulness for this great mercy.

I desire to be comended to Mr. Hawes. Sir H. Lingen came not to town before this night. Monday morning, God willing, I shall speak with him, and I hope secure both Mr. Hawes and some others from further troubles. I hope you have received before this time some letters I wrote since W. Reynolds coming up, who brought all things safe.

I pray God bless the children, who I hope will be glad of theyr new brother, for they shall be loved still . . . . peice . . . . . leg and thigh. My sister is much better in health than when she came up. I pray God be with you.

I am your most affectinat brother,   EDW. HARLEY.

Bow: Street, Dec: 7, 1661.

Directed—To the Worspl. Thomas Harley, Esq. at Bucknel.
Leave this with Mr. Edward Robinson, bookseller, at Ludlow.

No. II.

(1.)

The Protestation alluded to in Letter CVI. was no doubt that taken by the House of Commons 3rd May, 1641, to which is prefixed, in the Journals of that House, the following:—

"A Preamble, with the Protestation, made by the whole House of Commons, the 3 of May 1641, and assented unto, by the Lords of the Upper House, 4th of May.

"We, the Knights, Citizens, and Burgesses of the Commons House in Parliament, finding, to the Grief of our Hearts, that the designs of the priests and Jesuits, and other Adherents to the See of Rome, have of late more boldly and frequently put in Practice then formerly, to the Undermining and Danger of the Ruin of the true reformed Religion in his Majesty's Dominions established: and finding also, that there hath been, and having Cause to suspect there still are, even during the Sitting of Parliament, Endeavours to subvert the fundamental Laws of *England* and *Ireland*, and to introduce the Exercise of an arbitrary and tyrannical Government, by most pernicious and wicked Counsels, Plots, and Conspiracies: and that the long Intermission and unhappier Breach of Parliaments hath occasioned many illegal Taxations, whereupon the Subjects have been prosecuted and grieved: and that divers Innovations and Superstitions have been brought into the Church; Multitudes driven out of his Majesty's Dominions; Jealousies raised and fomented between the King and People; a Popish Army levied in *Ireland*, and Two Armies brought into the Bowels of this Kingdom, to the Hazard of his Majesty's Royal Person, the Consumption of the Revenue of the Crown, and the Treasure of this Realm: and lastly, finding the great Causes of Jealousy, Endeavours have been and are used, to bring the *English* Army into Misunderstanding of this Parliament, thereby to incline that Army by Force to bring to pass those wicked Counsels; have therefore thought good to join ourselves in a Declaration of our united Affections and Resolutions; and to make this ensuing Protestation:—

"I, A. B., do, in the Presence of Almighty God, promise, vow, and protest, to maintain and defend, as far as lawfully I may, with my Life, Power, and Estate, the true, reformed, Protestant Religion, expressed in the Doctrine of the Church of *England*, against all Popery and Popish Innovations, and according to the Duty of my Allegiance to his Majesty's Royal Person, Honour, and Estate; as also the Power and Privilege of Parliament, the lawful Rights and Liberties of the Subjects, and every Person that maketh this Protestation, in whatsoever he shall do, in the lawful Pursuance of the same: And to my Power, as far as lawfully I may, I will oppose and by good Ways and Means endeavour to bring to condign Punishment all such as shall, by Force, Practice, Counsel, Plots, Conspiracies, or otherwise, do any thing to the contrary in this present Protestation contained.

"And further, I shall, in all just and honourable Ways, endeavour to preserve the Union and Peace betwixt the Three Kingdoms of *England*, *Scotland*, and *Ireland;* and neither for Hope, Fear, nor other Respect, shall relinquish this Promise, Vow, and Protestation."

This protestation was immediately taken by the majority of the House then assembled, and directions were sent into the country for its being taken by sheriffs, magistrates, and others. It was not until 20th January, 1641-2, that Mr. Serjeant Wilde presented from his committee sitting at Grocers' Hall, the copy of a letter to be signed by the Speaker and sent to the several sheriffs of counties respectively, requiring "them and the justices of the peace of the counties to meet together in one place, as soon as possible they may, and then to take the protestation themselves; and then, dispersing themselves into their several divisions, to call together the minister, the constables, churchwardens, and overseers of the poor of every parish, and tender unto them the protestation, to be taken in their presence, and to desire them speedily to call together the inhabitants of their several parishes, both householders and others, being eighteen years of age and upwards, and to tender unto them the same protestation, and to take the names both of those who took it and of those who refuse, and to return them to the knights and burgesses, &c."

In consequence of this requirement, which was highly offensive to the gentry of Herefordshire, a declaration was got up and printed under the title of "The Declaration or Resolution of the County of Hereford:" on which occur the following notices in the Journal of the House of Commons:—

(2.)

"*Die Veneris*, 8° *Julii*, 1642. *Post meridiem.*

PROCEEDINGS OF THE HOUSE ON THE RESOLUTION OR DECLARATION OF THE COUNTY OF HEREFORD.

"*Resolved, &c.*—That the printed Paper intituled, 'The Declaration or Resolution of the County of Hereforde,' shall be referred to the Committee for Printing: Who are to sit To-morrow at Two o'clock, in the Exchequer Chamber.

"*Resolved, &c.*—That   Hammon the Printer shall be forthwith summoned to attend this House, and be brought up in safe Custody.

"Mr. Maddison was called in, and did aver that he, being at a Stationer's Shop, and reading a Pamphlet intituled, "The Declaration or Resolution of the County of Hereford," and saying, that this was a foul Scandal upon the Parliament, and that the Author of it deserved to be whipt; one Sir Will. Boteler told him, that he deserved to be whipt for saying so; and that he would justify every Word in it: and that, by God he would slash him; and while he was talking with him, one Mr. Dutton, a Minister, came to him, and likewise said, that he deserved to be whipt; and he asked, Wherefore? And he replied, For speaking Nonsense, and for saying it was a Libel.

"*Resolved,*—That Mr. Dutton, the minister, shall be forthwith committed a Prisoner to the Gatehouse, there to remain during the Pleasure of the House, for carrying himself in a scornful Manner in the House, and for as much as in him lay, justifying the foulest and most scandalous Pamphlet that ever was raised or published against the Parliament.

"Mr. Dutton was again called in; and Mr. Speaker told him, that, by his carriage here towards the House, one might well judge of his Behaviour towards the Parliament out of the House: and that, as much as in him lay, he had justified one of the foulest and most scandalous libels that ever was raised or published against the Parliament: and then the Speaker pronounced the sentence against him aforesaid.

"*Ordered,*—That Sir William Boteler's bail shall be required to bring him in to-morrow morning.

" Same day.—Message from the Lords, by Judge Foster and Judge Mallet:—

" That the Lords do desire a present Conference by Committee of both Houses, concerning a Printed Paper intituled, ' A Declaration or Resolution of the County of Hereford.'

" Answer returned by the same messengers:—

" That this House will give a present meeting, as is desired.

" Sir William Lewis, Sir Rob. Harley, Sir John Evelyn are appointed managers of this conference.

" Two constables were called in, Who informed the House, that they were sent by the Justices of the Sessions at Newgate with Two Persons that were taken divulging the Printed Resolution of the County of Hereforde.

" The Men were called in, and confessed the same; and that they bought them of one Hamond.

" Sir Rob. Harley reports, from the Conference had with the Lords, That the Lords had brought unto them a printed Paper, which is a scandalous and infamous Libel in the name of the county of Hereforde, and do desire that this House will join with their Lordships in desiring the Knights that serve for that County to send down to know who in that County will avow the same: And, if any do, that they shall be prosecuted to the utmost, for setting forth such an infamous Libel.

" *Resolved*,—That this is a most scandalous and infamous Paper.

" *Resolved*,—That Jo. Hubbard and Evan Lewis shall be sent back to the Justices of Peace at the Sessions at Newgate, to be there proceeded against according to Law, for publishing an infamous and scandalous Libel.

" *Ordered*,—That Sir Rob. Harley do bring into the House To-Morrow Morning Two Letters he received from some of the Gentry of the County of Hereforde.

" *Resolved*,—That Hamon the printer shall be sent for as a Delinquent.

" 11 July. *Ordered*,—That Mr. Venables be sent for forthwith to attend the House, and that he be examined at the Committee appointed for the Defence of the Kingdom concerning the printed Paper of the Resolution of Hereford; and that Sir Rob. Harley do attend that Committee with those letters he hath received from some Gentlemen of the county of Hereforde.

"20 July. *Resolved,*—That upon the humble petition of Evan Lewis and Rich. Hubbard, Prisoners in Newgate, by Order of this House, for selling about the Streets, a printed Paper, called '*the Resolution of the County of Hereford,*' they be forthwith released from any further Restraint."

The editor has been unable to find any copy of this declaration; but among Lady Frances Vernon Harcourt's collection, is the following paper, which embodies the views of Sir Wilm. Croft and others, who now more openly joined the King, and were shortly in arms against the Parliament.

(3.)

MS. endorsed, "Herefford Protestation."

THE PROTESTATION.

I—— beinge herevnto required doe willingly and in the presence of Almighty God solemnely vow and protest as followeth :—

1. That I beleeve noe power of pope or parliament can depose the soveraigne Lo. K. Charles, or absolve mee from my naturall allegiance and obedience vnto his royall person and successors.

2. That the two Howses of Parliament without the King's consent hath noe authority to make lawes, or to bind and oblige the subject by their ordinances.

3. Wherefore I beleeve that the Earls of Essex and Manchester, Sir Tho. Fairfax, Sir Will. Waller, Coll. Massie, together with all such as already have or hereafter shall take vp armes by authority and commission of the members of parliament of Westminster, pretendinge to fight for Kinge and parliament, doe thereby become actuall rebells, and all such ought with their adherents and partakers to be prosecuted and brought to condigne punishment.

4. That myselfe will never beare armes in their quarrell; but if I shal be thereunto called, will assist my soveraigne and his armyes in the defence of his royall person, crowne, and dignity, against all contrary fforces, vnto the vttermost of my skill and power, and with the hazard of my life and ffortunes.

5. That I will not discover the secretts of his Majestyes armyes to the rebells, nor hold any correspondence or intelligence with them. And all designes of theirs against our soveraignes armyes, or for surprizeinge or deliveringe vppe the cittyes of Worcester or Hereford, or of any other his Majestyes forts, I shall truly discover to whom it shall concerne, so soon as ever it comes unto my knowledge.

6. That his Majesties takeinge up of armes for the causes by himselfe so oft declared in print is just and necessary.

7. That I will endeavour all I may to hinder all popular tumults, riseings, randevous, meetings, confederancies, and associations of the people, townes, hundreds, and countyes which are not warranted to assemble by his Majesties express commission, or by power derived from him or by vertue of his comissions, and in the sense he meanes it.

8. I detest from my heart that seditious and trayterous late invented nationall covenant, and I promise never to take it.

All these particular articles I vow and promise sincerely to observe without equivocation or mentall reservation.

So helpe me God.

I doe strictly enjoyne, without exception, all commanders and souldyers, gentry, cittizens, ffree-holders and others within the county and cittye of Herefford to take this protestation, which is to be tendered vnto them by the High Sheriffe and Comissioners of the county, assisted with such a divine as they shall make choice of to that purpose; and that a scedule of their names who shall refuse to take the same is to be delivered vnto Sir William Bellendene, Comissary-Generall.

C. R.

(4.)

THE HEREFORD PETITION.

Die Mercurii, 4° May, 1642. *Journals of the House of Commons.*

The House being informed that divers Gentlemen of the County of Hereford were at the Door, who desired to present a Petition to this House:

They were called in; and did present the same, and then they withdrew; and their petition was read,—

The which being done, they were again called in; and Mr. Speaker, by the Command of the House, told them, that this House finds their Petition full of great Expressions of Duty to his Majesty, and of Love and Respects to this House and the Commonwealth, (for which they give you Thanks,) and full of great Concernment to the Commonwealth; which they command me to tell you, they will take into serious Consideration, so soon as may stand with * * *

The petition was as follows, here printed from a printed paper, endorsed in Sir Robert Harley's handwriting

"HEREFORDSHIRE PETITION, 1642."

"To the honorable, the Knights, Cittizens, and Bvrgesses of the Commons Hovse assembled in Parliament.

"The humble Petition of the High Sheriffe and divers of the Gentrey, Ministers, Freeholders, and Inhabitants of the county of *Hereford.*

"*Most humbly sheweth,*

"That with all thankfulnesse we acknowledge those many and great Blessings we have already received through God's mercy, the favour of our Gratious Soveraigne, the Wisdome, Councell, Sollicitation, and unwearied Paines and Patience of this Honorable Assembly, for the preservation of the Priviledges of Parliament, and liberties of the Subject, the removing of many of these Obstructions which hindred your good endevours; your zealous furthering of bleeding *Ireland's* Reliefe, earnest desire of disarming Papists, and securing of their persons; your prudent care in disposing the *Militia, Navie,* and places of Importance of this Kingdome to such persons of Trust as may (by God's blessing) give assurance of safetie to the King's Royall person, and good subjects of all his Majesties Dominions: your Pious Care to settle a Government in the Church according to the Word of God, your godly desires to prevent the Prophaning of the Lord's day; To take away pluralities and *Non Residents,* and your zeale to provide Preaching Ministerie throughout the Kingdome, whereof this County stands in great neede, it now abounding with insufficient, Idle, and Scandalous Ministers, whereby the people generally are continued in Ignorance, Superstition, and prophanenesse, and are ready to become a prey to popish suducers, which Idolatrous profession hath of late yeares with much boldnesse appeared in this County: And wheras one of our cheife Commodities is the Native Wooll of this County, the price whereof is much fallen through the excessive importation of Spanish woolls, to our great impoverishing.

May it therefore please this Honorable House to continue your Prudence and Pious intentions and indeavours in all the Premisses not yett Accomplished, to hasten the speedy releife of Distressed and Gasping Ireland, *To remove evill Councellors, To take away the Votes of Popish Lords, Speedily to disarme the Papists, To settle a Godly and Learned Ministery, and to restraine the excessive Importation of Spanish Wooll.*

And wee shall be ready with chearefulnesse to contribute all possible Assistance our Prayers, lives, and livelyhoods may afford for the defence of his Maiesties Royall person, this Honorable House; and the preservation of the priviledges of Parliament.

London, Printed for *John Francke.* 1642.

No. III.

(1.)

LETTER FROM DR. NATHANIEL WRIGHT TO SIR ROBERT HARLEY.

To his much honoured friend SIR ROBERT HARLEY, Knight of the Most Noble Order of the Bathe, present these in Westminster.

Sr—If you can conveniently spare it, I desire that favour from you as to furnish me with the remainder of that mony which I disbursed for our Brompton soldiers in distresse. The account I left with you, and if you please to satisfye my request herein, this bearer (my brother-in-law) will convey it to me at his returne into these parts, which will be speedy. Were not my condition such as to enforse me to call upon you, I had much rather be silent, then sollicite you in this nature. I shall not need relate my wants, nor yet tell you of my sufferings: the last you in some measure know, and the former I sufficiently feele. I beseeche you pardon this freedome of expression, and accept of the humble tender of mine and my wifes love and service to yourself and yours, from him who is in all conditions, Sr,

Your most affectionate and most humble servant,

NATH: WRIGHT.

Salop, 9bris 10, '45.

(2.)

MEMORANDUM OF RENTS PAID BY SIR ROBERT HARLEY. 1639.

(In Sir Robert Harley's handwriting.)

1639.   Rents yearly payd by mee.

		£	s.	d.
1.	To ye kg for Kgsland	85	16	00
2.	To ye kg for Wigmore parke	02	02	00
3.	To ye kg for Bucton, &c.	00	14	04
4.	To my Lo. Craven for Leintwarde	36	00	00
5.	To my Lo. Craven for Mocktree	84	15	00
6.	To ye kg for Burrington	21	10	11½
7.	To Sr Ro. Howard for Bucknill	00	00	00
8.	To hym for the forrest, &c.	00	00	00
9.	To Sr Wm Croft for my chiefe rent for Eyton	05	14	00
10.	To ye bishop for Wigmore teithe	03	06	08
11.	To hym for Leynthall Starks	04	04	00
12.	To hym for Bucton	03	06	00
		247	08	11½
13.	To my Lady Wake	200	00	00
		447	08	11½

(3.)

PARTICULARS OF LOSSES SUSTAINED BY SIR ROBERT HARLEY SINCE THE WARS.

A particular of what loss my master, Sir Robert Harley, hath sustained by the enemy in the county of Hereford since these wars.

	£	s.	d.
Imp.—The stock of cattle of all sorts at	940	0	0
The loss of £1500 per annum for 3 years	4500	0	0
The castle itself being utterly ruined	3000	0	0
All the rich furniture and household goods belonging to the castle	2500	0	0
Two mills, with brew-houses and stalls and other outhouses, together with corn and hay, valued at	950	0	0
A study of books, valued at	200	0	0
Two parks wholly laid open and destroyed	500	0	0
Timber and other wood cut down and destroyed, valued at	300	0	0
Destroyed at least 500 deer.			
Destroyed more in corn at least	100	0	0
	12,990	0	0

This was brought to Westminster by the 23rd July, 1646.

SAML. SHELTON.
WM. BAYLEY.

(4.)

RENTS PAID TO THE KING BY SIR ROBERT HARLEY.

Endorsed—" Rents paid to the King by Sr Robert Harley."

Sr Robert Harleys estate in Herefordshire was from anno 1642 till May 1646, vnder the power of the Kings souldiers.

Aprill 16th, 1642.—The halfe years rent for Kingsland, Burrington, and Wigmore Parke was paid to Mr. William Geears, then receiver.

Aprill 11th, 1643?—The whole years rent was paid to Mr. Gervase Blackwall, receiver.

Octob. 16, 1643, was paid the halfe years rent to the said Mr. Blackwall.

No. IV.

(1.)

LETTER 12 AUG. 1647, SIGNED, DENZELL HOLLES, WALTER LONG, WILL. LEWIS, JO. CLOTWORTHY, WILLIAM WALLER, PH. STAPILTON, ANTH. NICOLL, TO EDWD. HARLEY.

Noble Sr—The place where you lodge and the necessity of our priuacy have denied vs of the opportunity of visitinge you, which wee have very much desired. Wee haue now gotten our passes to trauell, and beinge as carefull of you as of our selves, haue procured yours also, which wee send you heere inclosed. Wee intend to goe away speedily, and the most of vs into the Low Countryes, from whence wee shall (God willinge) giue you notice in what place wee shall stay. Sr, wee hartily pray for your health, and much desire the happinesse of your company, as a person of soe much honnor and worth, that wee have a very greate obligation vpon vs to be for euer, Sr,

Your very affectionate freinds and humble seruants,
(Signed)

WILLIAM WALLER.	WILL. LEWIS.	DENZELL HOLLES.
PH. STAPILTON.	JO. CLOTWORTHY.	WALTER LONG.
ANTH: NICOLL.		

12th of Aug. 1647.

Endorsed—" From the 11."

(2.)

A Pass from the Speaker Lenthall, (11 Aug. 1647) for Col. Edward Harley to go beyond the sea.

Endorsed—" My pass to travel for six months."

By vertue of an order off the Howse of Commons, These are to will and require you to suffer the bearer hearoff, Collonell Edward Harley, a member of the Howse of Commons, wth his servants and twoe horses, to ship himselfe in any port wthin this kingdom to goe beyond the sea; heroff you may not fayle, as y^u will answer the contrary at your utmost perills. Dated ye 11th of August, 1647. This pass to continue for the space off six monthes, to be accounted from ye date of ye s^d order.

(Signed)   Wm. Lenthall,
                                                   Speaker.

To all comaunders, officers and soldiers, both
    by sea and land, and to all others whom
    these may conserne.

No. V.

The Protestation at the King's Head, 12 Dec. 1648.

Endorsed—" Protestation at the King's Head, &c."

Wee whose names are hereunto subscribed, being members of the House of Comons and free men of England, doe hereby declare before God, and angells, and men, that the general and officers of the armye, being raysed by authority of Plt, and for defence and mayntenance of the priviledges therof, have not, nor ought to have, any powr or jurisdiction to apprehend, secure, detaine, imprison, or remove or psons fro place to place, by any color or authority whatsoever, nor yet to question or trye us or any of us by martiall lawe or otherwise, for any offence or crime whatsoever which can or shall be objected or apprehended against vs. And that the present imprisonment and removall of or psons is a high violation of the rights and priviledgesof Plt, and of the fundamental lawes of y° land, and a higher vsurpation and exercise of an arbitrary and unlawful power than hath been heretofore appended to, or attempted by, this or any King [or] other Power whatsoever within these realmes. Notstanding w^h we and every of us doe declare our readynes to submit o^{r}selves to y° legall tryall of a free Plt for any cryme or misdemeanour that can or shall be objected agst us. In wittness whereof we have hereunto subscribed o^r names y° 12th of 10^{bris}, 1648.

(Signed)
    EDW. MASSIE.   WILLIAM WALLER.
    LIO. COPLEY.   JOHN CLOTWORTHY.

Att the King's Head in the Strand.

No. VI.

(1.)

LETTER FROM MAJOR WINTHROP TO COLONEL HARLEY AND MAJOR HARLEY, 3 AUG. 1650.

To my honoured ffriends Col. HARLOWE and Major HARLOWE these present.

Gentlemen—I have received some commands from the Commissioners for the militia of this countye concerning yourselves, grounded (as I believe) upon some information of your disaffection to this present government, and therefore that I should send for you to my quarters at Leominster; but I shall only at present lett you know that they expect you should appear before them at Hereford, on Tuesday next, and so I remain,
    Gentlemen,
      Your friend and servant,
  (Signed)   S. WINTHROP.

Leominster, 3 *August*, 1650.

(2.)

LETTER FROM COLONEL HARLEY TO MAJOR WINTHROP.

Colonel HARLEY to Major WINTHROP.

Sir—I received by this bearer a letter from you dated this day, and directed to myself and my brother Major Harley (who hath been gone out of this country now four days), in which you express that you have received some commands, grounded as you believe upon information of our disaffection to the present government, from the commissioners of the militia, to send for us to your quarters at Leominster, where for the present you are, and let us know that the commissioners expect our appearance before them at Hereford, on Tuesday next.

Sir—After giving you thanks for your civility, I must take liberty something to wonder, that the commissioners for the militia should in such manner summon myself and brother, who are members of Parliament, who have from the beginning of the late unhappy troubles constantly and faithfully served the Parliament, and I am sure cannot be justly taxed with the least disaffection to it. If our coming into this country, our birth-place, and where God hath disposed the means of our livelyhood, be ill interpreted, it is without reason; for, I assure you, no design brought me hither, but the dispatch of some necessary occasions, concerning my father's estate, which being once dispatched, I shall, God willing, returne to London. This being all my business in these parts, I hope that liberty which is not denied to those who have been in armes against the Parliament, shall not be grudged to us who have lost our blood and suffered so much for the Parliament. But if this, which is nothing but the truth, do not satisfy you, I will, if please God, visit you on Monday next at Leominster.

(3.)

COLONEL HARLEY'S PROMISE TO BE IN LONDON.

Endorsed—" Promise when I was a prisoner at Hereford, August 10, 1650."

"For ten years space after this, I was not permitted any residence in Herefordshire. E. H."

I will, by the help of God, if my life and health permitt, be at my father's house in Westminster, Saturday August 18, 1650, and continue there until the 1st day of September next following.

In witness whereunto I have put my hand this tenth day of August, 1650.

EDW. HARLEY.

(4.)

PASS FROM WROTH ROGERS TO COLONEL HARLEY TO TRAVEL FROM HEREFORD TO LONDON. 10 AUG. 1650.

Endorsed—" Pass from Wroth Rogers when I was disarmed and imprisoned. August 10, 1650. E. H."

These are to desire all officers and soldiers, and all others whom it may concern, to permitt and suffer the bearer hereof, Collonell Edward Harley, with his three servants and fower horses, quietly to pass from the cittee of Hereford unto the cittee of London, wthout any trouble or molestation, hee acting nothing prejudiciall to the commonwealth.

Given under my hand this 10th day of August, 1650.

(Signed) WROTH ROGERS.

(5.)

SIR ROBERT HARLEY TO SIR HENRY VANE, WITH SIR HENRY VANE'S REPLY, AND A LETTER FROM SIR ROBERT TO EDWARD HARLEY, ON ONE SHEET. 20 AUG. 1650.

Sir ROBERT HARLEY to Sir HENRY VANE.

S^r—This waits on you to receave the further manifestation of y^r good favour towards, Sr,

Your affectionat friend and humble servant,

RO. HARLEY.

Westminster, Aug. 20th, 1650.

Directed—To his honorable friend,
    Sr Henry Vane, Kt.
        at Whitehall.

Below which is returned, on the same paper:—

S^r—I have enquired into your busines, and finde that your sons are under greete suspecion and not like to be removed suddenly from thence, unlesse there be some more urgent occasion for it then yet appears, and I do perceave that the matter depending now as it does before the counsell, they will expect addresses to be made to themselves in this affair; so rests,

S^r,
Your affectionate freend and humble servant,
H. VANE.

On the same sheet:—

Ned Harley—The enclosed will tell you what I haue done upon the news of both your brothers being confined in Bristol. I pray you quitt Herefordshire as soone as you can, and the Lord blesse you and return you with safety to your most loving father.

RO. HARLEY.

Westminster, Aug. 20, 1650.

(6.)

MR. ROBERT HARLEY TO HIS BROTHER, FROM BRISTOL CASTLE.
9 Nov. 1650.

Major ROBERT HARLEY to his Brother THOMAS.

Deare Brother—I have receaved yours by my footman with Mr. Watts receipt and counsell of states letter, for doing the . . . the . . . I am not . . . but to gett suretys is the difficulty, I being not as yett prepared.

My love to my brother and sisters, and humble duty to my father: by the next you will heare of my continuance here or remouve, that, if please God, wee may see one another.

Your most affectionat,
RO. HARLEY.

Bristoll Castell, 9 Novr. 1650.
For Mr. Thos. Harley,
at Sir Robert Harleys house,
Tuttle Street, Westminster.

No. VII.

(1.)

Letter from Edward Harley to the Master and Fellows of Caius Coll. 14 Dec. 1658.

EDWARD HARLEY to the Reverend and Worthy the Master and Fellowes of Gonvil and Caius Colledg in Cambridg—present these.

Reverend and Worthy—The leas of the rectory of Folden in Norfolk, granted by your society to my wifes mother, the Lady Button, and by her death accrewing to us, wee desire in Gods fear, so far as lies in us, to restore that portion of the Lords to the seruice of the Lord. We would choos silently to discharge this duty; but we hope God will inclin the hearts of so worthy a school of the prophets, both to place a godly and lerned pastor at Folden, now voyd, and to perpetuat that mayntenance which I can only perform for a few years. In order to which we are willing to resign our leas upon these terms,—viz. That you wil promis under your hands to joyn your best endevors with ours, that assoon as may be, by act of Parlement, the profits of the rectory of Folden surmounting your rent reserued upon our leas, may be vnited to the vicarag, and settled for ever upon the incumbent minister at Folden; that until this vnion be effected, according to law, you will renew the leas for twenty-and one years future, either to myself or some other person of responsible estat and integrity, only in trust and for the use and benefit of the minister of Folden for the time being, which leassee shal also giv bond of 500 lb. penalty not to conuert the profits aforsaid to any other use then is expressed.

Concerning the next incumbent, I beseech you accept my thanks for your curteous offer by Mr. Naylor, of the nomination, of which favor I shall only desire this, that before you confer your presentation, the person may be aproved by my reverend friend Dr. Tuckney. I understand the benefit of my leas will augment the mayntenance to 100 lb. yearly, which wil be a comfortable subsistence for an able divine. To such an one I beseech God direct your choice, and bles your society, to send forth many faithful laborers into the vineyard of the Lord, who from thence may be transplanted to shine as the stars for ever. Thus prays

Your most assured friend to serve you,

EDW. HARLEY.

Decemb. 14, 1658.

(2.)

LETTER TO DR. TUCKNEY, MASTER OF ST. JOHN'S COLLEGE CAMBRIDGE.

EDWARD HARLEY to the Reverend Dr. TUCKNEY, Master of St. John's Colledg, and Regius Professor of Divinity in Cambridg, present these.

Reverend Sr—Whereas the Master and Fellowes of Caius Colledg have pleased in contemplation of some interest I hau in the impropriat rectory of Folden in Norfolk, to offer me the nomination of the next incumbent, now voyd, and in the colledges gift, of which favor I have only thus far accepted, to desire that the person the college intend to present may be first aproved by yourself, whom I beseech to be wel assured, that the person you shall approv, be orthodox in doctrin and disciplin, and of a godly conversation. Your acquaintance with my dear father, who is with God, encorages me in this boldness to trouble you, as your known worth gives me confidence to entrust you. I shal be most glad of any occasion to present you a thankful return from, Sr,

Your very faithful friend and servant, E. H.

Tawstok in Devon, Decemb: 14, 1658.

(3.)

MEMORANDUM SIGNED BY THE MASTER AND FELLOWS OF CAIUS COLLEGE, RELATIVE TO THE LIVING OF FOLDEN IN NORFOLK.

Endorsed—" Caius Colledge, concerning Ffolden."

July 2, 1662.

Whereas the vicarage of Ffoulden in the county of Norfolk is of so small value, that it is not a competent maintenance for a minister, We, the master and ffellows of Gonvil and Caius College (the undoubted patrons of the said vicarage), being desirous to add all possible encouragement to the future incumbent of the said vicarage, have jointly and vnanimously ordered and decreed the day and yere above written, that for the future the rectorie impropriate in Ffoulden aforesaid, belonging to the said college, shall be perpetually annexed to the said vicarage, and that the vicars thereof successively shall enjoy the same during their residence there, without payment of any ffiue or income. . . . . paying to the said college the ancient usually reserved rents. In witnesse whereof, we, the said master and ffellowes have subscribed our names, this 3rd day of July, in the year of our Lord 1662.

WILL. ADAMSON.	ROB. BRADY, Mr. or Keeper.
JO. FELTON.	WILLIAM BLANKE, ye Prd:
JO. ROBINSON.	JOHN GOSTLIN.
JO. ELLYS.	HENRY JENKES.
	WILLIAM LYNG.
	ED. GELSTHORP.
	WIL. NAILOR.
	. THRUSTON

No. VIII.

ORDER IN COUNCIL FOR THE APPREHENSION OF MAJOR ROBERT HARLEY. SIGNED HE. LAURENCE. 28 DEC. 1658.

Endorsed—" Copy of an Order of the Council of State for the apprehending Major Robert Harley. December 28°, 1658.

" By Richard Cromwel, (called) Protector.

" He was apprehended at Kynsham Court, at Mr. Thomas Blayneys. January, 1658-9."

In pursuance of an order of his Highnes and the Councell of the date hereof, These are to will and require you, immediately upon sight hereof, to repaire unto the lodgings of Major Robert Harlowe, or unto any other place or places where you shall understand the said Major Robert Harlow to be, and him the said Major Harlow to apprehend, and in safe custody to bring before the Councell to answer such matters as shall be objected against him. And all mayors, sheriffes, justices of the peace, constables, and other officers are required to be aiding and assisting in the due execution of the premises; and for so doing this shal be your sufficient warrant. Given at Whitehall this 28th of December, 1658.

Signed in the name and by order of his Highnes and the Councell.

(Signed)   HE. LAWRENCE,
Presdt.

To Edward Dendy, Esq. S^{rt}
  at Armes, or to his deputy
    or deputies.

No. IX.

(1.)

LETTER FROM SIR EDWARD HARLEY TO THE LORD CHANCELLOR CLARENDON. 12 DEC. 1665.

May it please your Lordship—I humbly address this to wipe off that breath would intercept the clearness of your Lordship's favor, wherein (in that degree became me) I thought myself happy. My Lord Bishop of Hereford since his return from Parliament told me that your Lordship had acquainted him you had received some late informations concerning me, as if I were not well affected, neither to the church nor state, and that I countenanced factious persons. Particular instances or proofs of this general accusation my Lord Bishop did not mention to me, and if such were given to your Lordship, I doubt not most clearly to disprove or refute them.

I shall therefore (after most humble thanks for the notice your Lordship hath pleased thus to give me, wherein I hope I mistake not your favors towards me) beg leave to rectifye myself before your Lordship.

As for my religion, I thank God I can truly say I have no opinion but what is consonant to the Catholic faith and the doctrines of the Church of England, but what I have learned out of the Scriptures and the writings of the ancient fathers; accordingly, through God's help, I endeavour to lead my life, which, to clear me from all suspicion of schism, hath not only the present and sufficient evidences of a constant and reverend attendance upon divine service, but in times of danger had the testimony of many hazards, and expences in behalf of reverend persons of the church. I could say more, but I forbear, least I speak like a fool. My Lord, I wonder not that I am now reported to be a countenancer of factious persons, for I well remember when I served his Majesty in Dunkirk, it was commonly said, that the chaplains I brought into garrison were factious persons. But the truth was, I discarded the factious, and introduced learned and pious persons, who are now, one of them a prelate, the others, reverend divines in the church. I can now also truly averr, that I have not countenanced any factious persons, nor have such persons resorted to me, nor hath there been in my family any factious or unlawful meeting.

As for my affection to his Majesty's service, it is now twenty years since, upon that account I have constantly lost, done, and suffered: and in order to his Majesty's happy restoration I did, without the vanity of comparison, employ all the poor ability of my estate and person. My Lord, what I did then, I did out of duty—I had not any other design. My Lord General knew how unwillingly I undertook the command of Dunkirk. In that employment, I thank God, I served his Majesty with all fidelity and affection, and with as much devotion as ever my life is always at his Majesty's service.

In the beginning of July, I was visited extreamly with the gout in both my legs, from which affliction I have not been wholly free for ten days space, that kept me from attending my duty in Parliament. But in this part of the country, where I reside, I can truly affirm the King's service, in all respects, hath been diligently and faithfully managed.

My Lord Bishop* told me that the like information was brought to your Lordship, concerning my brother Thomas as concerning myself. As for him, though I had not sooner opportunity to signifye, I had a most grateful sense of your Lordship's favor in making him a Master in Chancery. He doth most humbly profess the like, and what I have alleadged for myself, I can do the same for him; that both his religion and loyalty are most affectionately orthodox and sincere. Having said thus much, I beseech I may add the tender of most humble service to your Lordship from my brother Robert, who still remains with me in a very weak condition. I hope your Lordship will vouchsafe credit to these lines of truth, in behalf of a poor family, which hath not deserved ill, I am confident, of those who have misrepresented us. I heartily forgive all the injury, except the necessity of so long a trouble to your Lordship, from, my Lord,

Your Lordship's most obedient, most humble servant,

E. HARLEY.

Brompton Brian, Dec. 12, 1665.

(2.)

LETTER FROM THE LORD CHANCELLOR TO SIR EDWARD HARLEY.
18 DEC. 1665.

Sir—Though I am very glad always to hear from you, yet I am very sorry that you had such an occasion to give yourself the trouble of writing to me the 12th of this month, when it seems you thought my friendship was lessened towards you. I make no doubt but I might say any thing to my Lord Bishop, which his Lordship sayth I did say to him; and that he meant no ill, either to you or me in the representation; but I do as well know that I have received no late informations concerning you which made the least impression on me to your prejudice. I know too well the humours of this age, and how frankly they speak of things and persons, according as they like or dislike, and I do in some degree know the temper of Herefordshire; and, if any information had about that time been given to me, to your prejudice, it is very probable I might communicate it to my Lord

* Dr. Herbert Croft.

Bishop, to receive his good testimony of you, without the least doubt of your sincerity either to church or state, which in truth I never had, since I was acquainted with you, and upon my conscience the king is well satisfied in both. Truely, I cannot remember that ever any body spoke to me to the disadvantage of your brother Thomas, and therefore I must confess to you, I was in some amazement when I read your letter. You will give better reason to be ill thought of, than you have yet done, if you are much troubled with the licence men take of talking, of whom they please, and what they please. It is an even lay that they who are bold with you one day, will be as bold with the king himself another day. I pray be confident, when I have any thing that makes your affections worthy to be questioned, I will let you know it, and receive your answer. I am heartily sorry poor Robin continues still weak. I pray commend me to him, and believe, that you shall always find me to be,

    Good Sir Edward,

        Your affectionat, humble servant,

            CLARENDON, Chancellor.

For Sr Edward Harley, Knight of
the Bath, at Brompton Brian, in
Herefordshire.   [Per Ludlow post.]

St. John's Colledge, 18° *December*, 1665.

(3.)

LETTER FROM SIR EDWARD HARLEY TO THE LORD CHANCELLOR.
28 JAN. 1665-6.

I presume too much, to offer to your Lordship the trouble of reading so many lines of no better subject than myself. I see, it is too true, that it is very difficult to undertake one's own cause, without committing great faults. Of one I am extremely sensible—that I have occasioned your Lordship the pains of answering my humble paper. I beg your pardon in all sincerity, yet I cannot but reckon it a happy fault, by which I am possessed of so many noble expressions of your Lordship's goodness and kindness, as your lines bestow upon me.

I have many reasons to believe my Lord Bishop's friendship to me, and specially because he hath several times related to me your Lordship's favourable discourse to him of me; but when I shall have the honor to wait on your Lordship, I shall, with your leave, make appear what I said on my own behalf was not altogether without cause. Though your Lordship be allways above the endeavour, be pleased to accept the affection that devotes me, my Lord,

Your Lordship's most obedient, most humble servant,

E. HARLEY.

Brompton Brian, January 28, 1665-6.

To my Lord Chancellor Clarendon, &c.

No. X.

(1.)

EXTRACT FROM A LETTER OF ROBERT HARLEY, ESQ. TO HIS FATHER, 14 MARCH, 1699-1700, RELATIVE TO DUNKIRK.

Lord Clarendon's memoirs are coming out. There are some letters, &c. confirmed by Sir Stephen Fox, that General Monk agreed to and pressed the selling Dunkirk, because Sir Edward Harley was turned out. An account of that and E. Macclesfield's proposal would be very acceptable.

(2.)

Sir EDWARD HARLEY'S Answer, dated 19 March, 1688, wrote in my aunt Harley's hand.

I shall be very glad to see the memoirs you mention; but, as concerning your friend, once at Dunkirk, the sum of what he can say concerning himself is summed up in the 90th Psalm:—" We spend our years like a tale that is told." If the Lord please to spare his poor worm, an account shall be endeavoured for you, concerning that affair. What you mention concerning the Earl of Macclesfield's offer of 10,000*l.*; it is what many witnesses in several places, and upon several occasions, have heard his Lordship fully express, with undeserved regard and kindness, to the then governor of Dunkirk. What is said to be spoke by the Lord General Monk in relation to Colonel Harley and Dunkirk, hath many attestations, but it is hoped that, without mistake, it may be averred that the Earl of Montague was told by King Charles that he would not have parted with Dunkirk, if he could have been permitted to retain Colonel Harley in that post, which *he* would have preserved for his Majesty without extraordinary charge; but, said the king, " I am continually disturbed because he is represented to be a notorious Presbyterian." I shall not at this time add more upon that subject. I would be glad, if the Lord sees good, to represent to you that full scene.

No. XI.

Sir WILLIAM GREGORY to Sir EDWARD HARLEY.

Sir—Being sensible of the greate love that was betwene my Lord Scudamore and yourselfe, it makes me thinke it a necessary duty in me, to acquaint you of the time intended for his Lordship's interment, that soe, if your health and occasions will permitt, you may, if you please, performe your last civility to his Lordship's body, by accompanying it to the grave, wherein, I opine, it will be layed upon Thursday, the 8th of June, at Home Lacy church. We shall come that morning from Gloucester, and therefore I believe the funerall will not be, till about two of the clock. Sir, I begg your pardon for this trouble, and for my haste in it, but I have time only to subscribe my selfe,

Your most faithfull and humble servant,   W. GREGORY.

Grays Inn, ult: Maij, 1671.

No. XII.

(1.)

SIR EDWARD HARLEY'S RETROSPECT OF HIS LIFE ON ENTERING HIS FIFTIETH YEAR.   21 OCT. 1673.

I was born at Brompton Castle, 21st Oct. 1624.

I am now, through divine long suffering, at Brompton Brian, 49 years old.

O Lord! in thy hand is the breath of all mankind, and it is only God who holdeth our soul in life. But in most special manner I ought to praise my God, who preserved me from abortion at Burton-under-the-Hill. In this place, this day gave the light of life to poor clay, and for forty-nine years thou hast granted me life and favour, and thy visitation hath preserved my spirit. Lord, thou hast granted me life in the deliverances of life: when a child, from the chin-cough, measles, small-pox twice, and danger of drowning in the moat; when a man, from many perils in the wars, particularly when my horse was shot, when my arm was hurt, when a muskett-bullett, levelled at my heart, was bent flat against my armour, not reckoned of such proof, without any harm to myself. Many dangerous falls on horseback I have had, specially when I was wonderfully preserved, my horse stumbling and falling into a ditch near Orleton, in frosty weather, but was never by any fall much hurt. I have often been preserved in journeys and voyages from thieves; from waters, specially in a dangerous passage once at Newnham. Many times I crossed the sea between England and Flanders, allways safely; though once, in a great storm, constrained to lye at anchor 36 hours over against Graveling, 1661. I was delivered from the malitious accusation of the army, 1647, and my God made my speech in my defence in Parliament acceptable. That year I was preserved from the plague, of which my servant died, and at the same time recovered from a dangerous pestilential fever. In 1649 I had a long lingering distemper, which ended in a violent sickness with vomiting and purging at Wigmore; but, though the chastening was sore and deserved, I was not given over to death, but God restored me to health. Afterward I was preserved from the cruelty of that power which put to death holy Mr. Love. In 1654 I was recovered from a grievous ague, which had seized me in Devonshire. Some years I was visited with the gout, but through mercy the fits have been short, and my limbs restored to me; and now for above two years I have not been disabled with that disease. In 1640 God was pleased, with a fatherly wisdom and goodness, to visit me with a rupture, by which I was for many years kept humble and from many temptations. I used often many medicines and remedies prescribed by physitians and chirurgions, but without effect, yet after it had been upon me more than twenty years, it pleased God to heal that breach upon me, without the use of any remedy whatsoever, so that I have been perfectly well for several years. This is a most bountiful favour. O Lord! heal my soul of all vain desires, and accept my strength to serve the God of my life. O! let me never forget this signall blessing. Teach me, oh my God! to love thee with all my strength, and never to doubt the love of God Almighty, all sufficient, in whatever condition I shall be exercised, for my God is my life and the length of my days.

In all distress during the warrs, when my father lost all his estate, his houses burnt, and for three years had not any thing of his own for his family, we had allways meat to eat and raiment to put on. Praised be my God, that hath granted me the comforts of life, healthy constitution, usefull senses, money to pay my debts, power to build a convenient habitation, blessing to repair many ruins in the estate of my father, and to enjoy it peaceably. Gracious was my God in giving me my first wife, now I trust, a blessed saint, who was a most affectionate, prudent, pious person, by whom God gave me, besides a very considerable portion, the mercy of four daughters. Two sleep, I trust, in Jesus, and live with God. Two now survive, I hope, to glorifie God.

Gracious was my God, in giving to me my present wife, who hath been made the dear comfort of my life now above twelve years, and the mother of four sons and a daughter, of which God was pleased to take my youngest son, in infancy, to His mercy.

Blessed be God! that hath granted me favour in the affection of my father and my mother, who tenderly loved me, and wisely and carefully instructed and corrected me. What am I, a poor worm, to have any esteem in the world, or to be accepted by thy saints? O Lord! by thy favour I was chosen of several parliaments; chosen, unknown to myself, Governor of Dunkirk, and there honoured to be serviceable to thy servants, and to assist the sanctification of thy holy sabbath.

How pretious are all thy thoughts of love unto me, O God! How great is the sum of them! The visitation of thy Spirit, O Lord! hath taught me the precious wonders of thy laws. From my birth, the lines have fallen unto me in pleasant places, for I have always heard the joyful sound of thy divine jubilee. Nay, Lord! this place, which was greatly waste, and for divers years in the region of the shadow of death, for the sins and iniquities of my forefathers, who were idolators and sinners, and of me an unholy, vile wretch, now is made to me a goodly heritage; for we have a place of worship and a faithful dispenser of the Word of God.

Who is a God like unto our God, that pardons iniquity, transgression, and sin? O Lord! for thy name's sake, heal my backslidings, love me freely, subdue all my iniquities, and cast all my sins into the depths of the sea. My life is but a vapour. Oh! in Jesus Christ beget me, by the incorruptible seed of thy word, which liveth and abideth for ever, that I may do the will of God and abide for ever. Oh, Lord! I am the clay, be thou my potter. Fashion this house of clay to be thy temple. Make me a vessel of praise and service to thy Majesty. Be not ashamed to be my God! therefore make me holy, as my God is holy, in all manner of conversation and godliness. Forsake not the work of thy hands, but keep me by thy power through faith into salvation, for the sake of Jesus Christ, in whom make me accepted, and partaker of the riches of thy grace, which hath abounded towards me, in all wisdom and prudence. Amen.

(2)

Sir Edward Harley's Retrospect on the Completion of his Fiftieth Year.

At Brompton Brian, 21 Oct. 1674.

I am this day, through divine patience, 50 years old. O Lord! I am not worthy the least of thy mercies. I have recorded some of the manifold loving kindnesses of the Almighty in the memorial of my last anniversary.

This year is now concluded to me in health, though it hath in every month of it been full of sorrow. Many dear friends taken away. After the death of Sir Robert Moray and my cousin Froysell, it pleased God to put an end to the pilgrimage of my brother Sir Robert Harley, Nov. 1673. In January at Westminster I was visited sharply with the griping of the guts, but when I was under sentence of death it pleased God to cheer and raise me up. I returned from the Parlement in March. The weather being very bitter, I had no harm in that journey, but immediately after return, I was visited with the gout in both feet and hands. This fit was most painful and of longest continuance, yet now I am, blessed be God! comfortably free from that distemper. In November dyed my good friend Mr. Thomas Doughtie. In April, Sir Edward Massie; and, in a sad manner my cosin, Bartholomew Beal. In August, my dear neice Frances FitzJames, of the small-pox. Since that, my worthy friend Mr. Thomas Treherne, and my cosin Reads wife, both dead in the same day! and now my sister Palmer; while I, a poor unprofitable worm, am still spared. O, my God! the fiftieth year was in Canaan the year of Jubilee. Oh! that this may be to me the acceptable year of the Lord! wherein I may be released from the miserable chains of sloth and carelessness, which render me so vile in the eyes of the glory of my God. Lord! work in me for this same thing, by thy

Spirit, that I may be fervent in spirit, serving the Lord. I do not beg length of days, but with humble submission and resignation I beg to be spared to bring up my children, which in mercy are given me, to serve their generation according to the will of God, and that I may see the goodness of God to the Church in the land of my nativity, and be someway serviceable thereunto; that having seen the salvation of the Lord, I may depart in peace, my spirit being received by God who gave it, and my body sleeping in Jesus, until the last day, when both body and soul shall be glorified and be ever with the Lord, who loved and washed me from my sins in His blood. Even so, come Lord Jesus! come quickly. Amen.

NOTES TO THE LETTERS.

P. 1. *Lord Brooke.*—Fulke Grevile, Lord Brooke, was great-uncle to the lady Brilliana, her grandfather, Sir John Conway, having married his sister Eleanor. Collins, Peerage, vol. v. p. 225. Lond. ed. 1768.

Beaetham's Court.—Beauchamp Court, co. Warwick, the seat of Lord Brooke.

Tuddington.—Toddington, co. Gloucester, the seat of her grandfather, Sir John Tracy.

P. 2. *I hope the Parlament has spent as much time as will satisfy them in dooing nothing.*—Sir Robert Harley sat in the second Parliament of that year for the county of Hereford, from 6 Feb. 1625-6, to 15 June, 1626. (Willis, Notitia Parliamentaria.)

The payling of the nwe parke is made an end of.—The park adjoining Wigmore Castle was in a very decayed and neglected state, when it was granted to Sir Robert Harley.

P. 3. *I hope your clocke did you sarvis betwne Glostre and my brother Brays.*—Sir Giles Bray, of Barrington, in the county of Gloucester, son of Edmund Bray, Esq. by Dorothy, daughter of Sir John Tracy, who married, secondly, Sir Edward Conway.

P. 4. *Mr. Pirson.*—The Rector of Brampton Bryan.

P. 5. *Present my beest love to my sister Wacks.*—A contraction, probably, of Helegenwagh, the third daughter of Lord Conway, wife of Sir W. Smith, of Hill Hall, co. Essex.

P. 6. *Ragley.*—The seat of Lord Viscount Conway, in Warwickshire.

Lady Veere.—She was the third daughter of Sir John Tracy, of Toddington, and aunt to the Lady Brilliana. Collins, Life of Vere, p. 342.

P. 7. *Ned Smith.*—Son of Sir Wm. Smith, by Helegenwagh, sister of Lady Brilliana.

P. 8. *Mrs. Willkinson.*—Wife of Dr. Willkinson, Principal of Magdalen Hall, Oxford. See Notes to the Introduction, p. xlix.

NOTES TO THE LETTERS.

P. 10. *I had not hard of Duke Roberts and my Lord Crauens being taken.*—Robert third son of the Elector Palatine and Elizabeth, daughter of King James, better known as Prince Rupert. In the battle of Lingen, in Westphalia, between the Emperor and Palatine, the forces of the latter were overpowered, and Duke Robert and Lord Craven made prisoners.

William Craven, eldest son of Sir William Craven, Lord Mayor of London (1611), having distinguished himself in foreign service, was knighted 4 March, 1626, and, eight days afterwards, created Baron Craven.

P. 12. *A booke printed by authority from the King, in which he has forbid the Booke of Common Prayer, and granted them a public fast.*—In Sept. 1638, the Marquis of Hamilton published a royal Proclamation in Scotland, which is "the Book" here alluded to.

P. 13. *Mrs. Pirson.*—Widow of the Rev. Thomas Pierson, the Rector of Brampton Bryan.

I thanke you for the Man in the Moune.—The Man in the Moon, by Domingo Gonzales, was the title of a posthumous work by Francis Godwin, Bishop of Hereford 1617—1633.

P. 14. *At Loudlow wheare the caus was hard.*—In the Court of the Council of the Marches of Wales.

P. 18. *I hope theare will no such things be imposed upon your howes.*—That is, innovations in religious matters on Magdalen Hall.

P. 19. *By order of the Lords.*—The Lords of Privy Council, or the Lords Lieutenants of counties, issued orders to the magistrates and deputy lieutenants to take measures for keeping the peace and calling out and regulating the militia, in which Sir Robert Harley had a company: they were about this time usually trained by Low Country officers and soldiers. "Sargent Weare was one of these; he had been in Germany under Sir Thomas Conway."

Cousin Scriven.—Thomas Scriven of Frodesley, in co. Salop, colonel of a regiment of foot of the trained bands in that county: married Elizabeth daughter of Vincent Corbet or Moreton Corbet, and widow of Thomas Corbet. He was distinguished for his loyalty, and knighted, probably at Shrewsbury, soon after the battle of Edge Hill; and was buried in Condover Church, Salop.

For Forane newes, I beleeve you have hard that Brisacke is taken.—Old Brisach or Brisac, a town of the Grand Duchy of Baden, once included in the Brisgau: it formerly stood on the west side of the Rhine, but since the river changed its course it is near the east bank of it, between Basle and Strasburg. It was regarded as a strong place, and sustained several seiges; the most remarkable was that here alluded to, when it was taken by Duke Bernard of Saxe Weimar. (Encyc. Metrop.)

The Curantes are lisened againe.—Books of foreign news again licensed.

P. 21. *Mr. Penell: his mother was Sir Edwards Grevell's daughter, and so she was my cosen.*—Sir Edward Grevill being brother-in-law to Sir John Conway, his daughter was first cousin to Edward Viscount Conway, the father of the Lady Brilliana.

Mr. Scidamore that dwells hard by Heariford.—Mr. afterwards Sir John Scudamore, knight, eldest son of William Scudamore of Ballingham, co. Hereford, married Penelope sister of John, first Lord Scudamore. He was a distinguished traveller in Italy and other parts, a royalist, and took up arms in the King's cause, and was killed in a duel with Colonel David Hyde at Bristol, 12 May, 1645, and was there buried in the church of St. Werburgh.

P. 22. *Duke Robard and Lord Crauen prisoners.*—Prince Rupert was under restraint for upwards of three years: at length reluctantly liberated by the Emperor, through the mediation of Sir Thomas Roe, the English ambassador, upon solemn promise never again to bear arms against that prince.

P. 24. *Mr. Pirkins.*—Mr. Edward Perkins, under whose tutorage Edward Harley now was, at Magdalen Hall.

P. 25. *Lady Cope.*—Lady Elizabeth Cope, second daughter of Francis first Earl of Westmorland. She was wife of Sir John Cope, of Hanwell, Bart., and married secondly William Cope of Icomb, co. Gloucester. (Collins's Peerage, iii. p. 183.)

P. 27. *The holy Court.*—An English translation of "La Cour Sainte"—a devotional work of Nicholas Coussin, a learned jesuit, confessor to Louis XIII. This is perhaps the work alluded to in p. 13, where Lady B. says, "I would willingly have the French booke you write me word of .... for I had rather reade any thinge in that tounge then in Inglisch."

P. 31. *Theare is a booke which is rwitten by a papis that is conuerted; it discouers much.*—Probably "The Religion of Protestants a Safe Way to Salvation, by Will. Chillingworth, M.A." which was published in 1637 or 1638.

P. 32. *My Lord of Woster's sonne shall be generall of the hors.*—Edward Somerset, Lord Herbert of Ragland, afterwards known as Earl of Glamorgan, and second Marquis of Worcester, the author of "A Century of Inventions."

P. 37. *Good Mr. Stevenson.*—Vicar of Wigmore. The register of that parish records the baptism of one of his daughters by the name of Brilliana, in compliment to Lady Brilliana Harley.

P. 39. *The Act.*—Scholastic exercises at Oxford: again p. 45.

P. 46. *I haue sent some bessor stone, which you may take at a night when you goo to bede.*—Bezoars: concretions met with in the bodies of ruminant animals. They were celebrated for their supposed medicinal virtues, and considered as highly alexipharmic; so much so, that other medicines supposed to possess the same virtues obtained the name of bezoardics. So efficacious were they once thought, that they were eagerly bought for ten times their weight in gold. Besides being exhibited internally, they were worn round the neck, as preservatives against contagion. For this purpose, it is said, in Portugal it was customary to hire them at about ten shillings per day. It is needless to add, that the accounts of their extrordinary virtues must be now considered imaginary. See a further account in the Encyclopædia Metropolitana.

Orampotabely.—Aurum potabile. Another medicine rejected from the Materia Medica, but formerly much vaunted by empirics as a most powerful tonic. (Encyclopædia Metropolitana.)

P. 49. *Mr. Simons, a worthy minister, and three or fower more are gone into the Low Contreyes to shift for themselves.*—Escaping from the contributions required from ministers towards supplying the army: before alluded to in p. 37.

P. 51. *I thanke you for the King's booke.*—The large declaration concerning the tumults of Scotland, by the King, 1639, written by Dr. Balcanquall, Dean of Durham.

P. 63. *Letter* XLVIII.—Terminating the first series of Letters addressed to Edward Harley at Oxford.

P. 64. *Letter* XLIX.—Edward Harley returns again to Oxford.

P. 66. *I thanke you for the relation of the seae fight.*—A relation of the engagement between the Dutch and Spanish fleets in the Downs, which took place early in September.

P. 68. *Sir Richard Newport.*—Created Lord Newport 1642. Brother of Sir Robert Harley's second wife.

P. 69. *If the venter of the Corrantes be in prison.*—Vendor of foreign news.

P. 72. *There is a Duch imbasodr, Mounsire Arttson, come over to excuse the fighting of the Duch ships upon the Inglisch cost.*—Van Aersen, Lord Somnelsdyke. Another object of this embassy was the marriage of the Prince of Orange with the Princess Mary. (Baillie's Letters, 29 Jan. 1640-1, vol. i. p. 294.)

P. 81. *Sir William Pelham hath refused to be knight of the shire.*—For Lincolnshire, in the first parliament of 1640, which met on the 17th April, and was dissolved on the 5th May following,

P. 84. *Mr. Blineman is goon into New Ingland.*—One of the Puritan ministers.

P. 87. *On Tuesday next, if pleas God, your father will keep a day.*—In this parliament Sir Robert Harley and Sir Walter Pye represented the county of Hereford. He now sets apart a day for solemn prayer, in preparation for his duties in parliament.

P. 95. *On Sunday morning I receved a letter from your father, by which I found the nwes of the disolueing of the parlament to be true.*—On Sunday, the 10th May, Lady Brilliana hears from Sir Robert a confirmation of the rumour of the dissolution of parliament which took place on Tuesday (Die Martis) the 5th of May.

P. 100. *Letter* LXXXIII.—Ends another series of letters to Edward Harley at Oxford.

P. 101. *Letter* LXXXIV.—Finds Edward Harley with his father in London.

P. 103. *I heare that parlament is ajournded for ten days, but I defer my beleefe.*—A mere rumour. Parliament sat all December.

P. 105. *Mrs. Wallcote was with me this weake.*—The wife of Humphrey Walcot, of Walcot, Esq., whose funeral sermon, under the title of "The Gale of Opportunity," was published with that preached at the funeral of Sir Robert Harley, by Thos. Froysell, minister of Clun, in Shropshire.
Dr. Toby Mathue was with Mr. Plooden, wheare theare was great resort of papis, which makes some feare they haue some plots.—At Plowden Hall, near Walcot, the seat of a Catholic family who have enjoyed the estate, from which they derive their name, as far back as our records extend. Sir Toby Mathew was a Jesuit of the order of Politicians.

P. 106. *Mr. Tomms was at Brompton and helpt us in my family.*—In the religious exercises of the previous Wednesday. This was most probably John Tombes, B.D., a most eminent divine of his sect, settled at this time at Leominster, whom Calamy says, in his abridgment of Baxter's History of his Life and Times, "all the world must own to have been a very considerable man and excellent scholar, howsoever disinclined they may be to his particular opinions." See a list of his works in Calamy, and further particulars in Neal's History of the Puritans, and also in Wood's Athenæ, vol. iii. p. 1063.

P. 112. *I thought the Jesuet had bine acuesed of treson. I hope the King will yeald to the request of the parlament in that particular.*—The person alluded to was John Goodman, a priest and Jesuit, whose history is well known.

P. 117. *I hope my brother is not for Lord Straford: I hard my Lord Straford layed some of his actions to his charge.*—Lord Conway gave adverse evidence on Strafford's trial.

P. 118. *If you have bine to hear the Scots ministers, send me word how you like them.*—"The people throngs to our sermon, as ever yow saw any to Irwin communion: their crowd daylie increasses. Six of us, Mr. Blair, Mr. Henderson, Mr. Borthick, Mr. Gillespie, Mr. Smith, and I preaches our tour about on Sunday and Thursday. In my last tour on the 3d verse of the 126th Psalm, ' The Lord hath done great things for us," I spent much of an hour in ane historick narration, the best I could penn, of all that God had done for us fra the maid's commotion in the Cathedroll of Edinburgh to that present day: monie teares of compassion and joy did fall from the eyes of the English." Baillie's Letters, vol. i. p. 295.

I thanks you for the paper the Scots put into the Lords.—Many papers were put in for money on account of the 300,000*l.* granted in February to supply the wants of the army before it was disbanded. In the end of the following May 120,000*l.* of arrears were due. On the 19th June it was concluded that 100,000*l.* should be paid Midsummer 1642, and 200,000*l.* at Midsummer two years after. (May's Hist. of the Long Parliament.)

P. 121. *Letter* cvi. *misdated in the year.*—Letter cvi. 25 March, 1641, appears to be misdated and misplaced in the collection: it would naturally follow Letter cxliii (19 March, 1641), in which it is said, " I hear the justices have sent up their answer why they would not take the Protestation—Sir Will. Croft governs all of them," and should be dated 1642. The protestation mentioned in it was, no doubt, that taken by the House of Commons 3 May, 1641, which was considered by the parliament " a true test of every good subject," " a shibboleth to distinguish the Ephramites from the Gileadites, that whosoever was well affected in religion and to the good of the commonwealth would take, and on the other side who would not take it was not well affected " (Denzel Holles' Speech to the House of Lords): and which was designed to be taken by all well-wishers to the Parliamentary cause. It appears from Letter cxvii., 21 May, 1641, to have been taken with great willingness at Brampton, Wigmore, and Lentwardine, where Sir Robert Harley's influence predominated, but it was not well received in the country; and, on the 20 Jan. 1641-2, a few days after the King's attempt to seize the *five* members, Serjeant Wilde brought up from his committee, for the signature of the Speaker, a copy of a letter to the sheriffs, requiring the justices of the peace and others, of 18 years of age and upwards, to take it. (See Appendix, p. 222.) The petition alluded to in this letter was probably the Hereford Petition, afterwards presented to the House, and well received by it in May, 1642. This letter acquaints us also with the views of Sir William Croft towards the Parliament, and soon after the raising of the standard at Nottingham in August, although he had been for some time under the displeasure of the King, he joined his majesty's army, and was with the King, to his great admiration, at Edge Hill.

P. 124. *Sir William Croft.*—Sir William Croft, of Croft Castle, in the county of Hereford, was son of Sir Herbert Croft, and born 1593: he represented Malmesbury in Parliament in 1625-1627. He was a gentleman of the Privy Chamber to King Charles; but, having evinced his dislike to the Duke of Buckingham, he was suspended from his office for three years, and on his murder banished from the court and dismissed. This treatment did not destroy his attachment to his royal master, in whose army he held the rank of colonel, and particularly distinguished himself at the battle of Edge Hill. He was taken prisoner at the surrender of Hereford on April 25th, 1643, but soon afterwards recovered his liberty, and was killed gallantly fighting in the royal cause, in a skirmish near Hopton Castle, or, as others say, near Stokesay Castle in Shropshire, July, 1645, and was buried in the chancel at Croft, where there is a slab to his memory. See Memoir of Sir James Croft in Southern and Nicolas' Retrospective Review and Historical Magazine, vol. i. p. 496. London.

P. 129. *I am glad my Lord Saye is Master of the Wards.*—" 17 May, 1641. The Lord Cottington gave up his place of Master of the Wards, which the Lord Say had conferred on him." Whitelocke's Memorials, p. 44.

P. 130. *The Protestation was taken on Sabath day last at Brompton, Wigmore, and Lainterdine, with much willingness. I desire to know whether you took it.*—This protestation must have been that taken by the House of Commons on the 4th of May. The readiness with which it was taken marks the great influence of Sir Robert Harley in these places. It was much objected to and resisted in the country.

I have sent you a peace of angelica rooat, you may carry it in your pocket, and bite sometimes of it.—" A pious and learned schoolmaster, that ventured to stay in London in the Great Plague of 1665, and was much employed, as some friends of mine that knew him and commended him assured me, to visit the sick, and distribute alms and relief to them, went indiscriminately to all sorts of infected, and even dying persons, to the number, as he told me, of nine hundred or a thousand. . . . . . I enquired what antidote he used: he replied, that next the protection of God, which so many sad objects made him the more fervently implore, and a constant fearlessness, the only preservative he used, besides good diet, were, half a spoonful or a spoonful of brandy five or six times a-day, especially when he went into infected places, and the bigness of a small nut, or less, of a root of Spanish angelica, of which he held in his mouth the quantity of a pepper-corn, or somewhat less, as often as he thought there was need." Relation iii. of Strange Reports, Robert Boyle's Works, vol. v. p. 102.

P. 131. *I am glad that justice is exicuted on my Lord Straford, whoo I thinke dyed like a Seneca, but not like one that had tasted of the mistery of godlyness.*—Wednesday, 12 May. " The Earl of Strafford beheaded on Tower hill. Some doubted whether his death had more of the Roman or the Christian, it was so full of both." Laud's Diary.

P. 135. *Rwit me word how the pasage was of Mr. Harberde Pris his carage in the parliament, becaus theare is such rarious reports of it.*—Mr. Herbert Price was burgess for Brecon in both parliaments of 1640. He is noted in Cobbett's Parliamentary History as one who left the Parliament and joined the King at Oxford, and was among the forty-six members who, on the call of the House, 16 June, 1642, were absent, when it was resolved "that those absent members whose names were now read shall not sit in the House till they have made their excuse to the Committee, and their excuse reported to the House, and that the House hath allowed it." Journ. H. Com. 16 June, 1642.

P. 136. *I am glad Corenell Goreing did so well cleere himself. We heare of many plots, &c.*—Lord Strafford's escape, it is said, had been planned. Master Goreing, eldest son of the Lord Goreing, was implicated in the charge, but, upon examination, dealt so clearly with the charge, and so far purged himself from evil intentions, that he was not at all committed by the Parliament. May's Hist of the Long Parliament.

P. 140. *I thanke you for the acts of Parlament, and for Docter Dowing booke.*—This was probably a book of the notorious Colybute Downing, of whom an account will be found in Wood's Athenæ, vol. iii. p. 106, too long to abstract, and too curious and edifying not to claim the reading of all who have access to it.

P. 142. *I thanke you for the King's manifest.*—Journ. H. Commons, 5 July, 1641. "The King's manifesto touching the Prince Elector read, and *Ordered*, That the House be resolved into a Committee on Wednesday next, at nine o'clock, to take into consideration *the manifesto* now received concerning the Prince Elector Palatine." Sir Robert Harley was of this Committee. The manifesto will be found in Nalson's Collections, vol. ii. p. 383.

P. 144. *Letter* CXXXIII. *9 Aug.* 1641.—This letter terminates another series of letters addressed to Edward Harley, who now returns home from London.

Letter CXXXIV. *undated and misplaced.*—Letter CXXXIV. undated, contains allusions to Dr. Wright's exertions in the Hereford city election subsequent to the death of Mr. Weaver, Member for that place, which, it will be seen, took place in May, 1642: and also to a Proclamation in Shobdon church, which was most probably made after the receipt of the Speaker's letter to the sheriff; for Mr. Wigmore exercised at Shobdon a contrary influence to Sir Robert at Brampton. It would follow Letter CLXXIX., dated 2 July, 1642, which announces Sir W. Croft and Mr. Wigmore's intention of going to the King, or rather the previous letter, CLXXVIII. The original of Letter CLXXIX. is in a very decayed state, and the date in part obliterated: it was certainly written in the week of the 23rd, as it speaks of Wigmore fair to be held on the Monday following, which, according to the old style, took place on the 25th of July, which was on Monday, but before CLXXVIII. as it says Mr. Elton had not arrived to supper at 10 o'clock, whereas that letter says he came at four o'clock, no doubt of the following day. It would, there placed, terminate another series of letters addressed to Edward Harley before his return home: this it does as now printed.

P. 146. *Letter* CXXXV. *5 Feb.* 1641-2.—Commences a new series addressed to Edw. Harley in London.

NOTES TO THE LETTERS. 259

P. 147. *I doe much recoige in the King's answer to the petcion of both Houses, and that my brother was one of the sixe and threetie lords that voted against the bishopes.*—See Journ. H. Com. 7 Feb. 1641-2.

Answers to two petitions of the Lords and Commons, delivered 2 Feb. 1641, will be seen in the Appendix to May's Hist. of the Long Parliament. Oxford edition, 1854.

"Feb. 1641-2. The Lords pass the Bill for disabling persons in holy orders to have any place or vote in Parliament.

"Lord Conway was well affected to the Parliament and the Presbyterian discipline, and was one of the lords selected to be of the Assembly of Divines." (See the list in Neal's Hist. of the Puritans.)

"Sir Rob. Harley carried up this Bill with its amendments to the Lords." Journ. H. Com. 7 Feb. 1641-2.

P. 148. *In Hareford they have turned the tabell in the cathedroll, and taken away the cops and bassons and all such things. I hope they begine to see that the Lord is about to purg the Church of all such inuencions of men.*—See the Order of the House of Commons on divers innovations in and about the worship of God. Journ. H. Com. 1 Sept. 1641.

P. 149. *I am glad to hear that Sir Jhon Conyars is leftenant of the Tower.*—On the removal of Sir John Byron, Sir John Conyars was made Lieutenant of the Tower, Jan. 1641-2. Whitelock, p. 53.

They are now about a peticion to the Parlament, which I hope will be ready to send up next weake.—A petition was on the 4th May, 1642, presented for Herefordshire, and well received by the House of Commons. See the petition in Appendix, p. 226.

We heare of letters that weare intersepted from my Lord Digbe.—Letters intercepted from Lord Digby to the Queen and Secretary Nicholas, on which the Parliament moved the King, "that he would desire the Queen not to correspond with Digby, nor any other persons whom his great council had proclaimed traytors. Jan. 1642." Whitelocke, p. 52.

P. 150. *Many feares did aris in the cuntry because the Kinge gaue such a refusall to the requeste of both Howes.*—To the petition of both Houses concerning the militia, presented to his Majesty at Theobalds, 1 March, 1641.

It was a most remarqabell thinge that shipe was cast away in which thos fopperis weare.—See Journ. H. Commons, 2nd and 4th March, 1641-2.

P. 151. *Piner sends up 20l. to venture in the Irisch wars.*—24 Feb. 1641-2. The King assents to the votes of the Lords and Commons upon the propositions made for the speedy and effectual reducing of the Kingdom of Ireland. This was a scheme of adventure for raising money on the confiscated lands of the rebels in Ireland. See the scheme in Appendix to May's History, and in the Journals of the House of Commons.

260   NOTES TO THE LETTERS.

P. 152. *I did much long to receave the declaration to the King.*—"A new declaration of both Houses of Parliament sent to the King's most excellent Majesty, 16 March, upon his removall from Huntingdon to York." See May's Hist. Appendix, p. 493.

I heare the justices have sent up theare answer why they would not take the Protestation.— The Protestation of the 4th May, 1641, now demanded of all of eighteen years of age and upwards. See Appendix, p. 221, and note, page 121.

I hope shortly you will have the peticion from this county, but Sir Will. Croft disswaded it, as a thing unlawful to peticion.—See the petition in Appendix, p. 226. It was presented 4th May, 1642, and is again alluded to in pages 158—159.

P. 155. *Mr Gower is very well pleased that he is chosen on of the ministers.*—Journ. H. Com. 23 April, 1642. "Mr. John Green of Pencomb, and Mr. Stanley Gower of Brampton, were approved as divines for Herefordshire, fit to be consulted in the matters of the Church. The Bill for calling the Assembly of Godly and Learned Divines was read the third time 19 May, 1642." A list of them will be found in Rushworth Abridged, and Neal's History of the Puritans.

P. 158. *We hard the Kentiche peticion was brought by 3000 men, and that 3000 Loundoners meete them upon Blackeheath, and theare fought, and many weare killed.*—This was the celebrated Kentish Petition. Its reception is thus entered on the Journ. H. Com. 30 April, 1642: "The House being informed that divers gentlemen of the co. of Kent were at the door that desired to present a petition to the House, they were called in, presented their petition, and then withdrew. And their petition was read, and appeared to be the same that was formerly burnt, by order of both Houses, by the hands of the common hangman."

P. 159. *I hope something will be done to Docter Rogers.*—Dr. Henry Rogers, Canon Residentiary of Hereford Cathedral, and Rector of Stoke Edith, in Herefordshire. He was of Jesus College, Oxford, and became a famous preacher and schoolmaster. He was a member of the Convocation assembled with the Parliament of Nov. 1640, a decided Royalist, and, on the surrender of Hereford in April, 1643, was made prisoner. His preferments were sequestered, and his prebendal house, furniture, &c. bestowed on Dr. Timothy Woodroffe, a gifted chaplain, mentioned in the Introduction as having been promoted by Sir Robert Harley to the rectory of Kingsland, and a Parliamentary Preacher in Hereford cathedral. Wood informs us that Rogers had been acquainted with John Perse, alias Fisher, the Jesuit, with whom he had many disputes, and who, without authority, published an account of what had passed between them, which brought from Rogers an answer by way of Dialogue between Mr. Rogers and Mr. Fisher, 1633, to which Fisher published a reply, which was followed by Rogers in "The Protestant Church existent, and their Faith professed in all ages, and by whom. Lond. 1638." Wood's Athenæ, vol. iii, p 31. Walker's Sufferings of the Clergy, part 2, p. 35.

P. 160. *I desire to heare how Sir Jhon Conyars comes off for Onell's escape.*—O'Neile escaped from the Tower, 5 May, 1642. "On May 13th, it was ordered that Sir Walter Erle do report the business of Mr. Daniel O'Neile's escape to-morrow morning. 17 May, Sir Walt. Erle reports the business of the escape; that the greatest matter of suspicion fell on Mrs Sanders, who confessed she had once attempted it, but, being told of the danger of it, gave it over: notwithstanding that, many circumstances still stuck on her, for being at least knowing of his escape; and that therefore he had given order that she should put in good security for her appearance at such time as she should be required." See the Nicholas Correspondence, published with Diary and Correspondence of John Evelyn, vol. iv. p. 128.

Your father rwiteing to me by the post, and letting me knowe you weare to see the soulders on Tuesday last, I tooke it that that hindered you.—Journ. H. Com. Monday, 9 May, 1642. "*Ordered*, That the House shall meet to-morrow at eight, and adjourn at ten, to the end that such as please may see the militia of the city of London exercised."

They were assembled in Finsbury fields under the command of Philip Skippon, Major-General of all the city forces under the Parliament.

I thinke if Mr Schirbere be reproufed it would be very well.—William Sherbourn, D.D. Prebendary of Morton Parva, in the county of Hereford, suffered much for the King's cause, and lost all his preferments, to which he was re-admitted at the Restoration. He was Rector of Pembridge, where he died in 1679, aged ninety-two years. Walker says, "He had, at the persuasion of his old friend, the Earl of Essex, taken the Covenant, for which he was much disturbed in his last sickness." Walker's Sufferings of the Clergy, part 2, p. 36.

P. 161. *Sir Wm. Pelham rwites me word he has given up his liftenatcy, and his gooing to Yorke to the King.*—Early in May the Commons issued their ordinance for raising the militia, which the King commanded his subjects not to obey. On this, the Commons published a declaration, forbidding all persons to obey the King's proclamation. Orders were then sent into all the counties to muster the militia, and the King summoned the gentry of Yorkshire as a defence of his person.

P. 162. *The ocation of this letter is to let you knowe that Mr. Weafer is dead.*—Richard Weaver and Richard Seabourne, Esqs. were burgesses for the city of Hereford.

There had been previous rumours of Mr. Weaver's death, which had excited in the mind of the Lady Brilliana, a desire that her son Edward should succeed him. Dr. Wright had been actively engaged on that occasion, and is again now; but James Scudamore, Esq. appears to have been elected. Seabourne and Scudamore were Royalists, and, having joined the King at Oxford, were disabled by the House, when Edmund Weaver and Bennet Hoskins, Esqs. were elected in 1646. Willis's Notitia Parliamentaria, and Cobbett's Parl. History.

Sir Robert Harley's colleague was Fitzwilliam Coningsby, Esq. who was disabled 30 Oct. 1641 (Journ. H. Com.) as a monopolist, and was succeeded by Humphrey

Coningsby, Esq. who, having joined the King at Oxford, was also disabled, and made way for the election of Edward Harley in 1646.

P. 166. *I thinke we must all acknowledeg God's greate mercy that the plot for the takeing of Hull was discouered.*—Journ. H. Com. 27 May, 1642. "A letter from Sir John Hotham, concerning a treasonable attempt upon Hull, was this day read, and a letter from Beckwith, who was the great agent in that matter.

"*Ordered*, That this letter from Sir John Hotham of the 25 May, and the letter of Beckwith, and the other papers inclosed, shall be forthwith printed. *Resolved*, upon the question, That Thomas Beckwith, of Beverley, shall be forthwith sent for as a delinquent by the serjeant-at-arms attending this House." For particulars of the design upon Hull, see Rushworth Abridged, vol. iv. p. 851.

P. 167. *At Loudlow they sett up a May-pole and a thinge like a head vpon it, and so they did at Croft, and gathered a greate many about it, and shot at it in derision of Roundheads.*—Roundheads, the name imposed on the Parliamentarians. "The origin of this name is not certainly known: some say it was because the Puritans then commonly wore short hair, and the King's party long flowing hair. Some say it was because the Queen, at Strafford's trial, asked, who that round-headed man was (meaning Pym), because he spake so strongly." Baxter's Narrative of his Life and Times, quoted in Trench, on the Study of Words, p. 137.

In the Bishops' riot, Westminster, 1641, "Some cavaliers and discarded officers retained in the King's service who were walking near, indignant at the rudeness of the crowd, still more foolishly attacked the Roundheads with drawn swords." Buchanan's Hist. of Scotland, vol. iv. p. 66.

Journ. H. Com. 1 Feb. 1641. "*Ordered*, That the pamphlet entitled, The Resolution of the Roundheads, be referred to the Committee for Printing. Steph. Buckle, St. Martin's Lane, London, ordered to attend the Committee."

P. 169. *In my opinion it weare better to borrow money, if your father will give any, then to give his plate.*—Journ. H. Com. 10 June, 1642. An order for the bringing in of money, horses, and plate, to be repaid at 8 per cent. with full value of the plate, and consideration for the fashion, not exceeding 1s. per oz. Sir Robert responds to this order, and on 19th Sept. 1642 (Journ. H. Com.) saith, "he hath brought in three hundred and fifty pounds in plate, and will bring in one hundred and fifty pounds more, and provide two horses." Other notices, occur in the Journals, of moneys advanced by Sir Robert Harley. How zealously Lady Brilliana concurred with her husband appears from her readiness to send up the plate, and from this letter, in which she says, "This I doo not say, that I am unwilling to part with the plate, or any thing ells in this case: if your father cannot borrow money, I thinke I might finde out some in the cuntry to lend him some."

P. 173. *When Sir Will. Croft came to me, he came from my Lord Harbert.* 25 June 1642.—Lord Herbert was now busy in making levies in the King's cause under the Commission of Array.

I heare that Sir W. Croft has commanded the beackon nwe furnished and nwe piche put into it.—Into the beacon which formerly stood near the Beacon-gate, on Croft Ambry. Under authority of the Commission of Array, beacons were to be provided and other necessaries for better exercising the people and discovering sudden invasions and commotions.

P. 176. *The Kinge has sent a commistion to 12 of the justices to settele the milica.*—The Commission of Array for Leicestershire was issued 11 June, 1642. Rushworth Abridged, vol. iv. p. 401. On the 18th June, Serjeant Wilde reported that the Committee of Lords and Commons appointed to consider of the Commission of Array in Leicestershire were all of opinion, that it was against the law and against the liberty and property of the subject.

The Editor has not met with any copy of the Commission of Array for Herefordshire. Journal of the House of Commons, 21 Sept. 1642, "A warrant was read under the hands of Wallop Brabazon, Esq. Sir Will. Croft, Fitzwilliam Conningsbye, Thos. Price, Henry Lingen, Will. Rudhall, Esqs. Commissioners of Array for the co. of Hereford, directed to the high sheriff of the said county, requiring him thereby to raise such forces as he shall think fitting for the apprehending of Priamus Davies, who had been summoned by divers warrants from them, and had refused to appear, and for conveying him to his Majesty's gaol. On which, Mr. Davies having been called in and avowing it was a true copy of the warrant, it was *Resolved*, That Wallop Brabazon, Esq., Sir Wm. Croft, Knt., Fitzw. Conningsbye, Esq., Mr. Thos. Price, Mr. Henry Lingen, and Will. Rudhall, Esq. be forthwith sent for as delinquents."

The name of Priamus Davies occurs in the Register of Brampton Bryan.

The militia summoned to meet at Hereford on the 15th July was, no doubt, under the authority of the Commission of Array.

P. 180. *The captaine of the voluntiers is one Barell.*—James Barroll was Mayor of Hereford, 1639. Price's Hist. of Hereford, 1796.

P. 182. *My cosen Tomkins is as violent as ever, and many thinks that her very words is in the Heariford resolutions. I beleeve it was Mr. Mason's penning.*—Mary, the daughter of Sir Herbert Croft, and sister to Sir William Croft, was baptized at Croft, 21 Dec. 1598, and married Richard Tomkyns, of Monnington, in the county of Hereford.

Sir Herbert Croft having joined the Roman Catholic church, and taken up his residence at Douay, addressed "letters persuasive to his wife and children in England to take upon them the Catholic religion. These letters appear to have been answered, if not by his daughter Mary, in her name, as he afterwards printed a reply to the answer of his daughter M. C., which she made to a paper sent to her concerning the Roman church." Wood's Athenæ, vol. ii. 318.

By referring to the Appendix, p. 223, it will be seen that the declaration or resolution of the county of Hereford was regarded by the House of Commons as a most libellous paper. The copies of it most probably shared the fate of Lord Digby's speech, the Kentish petition, and other offensive papers, which were burnt by the common hangman. The researches of James Edward Davis, of the Middle Temple, Esq. have brought to light a copy of it, "imprinted at London by a printed copie, 1642." It is found in vol. ii. of the folio collection of Civil War Tracts, presented by King George III. to the British Museum.

P. 182. *Letter* CLXXIX. *misplaced.*—See p. 258, for a note on this transposition.

P. 186. *I would have rwite to him, but I durst not rwite upon papaper. Dear Ned, rwite to me, though you rwite upon a peace of clothe, as this is.*—Letter CLXXXII. commences the last series of letters addressed to Edward Harley. It is written upon cloth for facility of concealment about the person.

Thears a 1000 dragonears came into Harford 5 owers offther my Lord Harferd.— William Marquis of Hertford, under the Commission of Array, was appointed Lord Lieutenant-General of Devon, Cornwall, Somerset, Dorset, Wilts, Southampton, Gloucester, Bucks, Oxford, Hereford, and seven counties within the principality of Wales. May's Hist. of the Long Parliament, p. 223.

P. 189. *The soulders are goon before Gloster: theaire randevous is Sir Ro. Cookes howes. 25 Feb.* 1642-3.—"In Feb. the troops, 1500 foot and 500 horse, collected by Lord Herbert, advanced towards Gloster, and were intrenched at Highnam, within 2 miles of the city, where, on the 22nd and 23rd March, they were completely routed by Sir Will. Waller and Genl. Massey." Introduction to Bibliotheca Gloucesteriensis, pp. xxxiv. xxxvi.

P. 196. *I know not wheather this sessation of armes will stay them.*—In the propositions for peace presented from the Parliament to the King at Oxford, in 31 Jan. 1642-3, and in those sent back by the Commissioners to the Parliament, one was, that there be a cessation of arms during the treaty. The treaty was still in debate. After many messages between London and Oxford, the Commissioners were recalled, and returned to London, 17th April, 1643. May's Hist. of Long Parliament, 277-278.

P. 198. *I heare some say you have an imployment.*—Edward Harley was, about this time, made Captain of a troop of horse in the Parliamentary army.

The report in the cuntry is that my Lord Capell comes very shortly to be Governor of Shrewsbury.—Sir Francis Ottley was at this time Governor of Shrewsbury, but the Prince of Wales was commander-in-chief, assisted by a council, and Arthur Lord Capell was constituted Lieut.-General under His Royal Highness, and took up his abode at that place. Owen and Blakeway's Hist. of Shrewsbury, vol. i. p. 433.

Honnest Petter taken. 6 May, 1643.—After the surrender of Hereford, 24 April, Sir W. Waller made a visit to Leominster, where there was some skirmishing. Petter probably had been sent to pick up what information he could of events in that neighbourhood, and, in returning home, fell in with some of Sir W. Croft's friends about Mortimer's Cross, and was there made prisoner.

God has mightily been seen in Hearcfordsheere.—In the success attending Sir William Waller's attack upon Hereford, which surrendered to him on quarter, 24 April, 1643. Lord Scudamore, James Scudamore, Esq. M.P. for Hereford, Col. Herbert Price, M.P. for Brecon, Sir Rich. Cave, M.P. for Lichfield, Lieut.-Col. Coningsby, and his son, Humphrey Coningsby, M.P. for Herefordshire (five revolted members of the House of Commons), Sir Will. Croft, Sir Walter Pye, Sir Saml. Amby, and Drs. Rogers, Goodwin, and Evans of the cathedral, and many others, were made prisoners, and all carried to Gloucester. May's Hist. of the Long Parliament, p. 315.

Within three days, Sir W. Waller surprised Leominster, where he took good prize, and disarmed many of the royal party, and placing a garrison there, scoured the country to the gates of Worcester, where meeting with an unexpected repulse, he withdrew to Reading. Webb's Introduction to Bibliotheca Gloucesteriensis, p. xxxix.

P. 199. *I have sent you on to be of your troope, and have furnished him with a hors. The hors coost me 8l.*—Journ. H. Com. 22 March, 1642-3. "Ordered, That the four horses of the Lady Petre, three of Mr. White's of Bacons, three of Barnard's of Westland, one of Robert Goodyere, be all sent to my Lord General, to be employed for the publick service, but one, which is to be given to Edm. Brasier, who seized them; and that it be recommended unto my Lord General, that Capt. Harley may have the horses for the furnishing of his troop, and that Mr. Pym write a letter to my Lord General to this purpose."

P. 202. *We are still threatened, some soulders are billeted at Pursla.*—5 or 6 miles north of Brampton Bryan.

Lef.-Couxenell Massey is commanded to be Gouernor of Gloster.—Soon after the surrender of Hereford. See Corbet's historical relation of the military government of Gloucester; also, notice of Col. Massie in Notes to Webb's Introduction to the Bibliotheca Gloucesteriensis, pp. clxxxix.—cciii. It will be seen by Edward Harley's retrospect on the completion of his fiftieth year, in the Appendix, p. 249, that Sir Edward Massie died in April, 1674.

In Lady Frances V. Harcourt's collections is the following letter, which, it is supposed, was written by Col. Massie's wife: the circumstance of his flight into Holland in the spring, 1648, makes it probable that she was left, like others in these sad times, in distress:—

"Noble Sir,—I lately receaved a letter from Capt. Blayney, in wch hee writes mee that hee hath given unto you, for my use, the sume of ffive pounds, wch ffive pounds I entreate you will bee pleased to sende unto mee by this bearer, my brother's servant, whereby you will oblige, Your friend and servant,

"CHRISTIAN MASSIE.

"To my honnord ffriend, Collonel Edward Harley, these, at Sr Robert Harley's house, in Tuttle Street, near the New Church, these present."

Endorsed, "Mrs. Massie's recept of 5*lb.* 25 Sep. '48."

P. 203. *I hard from Loundoun that you, with Sir Arter Hasellrike, left Loundoun on Friday was senight, and that your intentions weare to hast to Sir William Waller.*—Edward Harley now enters upon his military services. Lady Brilliana hears of his safe arrival with Sir William Waller, where, says she, "the Lord of heaven and earth bless you and presarue you. My hart is with you, and I know you beleeue it, for my life is bound up with yours."

P. 204. *I am very sorry that my brother has doun what he has.*—"10 June, 1643. The Earl of Portland and Lord Viscount Conway, being accused by the Commons of being concerned in Edmund Waller's plot, were sequestered from the Lords, and committed, the one to the custody of the Lord Mayor and the other to one of the sheriffs, but their lands and goods not to be seized on till upon trial it appeared they were guilty. Not being proved, they were soon discharged." Cobbett's Parl. Hist. vol. iii. p. 131.

P. 205. *All Lancaschere is cleered, only Latham howes. My Lord of Darby has left that county, which they take ill.*—Lord Derby about this time was ordered off to the defence of the Isle of Man, leaving Lady Derby in the possession of Latham House, now threatened by the Parliament army. The siege of Latham House commenced in February, 1643-4. The Journal of this memorable siege has been several times printed from a MS. in the Ashmolean Museum, Oxford.

P. 206. *I acknowledge the greate mercy of my God that He presarued you in so sharp a fight when your hors was killed.* 11 July, 1643.—This was probably in Edward Harley's first conflict, which must have been that which took place at Lansdown on the 5th July, 1643, between Sir William Waller and Prince Maurice and Sir Ralph Hopton.

P. 207. *Sir William Vavasor has left Mr. Lingen with the soulders.* 25 Aug. 1643.— "Friday, August 11th. The Welsh forces, under Sir William Vavasor, advanced to the Wineyard, where after two houres solemnity they with great valour tooke it, nobody being there to make a shot against them." Dorney's briefe and exact relation of the most materiall and remarkeable passages that hapned in the late well-formed (and as valiently defended) seige laid before the city of Gloucester. Bib. Gloucesteriensis, p. 212.

209. *There are some souldiers come to Lemster and three troopes of hors to Hearsford with Sir William Vauasor, and they say they meane to visit Brompton agoine.*—Lady Brilliana's troubles at Brampton began in the spring of 1642. In the absence of Sir Robert Harley, then engaged busily in Parliament, she had the anxiety of the management of his country affairs upon her mind. The payment of certain rents and charges upon his estate, as stated in page 229, due to the King, had been enforced in April of this year. The calling out of the militia by the Parliament, and issuing of the commission of array by the King, brought matters to their ripeness, and made it necessary that every man should now select his ground. Herefordshire stood well affected to the King; Sir William Croft and others

of chief influence immediately joined the royal standard, and in the autumn a strong muster in that cause was made in Herefordshire, and many outrages committed on each side. Communications took place, between the Marquis of Hertford, when at Hereford in December, and Lady Brilliana, who had already been kept under much annoyance and daily expectation of a siege. A council of war was held at Hereford in February, when it was decided to bring some Welsh soldiers against her, and blow up the place. Matters of more importance were going on at Gloucester, in the neighbourhood of which there was a rendezvous of Lord Herbert's forces, to which those from the country about Brampton were now ordered; but, notwithstanding their removal, a summons and threat of 600 men were sent to her. At this juncture (22 and 23 March, 1642-3) Sir William Waller, with Colonel Massey, attacked and completely defeated Lord Herbert's forces at Highnam, and, following up his success, shortly afterwards laid siege to the city of Hereford, which surrendered on 24th April, from which place he scoured the country, by way of Leominster, to Worcester. These events dismayed the royalists, and gave a little quiet to Brampton; but in June, Sir William Croft, Sir Walter Pye, and others, taken at Hereford, and recently prisoners at Bristol, were liberated, and soldiers again collecting in the neighbourhood, demanding free quarter and an assessment on the county of 1,200*l.* a-month, she was again under alarm. In the end of June, Lord Herbert and Colonel Vavasor went into Montgomeryshire to muster new levies, and on their return the siege of Brampton Bryan was commenced by Colonel Vavasor. By the letter of the 25th August it appears that, having done much injury to the place, he had then left it, and the soldiers there under the charge of Mr. Lingen (Colonel Lyngen), who must himself have quitted it within a fortnight, as this first siege commenced on the 26th July, and continued but six weeks.

The last letter, of the 9th October, shews that she was again threatened by Sir William Vavasor; within a few days of which, having "taken a greate coold," she departed this life.

Under the danger which threatened the church at Brampton, and which was very much injured in the siege, the Register had been most probably put away in safety, as it does not contain any record of Lady Brilliana's death or burial. Sir Robert was at this time much engaged in Parliament. The Journals of the House of Commons record his presence on the 7th, 9th, 17th, 19th, and 26th of October. On the 27th of this month it is ordered, That the Committee for the Western parts do meet this afternoon, at 3 o'clock, at Sir Robert Harley's house; and again on the 30th there is a similar order. No doubt the tidings of her death had then reached him.

INDEX.

Acton, Mr. 64
Adams (Lady Brilliana's cousin), 56, 64, 180.
Adamson, William, 239.
Aersen, Van, 72, 254.
Alldern, Mr. 164.
Ancram, Lord, 25.
Angelica root, 130, 257.
Arundel, Earl of, 25, 39, 74.
Ash, ——, 58.
Ashby de la Zouch, 37.
Ashley, Sir Jacob, 39.
Aurum potabile, 46, 254.

Bagly, ——, 146.
Balham, Mr. 78, 79, 84, 88, 108, 117, 118, 119, 125, 128, 130, 132, 133, 135, 137, 138, 141, 143, 144.
Ball, Mr. 84.
Banbury, 54.
Bardlam, 186.
Barker, Dr. 1, 5. 6, 27, 94.
Barrington, 17.
Barroll, James, 180, 263.
Barthy, Mr. 67.
Barton, Mary, 35.
Bath, 64.
Burgess, Mr. 167.
Baughly, Mr. 195.
Bayley, Mr. 190.
—— William, 230.
Beal, Bartholomew, 249.
—— Dr. 96.
—— Mr. 193.
Beauchamp's Court, 1.
Beeb, Roger, 94, 132.
Bellenden, Sir William, 226.
Berwick, 45, 48, 52, 57, 83.

Beverley, 215.
Bezoar stone, 46, 253.
Bishops, proceedings against the, 119, 135, 140, 143, 146, 147, 148.
Bishop's Castle, 6; election of members for, 87.
Blackfriars (London), 1.
Blackheath, 158.
Blackwall, Gervase, 231.
Blanke, William, 239.
Blayney (Lady Brilliana's cousin), 105.
—— Thomas, 239.
Bletchly, ——, 68, 72, 83, 94, 119.
Blineman, Mr. 37, 76, 84, 254.
Bond, ——, 189.
Borough, ——, 32, 45, 49, 61.
Boteler, sir William, 223.
Bower, Dr. 119.
Brabazon, Mr. 205.
Brady, Robert, 239.
Bramley, Mrs. 64.
Brandsheave, Capt. 51.
Bray, Sir Giles (Lady Brilliana's brother), 3, 8, 11, 17, 23, 24, 25, 36, 41, 44, 59, 65, 105, 128, 251.
—— Lady, 17, 41, 85.
Brereton, Sir William, 205, 207.
Brisack, 19, 27, 252.
Bristol, 4, 236.
Brompton (now Brampton) Bryan, co. Hereford; most of Lady Brilliana's letters are dated from this seat of Sir Robert Harley, and there are many references to news of Brompton and its neighbourhood; siege of Brompton Castle, xix. 207—209; protestation taken at, 130.
Brocklesby, 107, 130.
Brooke, Lord, 1, 49, 170, 251.

INDEX.

Broughton, Mr. 47, 49, 57, 63, 67, 69, 70, 71, 109, 116, 152, 153, 159, 161, 168, 212.
Buckle, 84.
——— ———, 6.
Bucknell, 67, 84, 135, 171, 229.
Buckton, 190, 229.
Burrington, 229, 231.
Bursell, Mrs. 141.
Burton, Mr. 104.
Button, Capt. 94.
——— Lady, 218, 219, 237.
Bytheway, Richard, 186.

Caius College, 237—239.
Calvin, 20, 52, 69.
Capel, Lord, 198, 200, 201, 205.
Carlisle, 45.
Casimir, Prince, 75.
Charles I. his expedition against the Scots in 1639, 30, 32, 35, 37, 45.
Chester, 207.
Child, Anthony, 41, 164.
Chillingworth's Safe Way, 31, 253.
Chokes *(sic)*, Lady, 48.
Clanver, 74, 78, 140, 141, 142, 144.
Clare, Lord, 172, 177.
Clarendon, Lord Chancellor, letter to Edward Harley, 242; publication of his memoirs, 244.
Cloggie, Mr. 219.
Clogie, Rev. Alexander, l—li.
Clotworthy, Sir John, 231, 233.
Colborne, ———, 45, 50, 96, 205.
——— John, 89, 146.
Collins, Capt. Increse, 215, 216.
Coningsby, Mr. 186, 187, 189, 191, 198, 205, 261.
Convocation, proceedings of, 96.
Conway (Edward Harley's cousin), 151.
——— Lady, 32, 33, 43, 128.
——— Ralph, 6.
——— Sir Thomas, 19.
——— 1st Viscount, 2, 3, 4.
——— 2nd Viscount, 12, 24, 117, 139, 147, 204, 255, 266; letter of to Edw. Harley, 213.
Conyers, Sir John, 146, 149, 160, 259, 261.
——— Lady, 150.
Cooke, Sir Robert, 189, 264.
——— Secretary, 73.
Cope, Lady, 25, 253.
Copley, Lionel, 233.

Corbet (Edward Harley's cousin), 35, 55.
——— Andrew, 86.
——— Sir Andrew, 34.
——— Sir Jhon, 86.
——— Lady, 34.
Cornwall (Lady Brilliana's cousin), 89, 105, 108, 148, 168.
——— (Edward Harley's cousin), 146.
——— Sir Gilbert, 14, 21.
——— Lady, 21.
Courants, the Weekly, 19, 32, 69, 252, 254.
Coxall, 178.
Cradock, Mr. 26, 31, 74, 78.
Craven, Lord, 10, 22, 229, 252.
Croft, 167.
——— Capt. 199.
——— (Edward Harley's cousin), 38, 43.
——— Sir James, xlii.
——— Robert, 182.
——— Sir William, 121, 122, 124, 133, 152, 156, 162, 163, 164, 173, 183, 192, 198, 225, 229, 256.
Cromwell, Richard, 239.
——— Oliver, riding in state through the city of London, 218.

Dale of Leintwardine, 193.
Dally, 139, 184.
Daniel (Lady Brilliana's cousin), 115.
Davies, Thomas, 213.
Davis (Lady Brilliana's cousin), 65, 68, 80, 97, 110, 116, 117, 127, 135, 136, 150, 171, 181, 206.
——— Mr. 2, 162, 163, 164, 170, 173, 178, 193, 219.
——— of Coxall, 178.
——— of Wigmore, 124, 178.
Dean, forest of, 188.
Deodate, Dr. 26, 32, 37, 38, 40, 41, 42, 78, 80, 97, 98, 134.
Derby, Lord, 205, 266.
Devereux, Sir Francis, 82.
Dewe, Mr. 145.
De Wort, John, 75.
Digby, Lord, 149, 259.
Doughty, Mr. 136.
——— Thomas, 249.
Dover, 215, 216.
Downing, Rev. Colybute, 140, 258.
Dunkirk, sale of, 241, 244, 245.
Dutton, Mr. 223.

Eatcham, 219.

INDEX.

Eaton, Mr. 205.
Edinburgh, 40.
Edwards, Mr. 84, 117, 135, 171.
Elector, Prince, 72, 75.
Ellis, John, 239.
Elton (Lady Brilliana's cousin), 163, 164.
——— Mr. 162, 164, 165, 182, 183.
Erasmus, 52, 53.
Essex, Earl of, 39, 45, 48, 179, 225.
Eure, Mr. 43.
Evelyn, Sir John, 224.
Eyton, 229.

Fairfax (Lady Brilliana's cousin), 114.
——— Lord, 215.
——— Sir Thomas, 225.
Felton, John, 239.
Fiennes, Mr. 125.
Finch, Lord Chief Justice, 32.
Fisher, Mr. 208.
FitzJames, Frances, 249.
Floyd, Mr. 168.
Folden, 237, 238.
Foster, Judge, 224.
Fox, Mr. 156.
——— Somerset, 32.
——— Sir Stephen, 244.
Foxe (Lady Brilliana's cousin), 39.
Froysell, Thomas, xlvi.
——— Rev. Thomas, xii. xxxi. 249.
Fumdwen, J. 185.

Gardnas (sic), ———, 205.
Gears, William, 231.
Gelsthorp, Edward, 239.
Gloucester, 3, 189, 198, 202, 246, 264.
——— Bishop of, 96.
Goodwin (Lady Brilliana's cousin), 93.
——— Mr. 86, 202.
Goodman, the Jesuit, 112, 255.
Goring, Colonel, 136.
Gostlin, John, 239.
Gower, Mrs. 47.
——— Rev. Stanley, Rector of Brampton Bryan, xvii.—xviii. xlviii. 18, 26, 35, 37, 53, 62, 86, 97, 98, 99, 100, 103, 106, 108, 109, 110, 111, 112, 113, 115, 118, 121, 126, 128, 141, 155, 158, 160, 189, 193, 260.
Graveling, 247.
Gray's Inn, 130.
Green, Mr. 208.
Gregory, Sir William, 245.

Greville, Sir Edward, 21, 253.
Griffiths, George, 15, 21, 35, 86, 88, 114, 135, 187.
——— Jack, 206.
——— Mr. 67, 105, 114, 134, 137, 142.
——— William, 178, 190.
Grocers' Hall, 218, 222.
Gwyn, Mr. 113, 118, 130, 139, 140, 141.

Hackluyt (Lady Brilliana's cousin), 41, 42, 61, 84, 118, 154, 155, 167, 189.
——— Richard, xlvii.
Hall, ———, 11, 14, 27, 73, 93, 151, 152.
Hamilton, Marquess, 51.
Hammon (the printer), 223.
Hanmer, 205.
Harley family, descent of, xli.
——— Brilliana, Lady, her parentage and connection, xii.; marriage, 24, 25; character, xiii.; her letters to Sir Robert Harley, 1—7; to her son Edward, 7—183, 185—209; to Mrs. Wallcot, 183—185; besieged in Brompton Bryan, xviii.—xix.; her children, xlix.; her death, xx. 267.
——— Brilliana, daughter of Lady Brilliana, 5, 18, 29, 42, 111, 126; journey to London, 153—158; enters the household of Lady Vere, 160, 161, 168, 172, 190, 192, 195, 201.
——— Dorothy, 60, 82, 161, 165, 167, 168, 169, 173.
——— Edward (afterwards Sir Edward), biographical notice of, xx.—xxix.; letters to at Oxford, 7—104; in London, 105—183, 185—209; services under the parliament, xxi. l. li.; letter inclosing his pass to travel, in 1647, 231; copy of pass, 232; further pass in 1650, 235; letters to Caius College, 237; to Lord Clarendon, 240, 243; to his brother Thomas, 216, 220; to his father, Sir Robert, 217, 218; answer to his son Robert about the sale of Dunkirk, 245; his retrospects of his life, 246, 249.
——— John, xlii.
——— Margaret, 57, 110.
——— Mary, letter to Edward Harley, 219.
——— the first Sir Robert, his parentage, vi.; education, ib.; knight of the Bath, ib.; returned to various Parliaments, vii. xliii. 251; his character, vii.; public

employments, vii. xliii. xliv.; letters to whilst in London, 1628, letters i. to viii. and xxvii.; references to in 1638, 14—36; in 1639, 38—82; his return to the Short Parliament, 1640, 84—87; references to whilst in London on that occasion, 88—95; other references in 1640, 96—101; attends the meeting of the Long Parliament, 100; references to his occupations therein and its proceedings, 100—206; a letter, from to his son Edward, xlix.; letter to, from his son Edward, 218; proceedings as to Herefordshire Declaration, 224—230; letter from Dr. Wright, 228; rents paid by, 229, 230; letter to Sir Henry Vane, and his reply, 235; losses in the civil war, x. 230; death, 11; funeral sermon, xii. xxxi.—xxxix.; marriages, xii.

—— the second Sir Robert, allusions to in Lady Brilliana's letters *passim*, 233; letter to his brother Edward, 236; order for his apprehension, 1658, 239; his death, 249.

—— Robert (afterwards first Earl of Oxford), 244.

—— Thomas, father of the first Sir Robert, xlii.

—— Thomas, son of Lady Brilliana, 5, 15, 18, 37, 115, 117, 119, 120, 122, 125, 126, 127, 128, 129, 172, 173.

Harvey, Mr. 95.
Haselrig, Sir Arthur, 203.
Haughton Castle, 207.
Havor, Mr. 145.
Hawes, Mr. 220.
Heath, Mr. 99.
Henrietta Maria, Queen, 40, 143, 198.
Herbert, Lord, 32, 173, 188, 196, 205, 253.
—— Mr. 86, 90, 100.
Hereford, City of, allusions to in Lady Brilliana's Letters, *passim*; musters and conduct of soldiery there, 3, 44; puritanical alterations in the cathedral, 148, 259; unpopularity of the parliament party there, 170, 179; surrender to Waller, 198, 265.

—— Bishop Coke of, 27, 36, 43, 44, 67.
—— Bishop Croft of, li. 240.
Herefordshire, anti-parliamentarian declaration of, 148, 158, 159; proceedings in parliament respecting, 223—225; reference to copy of this declaration, 264.

Hertford, Marquess of, 186, 264.
Hibbons, Mr. 79.
Hill, Mr. 176, 189, 192, 199, 204, 206.
Holland, Earl of, 57, 73.
Hollingworth, ——, 54, 83.
Hollis, Denzell, 231.
Holy Court (The), 27, 253.
Home Lacy, 246.
Hopkis, ——, 187, 193; (of Downend), 193.
Hopton, Sir Richard, 182.
Hoskins, Mr. 164.
Howard, Sir Robert, 87, 229.
Hubbard, John, 224.
—— Richard, 225.
Hubbins, Mrs. 141.
Hull, 166, 215, 262.
Hullsy, ——, 59.
Hunks (Lady Brilliana's cousin), 6.
Hurse, ——, 219.
Husband, Mr. 141.
Hyde Park, 138.

Ireland, 58.

James, Mr. 104, 106, 170, 174, 188, 193.
Jeffreys, Capt. 195.
Jenkes, Henry, 239.
Jones, ——, 47, 50.

Kentish Petition, presentation of, 158, 260.
Kettleby, Nehemiah, 185.
Keynsham Court, 239.
King, Mr. 209.
King's Book, the, 51, 254.
Kingsland, 139, 148, 205, 229, 231.
Knight, ——, 196.
—— Mr. 137.
Knightly, Mr. 76.
Knighton, 203.
Kyrle (Lady Brilliana's cousin), 111.
—— Sir John, 64, 182.
—— Mr. 121.

Lacy, Mr. 2, 218.
Lane, Mr. 171.
Laneford, Mr. 122.
Lathom House, 205, 266.
Laud, Archbishop, 91, 129.
Lawes, Mr. 97.
Ledbury, 164, 179.
Lee, Sir Richard, 86.
Legg, ——, 190.

INDEX.

Legg, Mr. 196, 200.
Leintwardine, 43, 130, 213, 229.
Lenthall, William, 232.
Leominster, 6, 18, 98, 178, 209, 233, 234.
Lewis, Evan. 224, 225.
―――― Sir William, 224, 231.
Lewson (sic), Lord, 1.
Leynthall Starks, 229.
Lincoln, Earl of, 218.
Lincoln's Inn, 127, 130, 155.
Ling, William, 239.
Lingen, Sir H. 220.
―――― Mr. 205, 207.
Liquorice, 16.
Little, Mr. 7.
Littleton, Mrs. 172.
―――― William, ib.
Long, Walter, 231.
Longford, ――, 56.
Longly, Mr. 12, 177.
Looker, ――, 11, 12, 85, 90, 129, 199.
Love, Mr. 247.
Lowe, Mr. 190, 193.
Luddington, 77.
Ludlow, 64, 86, 88, 123, 125, 137, 138, 167, 172, 174, 198, 201, 202, 218, 252.
Luke, Philip, 206.
Luther, Life of, 52.

Macclesfield, Earl of, 244, 245.
Macklin, ――, 189.
Mackworth, Mr. 114.
Maddison, Mr. 223.
Maidstone, 216.
Mainwaring, Lady, 6.
Mallet, Judge, 123, 224.
Man in the Moon, 13, 252.
Manchester, Earl of, 225.
Marrow, Lieut.-Col. 202.
Martin, ――, 17, 23, 102, 169, 175, 181.
Martyrs, Book of, 52.
Mason, Mr. 170, 182.
Massey, Col. 202, 205, 225, 265.
Massie, Edward, 233.
―――― Sir Edward, 249.
Mathew, Dr. Toby, 105, 255.
Meyrick, Mr. 43.
Middlesex, Lord, 12.
Militia, musters of, 2, 18, 35, 36, 37, 48; King's commission for the, 176, 178.
Miller, Sir Nicholas, 215.
―――― Thomas, 58, 61, 62, 76, 77, 81, 82, 107.
Mint, the, 216.
―――― Mastership of, x. xlv.

Mocktree, 229.
Moene (sic), 60.
Monk, General, 244, 245.
Montague, Earl of, 245.
Montgomeryshire, election of knights for, 86.
Moore, Mr. 87, 108, 116, 123, 142, 143, 151, 153, 174, 200, 201, 204, 208.
―――― Robert, 26.
―――― Thomas, 147.
Moray, Sir Robert, 249.
Morgan, ―― 104, 117.
―――― Mr. 67, 200.
Mortimer's Cross, 198.
Morton, Lord, 25.

Nailor, William, 239.
Napier, Sir Robert, 86.
Naylor, Mr. 237.
Nelham, Mr. 86.
Newcastle, Lord, 215.
Newgate, 224, 225.
Newnham, 247.
Newport, Francis, 86.
―――― Lady, 155.
―――― Lord, 39.
―――― Mr. 155.
―――― Sir Richard, 68, 69, 254.
Nichol, Anthony, 231.
Northampton, Earl of, 102.
Northumberland, Earl of, 64.

Old, Mr. 155.
Old Bailey, 178.
Orleton, 247.
Osberson, Mrs. 138.
Oxenstiern, 109.
Oxford, Magdalen Hall, a Puritanical College, xx.; letters to Edward Harley whilst there, 7—104; few noblemen's sons there, 8; books cheaper there than at Worcester, 20; fire there, 22; people there inveigh against the Puritans, 40; Oxford apples, 65; plague there, 113; act at, 34, 39, 45, 61, 62, 63, 99, 253.

Paget, Lord, 170.
Palmer (Sir Edward Harley's sister), 249.
Parliament, meeting of the Long, 100.
Peacock, Rev. Thomas, Rector of Brampton Bryan, xv.
Pelham (Lady Brilliana's cousin), 59, 60, 111.
―――― (Lady Brilliana's nephew), 38, 96, 104, 106, 201.

Pelham, Harry, 101, 114, 130.
——— Lady (Lady Brilliana's sister), 9, 27, 30, 32, 68, 81, 87.
——— Ned, 102.
——— Sir William (Lady Brilliana's brother-in-law), 32, 81, 102, 107, 130, 161, 254, 261.
Pennell, Mr. 21, 253.
Perkins, Edward, tutor to Edward Harley at Oxford, 9, 14, 24, 26, 31, 32, 33, 37, 38, 40, 41, 43, 49, 54, 56, 60, 63, 83, 95, 99, 253.
Petter, honest, 198, 200, 201, 202, 203, 208, 264.
Phillips, Mr. 179, 186, 189, 195, 200, 203, 208.
Piedmont, Collection for, xl. xlvi.
Pierpoint, Mr. 86.
Pierson, Mrs. 13, 22, 26, 29, 158, 252.
——— Rev. Thomas, Rector of Brampton Bryan, xv.—xvii. xlviii. 4.
Pinner, ———, 6, 43, 44, 139, 150, 151, 154, 155, 159, 190, 213.
——— Edward, 90, 91, 92, 93, 94, 190, 194.
——— Samuel, 83, 118, 128, 190.
Pitts, Mrs. 48.
Plowden, Mr. 105, 255.
Potter, ———, 154.
Powell, ———, 190, 197.
Powis, Mr. 218.
Presteign, 95, 188.
Price (Lady Brilliana's cousin), 6, 14, 18, 32, 37, 39, 40.
——— Herbert, 135, 257.
——— Mr. 164.
Pritchard, ———, 98, 155.
Prosser, ———, 186, 197, 208.
——— Thomas, 185.
Protestation of 3rd May, 1641, 130, 221, 257.
Prynne, William, 104.
Pursla, 201, 265.
Pye, Robert, 95.
——— Sir Walter, 84, 87, 198, 205.

Queen Mother's arrival, 9, 10.

Ragley, 1, 6, 251.
Ratesford *(sic)*, Lord, 56.
Read (Sir Edward Harley's cousin), 249.
"Return of Prayer," 65.
Reynolds, W. 220.

Rice, ———, 107, 110, 143.
Richards, ———, 196.
Robert (Lady Brilliana's brother), 105.
Robinson, John, 239.
Rogers, Rev. Dr. 159, 171, 174, 260.
——— Mr. 87.
——— W. 235.
Roundheads, derision of, at Hereford, 170; at Ludlow, 167, 172, 262.
Rous, Mr. 211.
Rudall (cousin of Lady Brilliana), 48, 176.
Rupert, Prince, 10, 22, 252, 253.
Rutley, ———, 219.

St. John (Lady Brilliana's cousin), 117, 119. .
Salisbury, Lord, 172.
Sallwells, Mr. 99, 103.
Sankey, ———, 143, 165, 178, 206.
——— Capt. Lieut. 205.
Sanky, Richard, 94, 106, 118, 182.
Savile, Lord, 170.
Saxe Weimar, Duke of, 72.
Say, Lord, 49, 90, 129, 257.
Scotland, troubles in, 10, 12, 40, 45, 51, 57, 58, 72, 75, 99, 117, 118.
Scriven, Colonel, 19, 252.
Scudamore, John Lord, li.
——— Sir John, 2.
——— Lord, 124, 165, 166, 245.
——— Mr. 21, 48, 64, 124, 253.
Scurvygrass, 53.
Seaborne, Mr. 162, 164.
Shelton, Samuel, 230.
Sherborn, Rev. William, 160, 179, 261.
Sherwin, Mr. 218.
Shilton, Mr. 219.
Shobdon, 145, 176.
Shrewsbury, 15, 90, 123, 155, 171, 198, 203.
Simmons, Mr. reports of his health, 26—53; other references to, 49, 65, 69, 74, 76, 77, 84, 135, 254.
Smallman, ———, 14, 197.
——— Mr. 205.
Smith, *vide* Smyth.
Smith, Mr. 88, 153, 159, 178.
——— Edward, 7, 18, 22, 28, 31, 251.
Smyth (Lady Brilliana's cousin), 39, 40, 45, 101, 107, 110, 251.
——— (Edward Harley's cousin) 28, 35, 53, 55, 76, 86, 91, 121, 122, 128, 134, 137, 140, 151, 152, 154, 155, 158, 212, 213.

Smyth, Helengewagh Lady (sister to Lady Brilliana and referred to under the name of Wacke), 5, 48, 102, 105, 110, 128, 139.
Soldiers, misconduct of those of Shropshire, 97; of Hereford, 98.
Spain, King of, death of, 115.
Stanly, ——, 219.
Stanton, Elizabeth, 83.
Stapleton, Philip, 231.
Stevenson, Mr. 37, 108, 253.
—— Mrs. 14, 29, 37.
Stiche of Walford, 62.
Stiles, Mr. 205.
Storton, Dr. 49.
Strafford, Earl of, 104, 105, 114, 117, 125, 126, 127, 131, 257.

Taylor, Mr. 71, 72, 189, 195.
Temple, the, 127, 130.
Temple Bar, 218.
Tewkesbury, 53.
Thruston, ——, 239.
Toddington, 1, 251.
Tolson, John, xliii.
Tombes, Rev. John, 106, 255.
Tomkins (Lady Brilliana's cousin), 3, 30, 121, 182, 263.
—— Mr. 109.
Tracy, Sir John, 251.
—— Sir Robert, 8.
Trafford, Mrs. 26, 29, 32.
Traherne, Thomas, 249.
Tuckney, Dr. 237.
—— Dr. Anthony, li.

Vaughan (Lady Brilliana's cousin), 26, 45, 97, 99, 111, 113, 124, 164.
—— Mr. 2, 24, 64, 164.
Vavasour, Colonel, 205.
—— Sir William, 207, 209, 266.
Venables, Mr. 224.
Vere, Lady, 6, 76, 105, 114, 119, 126, 132, 157, 158, 160, 168, 172, 251; letter of, to Edward Harley, 213.
Voile, Mr. 107, 108, 137, 159.

Wacke, see Smyth, Helengewagh Lady.
Wake, Lady, 229.
Walcot, 76, 140.
—— Ann, 184.
—— Humphrey, 184.
—— John, 184, 185.
—— Mary, 184.

Walcot, Mr. 26, 31, 184, 185.
—— Mrs. 6, 26, 38, 91, 105, 144, 255; letters to, 183, 184.
Walker, Mr. 15.
Waller, Sir William, 202, 203, 204, 225, 231, 233.
Walls, John, 5, 83, 117.
Weare, ——, 19.
Weaver, Mr. M.P. for Hereford, 122, 154, 156, 162, 163, 165, 267.
Weobly, 109.
Westmoreland, Earl of, letters of to Ed. Harley, 214, 215.
—— Countess of, letter of, to Edward Harley, 215; other references to, 76, 105.
Whateley, 49, 54.
Whitchurch, 44.
Whitney, Lady, 79.
Wigmore, 36, 105, 122, 124, 130, 178, 209, 219, 229, 231.
—— Mr. 176, 182, 183, 186, 187, 205, 209, 213, 258.
—— (Lady Brilliana's cousin), 136, 138.
Wilde, Mr. Serj. 222.
Wilkinson, Rev. Dr. xlix. 31, 38.
—— Mrs. 8, 15, 27, 29, 36, 37, 66, 67, 72, 251.
Windebank, Secretary, 105.
Winthrop, S. 233.
Wistanstone, 164.
Witney, Mr. 124.
Wood, Mary, 6.
Woodhouse, ——, 42, 98, 117.
Worcester, 56, 64, 82, 178, 181, 182, 226.
—— Lord, 32.
Wortley, Sir Francis, 158.
Wright, Dr. Nathaniel, xlix. 80, 91, 92, 97, 98, 104, 105, 117, 119, 120, 121, 122, 124, 125, 127, 140, 144, 145, 151, 154, 155, 161, 162, 163, 164, 165, 170, 172, 174, 189, 192, 195, 196, 198, 201, 202, 206, 208; letter to Sir Robert Harley, 228.
—— Mrs. 192, 196, 198, 201.
Wycombe, High, 155, 156, 158.

Yates, Mr. 108, 112, 131, 153, 154, 155, 171, 172, 190, 193.
—— Mrs. 43, 104, 105, 108, 112.
York, 161, 170, 182.

LONDON:
J. B. NICHOLS AND SONS, PRINTERS,
PARLIAMENT-STREET.

CPSIA information can be obtained at www.ICGtesting.com
Printed in the USA
BVOW07s0914110314

347293BV00009B/573/P